Mike Pap

By the same author:
The Power of Ch'i

VISUALIZATION

The key to fulfilment
MICHAEL PAGE

THE AQUARIAN PRESS

First published 1990

© MICHAEL PAGE 1990

The extract from *Through the Time Barrier* by Danah Zohar is
reprinted by permission of William Heinemann Limited.

*All rights reserved. No part of this book may be reproduced or utilized in any form
or by any means, electronic or mechanical, including photocopying, recording or by
any information storage and retrieval system, without permission in writing from the
Publisher.*

British Library Cataloguing in Publication Data

Page, Michael
Visualization: the key to fulfilment.
1. Self — realization
I. Title
158.1

ISBN 0-85030-928-X

The Aquarian Press is part of the Thorsons Publishing Group,
Wellingborough, Northamptonshire, NN8 2RQ England

Typeset by Harper Phototypesetters Limited, Northampton, England
Printed in Great Britain by Mackays of Chatham, Kent

1 3 5 7 9 10 8 6 4 2

Contents

Introduction   7

1 **To See Ourselves**   15
 The self-concept; visualization dissected; slimming; sports performance; successful visualization; summary.

2 **To Heal Ourselves**   28
 Thought as energy; general health; causes of disease; controlling pain; self-healing; some examples of visualization in the cure of disease; emotional programming; mindfulness; self-hypnosis; Autogenic Training; think-see.

3 **How it works**   45
 Psycho-cybernetics; mystico-religious explanations; summary.

4 **To Heal Others**   52
 Hypnosis; psychic healers; psychic healing; distant healing; group healing; ethical questions; the problem of proof; conclusion.

5 **To Love Another**   62
 Behind the chemistry; beginnings; repairing relationships; sexual relationships; controlled visualization; forgiveness; improving normal relationships.

6 **Preparation**   77
 Obstacles to success; the mental gymnasium;

breathing; mindfulness; relaxation; getting and giving help; distractions; posture; meditation.

7 **To Love Ourselves (Part I)** 92
Guru therapies; ashram therapies.

8 **To Love Ourselves (Part II)** 105
Biofeedback; tapes; focusing; psychosynthesis; ideal scenes; sub-personalities; best therapist; dreamworking.

9 **To Woo the Muse** 114
Theft of innocence; rainbow bridges; intuition; *Wu wei* and the creative act; fostering intuition; striking the creative spark; visualization in the creative act.

10 **Towards Wider Horizons** 131
Some uses of paranormal faculties; scientific hints; learning to be psychic.

11 **Wider Horizons** 145
Science and the occult; self-transformation; the occult path; witches and shamans; working magic; healing; visualizing; affirming; pathworkings; odds and ends; warning notes; conclusion.

12 **Eastern Horizons** 162
The central channel; a diversion into fairyland; aids to meditation; identification with deities; mind substance; implications for the West; preliminary practices; conclusion.

13 **Beyond the Horizon** 178
Western ways of death; near-death experiences; life after death; rebirth, reincarnation; *karma*; death paths; do-it-yourself death path; choosing future life.

A Final Vision 193
Appendix 201
Bibliography 202
Index 205

Introduction

> He was a wonderfully equipped person. Intelligence and cunning emanated from him like energy from radium, with the same silent and penetrating continuity, without effort, without a pause, without a sign of exhaustion, in all directions at once. It was clear from the first that he was an excellent doctor. But I was never able to discover if his professional excellence was merely one aspect, one side of his high intellect, or if it was itself his instrument of penetration, his secret weapon to turn enemies into friends, to render prohibitions null, to change no into yes; this too formed part of the cloud in which he wrapped himself and which moved with him. It was an almost visible cloud, which made his looks and the lines of his face hard to decipher, and which led one to suspect, beneath every action of his, every phrase, every silence, the existence of a tactic and a technique, the pursuit of unperceivable ends, a continual shrewd labour of exploration, elaboration, penetration and possession.
>
> Nevertheless, Dr Gottlieb's intelligence, aimed though it was at practical ends, was not inhuman. So abundant was his self-assurance, his expectancy of victory, his faith in himself, that a large portion remained to bestow on assisting his less gifted neighbours . . .

So wrote Primo Levi of an inmate of a death camp in *If this is a Man and the Truce* (Sphere, 1987). The reader is invited not only to consider the question of how some survived the holocaust, but also what it is to be an autonomous human being, possessed, even in hell, of a key to fulfilment. Is the ability to survive and prosper a gift of the gods, is it an atavistic throwback to animal life — red in tooth and claw — or is it something in between and peculiarly human? What makes some people survivors, saints, successes, heroes, mages, millionaires, while others are beaten down, losers, cowards, weak? Is it a natural gift, a throwback to a previous existence, an accident or is it something that can be learned?

There is a technique that can help to make each individual more of a worldly success if that is what that person chooses. More importantly, it is a technique that can be used to raise individuals to the greatest heights of fulfilled human development.

Amazingly it works by means of an ordinary human ability and is therefore freely available to all of us. This is the power we have to reshape our picture of ourselves, that is, our ability to modify our self-concept by using our imagination. It also involves reshaping the mental pictures we have of our environment. By doing this, we gain access to our well-being and happiness.

We are much more at the mercy of our imaginations than we realize and too often we fall prey to the idea that we are at the mercy of fate, that we are at the mercy of unseen powers and other people. However, we need to see that it is *we* who make ourselves and our environment.

Consider the following. A woman may look out of her office window on two successive meteorologically identical days and 'see' two entirely different scenes. The first day she is head over heels in love, the next, she has had a flaming row with her lover. These affairs of the heart will affect the way she sees the view out of the window. On the first day, she will have seen the sun shining brilliantly from a cloudless sky, its heat a foretaste of the joys of the weekend to come, the pavements filled with happy and attractive people, whereas today, the sun will shine less brightly, the heat be oppressive, the pavement below covered with trash. Today, too, she will look in the mirror and wonder how anyone could have found the dowdy figure staring back at her at all attractive.

Such changes in the way we view the world are commonplace, of course, and, as such, are easily ignored, but they can provide valuable insights. That the change of view came about entirely because of the mental state of the woman is most important — *she* was creating her *own* world.

Equally, down the street today, her ex-lover will be whistling and smiling, whereas yesterday he had been taciturn, glum and prickly because, for him, the relationship was going sour, but today he has ended it.

Change, of course, is inevitable and so it is certain that each of these people will soon be feeling quite differently. The woman will remember that there's a women's group meeting that night that she will now be able to go to and the man will see an empty evening stretching out uninvitingly in front of him. For her, the sun will then recover some of its brightness, but for him, the temperature will seem to have increased unbearably.

Again, nothing has actually changed externally — it is all in the mind. This, though, is a good thing because with it comes the realization that it is easier to change ourselves than to change our surroundings. So let us now try a little exercise or two to illustrate just how much we create our worlds.

Take a look at a cream bun. Now. There may not be one in the cake tin, but there is one in your head — even if you are on a crowded, cakeless commuter train! Look at it clearly, this ideal cream bun you carry in your head. Are you merely seeing it or can you also smell it a bit, feel the tiny grains of sugar, taste it a bit, feel it in your mouth? Go on, swallow a piece.

We seem to be having a bit of a feast together, you and I. Is your mouth watering as mine is? I'm enjoying the feast and I hope that you are.

This exercise shows you that your mind and its imaginative faculty is truly a creator of your world, but its imaginative faculty does not operate in a vacuum. It has to have some raw material on which to work — in this case a few previous cream buns in your life. It is also dependent on the attitudes you may have developed towards cream buns. If they have ever made you sick, your attitudes are likely to be pretty negative, and you may now be feeling quite angry with me for suggesting cream buns to you, in which case I apologise.

What I hope you will have seen, however, is the undoubted power of your imagination. I hope you will also have seen how, uncontrolled, it can make you do things you don't necessarily want or need to (for example, if you like them, you may already have decided to get a bun to have with your next coffee, but if I had not suggested them to you, you would not be doing this).

Your uncontrolled imagination may make you do, and say things, that another part of your mind tells you you should not be doing. Take sex, for example. We are all, in our culture, slightly or very neurotic about sex. What does the word conjure up in your mind? Can you make yourself happy by thinking about it, by fantasizing, perhaps, can you arouse yourself? How are you feeling now as you read those words? Shocked, amused, aroused, indifferent? My words are only ink on paper: it's your own imagination that's making you feel whatever you are at this moment.

At this point in the proceedings, it's worth remembering the story of the two Zen monks on their travels. They came one day to a fast-moving stream and there, hesitating on the bank, was a pretty young girl. Without pausing, the first monk swept her off her feet, carried her across, set her down on the other side and strode on. The second monk, as they proceeded on their way, was strangely silent for a while, then he burst out, 'You shouldn't have touched that girl, it's not right.' The first monk replied, 'Are you still carrying that girl? I put her down at the stream back there.'

We can be like either of the two monks in the story — we can choose the way we behave by directing our controlled imagination the way we want to, unless, that is, our underlying attitudes to the subject are so strong as to immobilize us or make our uncontrolled imaginations work overtime. In the latter case, we have been taken over by something outside our own control, we have lost our grip on autonomy.

Too much of the behaviour of too many people is heteronomous, that is, under the control of forces outside them and too many people live lives controlled by others. Such forces may be cultural or familial, though the two are often the same. There is the hackneyed example of the spinster tied to the perceived or actual demands of an elder relative, the anxious adolescent falling in with the mores and customs of a local gang to be part of the group. There are, too, acts of racism, sexism and so on when cultural or group solidarity override the greater human solidarity.

It will now be clear that there are ways of using the mind that enable us to direct the inherently great power of our imaginations more effectively, to direct it in a way that maintains our *own* control and so leads to greater autonomy of action, greater control of our bodies, our minds, our relationships and therefore our happiness.

The examples I have given show that there is a very real sense in which it can truly be said that people do create their own worlds. They develop positive or negative feelings towards themselves, towards one another and towards the objects in the world around them.

The early chapters of this book look at how we can go about changing those feelings and attitudes by success-programming in physical and mental health and relationships.

There are many many self-help books, books that aim to improve the reader's worldly success, and the first chapter of this book describes and evaluates techniques that are aimed at success-programming in such activities as sport, slimming and dating. As regards money, so often seen as the basis of worldly success, we might note these words of a specialist in self-programming:

> It can be very liberating, personally and financially, to understand that creating money and creating abundance are often two very different things — and abundance is relatively easy to create. Many people who

have a substantial amount of money still have not created a feeling of abundance for themselves, and they are often worried about inflation, taxes, investments, the future, etc. And yet there are people with very little money who have a feeling of abundance, and who live in a world where there is always more than enough of everything. For *abundance is a state of mind* — a state of mind which can consciously be created by you, with the power of your mind.

We live in an abundant universe: look at the number of stars in the sky — 100 billion known galaxies, with an average of 200 billion suns each — look at the number of seeds in an oak, or a eucalyptus tree, or a dandelion. We are surrounded by infinite abundance, if we stop cutting ourselves off from it, open up to it, and let ourselves be a part of it.

Marcus Allen, Tantra for the West
(Whatever Publishing, 1981)

Maxwell Maltz — an American plastic surgeon and well-known exponent of the importance of the self-concept — puts a scientific gloss on the matter when, for example, he sees the self-concept as the guidance mechanism that directs our minds and bodies towards achieving the goals we consciously and unconsciously set ourselves and as the root cause of failure or success. I shall also look at the place of the self-concept in health and sickness. Maltz indicates that if we see ourselves as failing or ill, then fail we will and sick we shall be. By revising our self-concepts, however, we can turn ourselves into fit successes.

Similarly, in our relationships we almost never see other people quite purely — we all bring some underlying prejudgements based on experience or social pressures to our perception of them. When another person is of an easily recognized group that our culture or personal prejudices regard as not to be mixed with, then what we see (rather than *who* we see) is almost entirely a product of our imagination. 'We see what we want to see' has a modicum of truth in it, but is nevertheless not an absolutely accurate statement. To say that we see what our imagination is *pressured* into seeing is nearer the truth. Pressured? Pressured by whom or by what? Pressured by family, friends and early experiences. Pressured by mass media, religious groups, social groups, political parties.

We have also allowed ourselves to be pressured into a certain way of seeing what we are, and to realize this is fundamental if we are to change. If you see yourself as a put-upon spinster, for example, then you become more and more what your imagination puts before you. Perhaps your posture gradually becomes more slumped, you become less careful about your appearance, less able to meet men confidently and so on. If you admire a group leader, then you hope to be like them in appearance and mannerisms. We use our imaginations probably unconsciously and without realizing the power of what we are doing. We see ourselves as like them in our mind's eye and then become like them in reality.

The mind behaves like an ill-disciplined monkey: as soon as we try to concentrate on anything, it will flit away and away, going over yesterday's events, hopes of tomorrow, the menu for dinner, the twinge of a tummyache — anything, indeed, except the subject we have chosen for it. Another of the topics I cover in this book, then, is how to gain control of your restless mind — for it is through such control that any kind of success is gained. I shall describe many ways in which daily activities can be enhanced and, most importantly, ways in which you can change your life permanently for the better.

Practice in also achieving the more mundane goals of ordinary everyday life serves two incidental purposes: it gives confidence that visualization does work and opens the door to higher goals, for it is my belief that such ways can also be used to achieve mystical consciousness, spiritual realization and, indeed, ease the fear of death itself.

The latter part of the book turns, then, towards the use of visualization in those other potential powers of our minds, the psychic, the occult and the spiritual. Much religious practice, particularly at the higher levels of Buddhism and Hindu Tantra, depends upon the visualization of light and the visualization of deities as a means to an individual's spiritual development. Similar techniques are used in Taoism and other traditions, not excluding some of the more esoteric Western ones.

The book concludes by considering guided visualizations as a means of helping people at the time of death: the *Tibetan Book of the Dead* is a historic example of such practice and, on the basis of such examples, I suggest ways in which similar procedures may be used today. My hope is that the content of this part of the book will be useful to people who look after terminally sick and dying people, as well as the sick and dying themselves.

The book draws together, then, a large number of aspects of the same subject: the use of the mind to visualize changes in oneself, one's relationships, and in one's material and spiritual worlds, showing you how people succeed in changing their lives and destinies in ways ranging from the most mundane to the highest of which men and women are capable.

At a time when people's abilities to take control of their lives and destinies seem actually to be declining for a variety of reasons, it seems to me that an increased awareness of a relatively simple means by which we may increase our autonomy is to be welcomed. Such autonomy is described by Levi when he describes another death-camp survivor, a child of five years of age whose response to the situation is in its own way as appropriate as that of Dr Gottlieb.

> Peter Pavel spoke to nobody and had need of nobody. He was a beautiful blond and robust child, with an intelligent and impassive face. In the morning he climbed down from his bunk, which was on the third tier, with slow but sure movements, went to the showers to fill his bowl with water and washed himself meticulously. Then he disappeared for the whole day, making a brief appearance only at noon to collect his soup in the same bowl. In the evening he came back for dinner, ate, went out again, re-entered soon afterwards with a chamber-pot, placed it in the corner behind the stove, sat there for a few moments, left again with the pot, came back without it, climbed up quietly to his own place, punctiliously adjusted the blankets and pillow and slept until the morning without changing position.
>
> Primo Levi *If this is a Man and the Truce* (Sphere, 1987)

Again, I have found Levi illuminating something fundamental: somewhere along the line in his short life, Peter Pavel had worked out a consistently businesslike and detached stance to prevailing circumstances. It is difficult to say what sort of self-image he had developed, but it is likely that while it was reinforced by the regard of other inmates it was sufficient in itself. There is often a similar child-like naïveté about fulfilled men and women who have approached — or even attained — full autonomy and realization. A few — like Peter — arrive at that state without apparent effort. For the rest of us, we have to work at it.

1.
To See Ourselves

The self-concept

The self-concept is the total picture that one has of oneself and is probably created by our observations of how others — especially those who are important to us in early life — perceive us. We come to see ourselves as others see us.

If parents tell a child — overtly and covertly in all those ways parents have — that she is bright, then she will, in all probability, see herself as bright and behave as such. Similarly, people who are told that they are unattractive, will no doubt eventually see themselves as being unattractive, even if they are, in fact, quite the opposite, and will behave as if they are ugly, conforming more to their *imagined* picture of themselves than to the *reality*. They visualize themselves in a certain way and so their mental image affects all that they do. Such a mental picture will affect various images of self-esteem. As I shall show in later chapters, much of a neurotic person's low self-esteem is to do with extreme conflict between the ego ideal (the ideal person you would like to be) and the way they *actually* perceive themselves to be.

Maxwell Maltz, mentioned earlier, stresses the importance to the individual of his or her self-concept in his book, which has the somewhat awesome title *Psycho-cybernetics* (Prentice-Hall, 1960).

He had found that many of his patients who came to him because they believed that some cosmetic surgery would give them new hope for happiness and success in life were, in fact, quite unchanged in any psychological sense by the surgery. He compares the phenomenon to that of the 'phantom limb' that continues to feel very real pain long after the real leg or arm has been amputated. The picture that patients carried about in their heads of themselves as ugly and disfigured was more real to them than the new image they saw in the mirror after a cosmetic operation. As he writes in the book, 'When a facial disfigurement is corrected by plastic surgery, dramatic psychologic changes result *only* if there is a corresponding correction of the mutilated self-image.' Much of Dr Maltz's book is then to do with the correction of the mutilated self-image in the mind as a better alternative to plastic surgery of the body.

Cybernetics, from the Greek *kybernetes*, a steersman, is the science of feedback, of automatic control and self-regulation in machinery and bodies. Just as a ballistic missile will guide itself to a distant target once it has been programmed so to do, so, says Maltz, the human mind will direct itself and its vehicle body unerringly towards a target.

One of the most important insights in the book is that the mind first visualizes the desired outcome and that this mental picturing provides the target towards which the whole psycho-physical mechanism is then directed. Even deciding to pick up a cup of tea, for example, brings into play many muscle movements and many estimates of distance and weight. The action of achieving the target (picking up the cup) is achieved by the use of unconscious and delicate neural and muscular feedback loops in the body, all set in motion by the mental visualization of the goal.

In the same sort of way, once a mental picture has been formed of the self, whether of its physical or its mental attributes, so the mind will unerringly work towards the concrete achievement of that image. If I see myself as ugly and unattractive, then, for sure, I shall behave as if I am, and will turn out to be, unattractive and my face and body will, indeed, become less handsome than otherwise might have been expected. The mental target, the ugly self-image, remains even after a plastic surgeon has altered any physical blemishes.

Roberto Assagioli in his book *Psychosynthesis* (Turnstone Press, 1965) says, 'Every image has in itself a motor-drive.' In other words, '... *images and mental pictures tend to produce the physical conditions and the external acts corresponding to them*' (my italics).

Visualization dissected

Visualization is a means of altering the self-concept. Let me explain. In most people, the visual sense is the preferred sense and that is why visualization is the most used way to improve self-concepts, performance and the general quality of our lives.

According to the dictionary, one of the definitions of visualization as a noun is 'a mental picture'. As a verb, the definition is 'to call up a clear visual image'. As you can imagine from this, we spend much of our time visualizing. Some of the effects are bad, some good and some indifferent. In the main, only controlled visualization will have beneficial effects.

Uncontrolled visualizing
Our thoughts affect our bodies and our destinies because thoughts are energy and that energy, small though it is, can be transmuted into material form — thoughts can become facts and not always welcome ones. As Harvey Cox writes in *The Church in the Secular City* (Penguin, 1962):

> Anthropologists who investigate magical beliefs among tribal peoples today report that violating a taboo can cause death and that people who have been killed in effigy by voodoo techniques do in fact die with more than accidental frequency. The reason for this is that a personality system includes organic, social and cultural components. A person whose whole view of himself includes the cultural meanings inherent in a magical society will die if that culture indicates he should.

Such strength of cultural beliefs is no less strong in our own society.

Life-scripts and trips
As we have seen, we all have a mental picture of ourselves, a curious amalgam of what we were as children and as we are as spouses, workers, church-goers or whatever. We should really try to take care that we have control of the picture, otherwise some unwanted aspect of the picture may come true. For instance, Berne and other Transactional Analysts suggest that we all have 'life-scripts' to which we may respond throughout all our lives. Indeed, even the age at which we die may be part of such a script laid down in early childhood. If, for example, I have a parent and a grandparent who both died at the age of 75, that may become part of my life-script and the chances are high that I shall also die at that age. Similarly, if a woman believes on the basis of a life-script perhaps created for her by her parents that she will lose a husband when she reaches the age of 40, then it seems likely that those very thoughts cause her to behave in ways that are likely to make that happen. Janette Rainwater in *You're in Charge* (Turnstone Press, 1979), cites a case of a woman who had such a script and who made herself sexually unavailable at the very time that her husband was thrown into the company of a lonely woman friend. Her self-concept was of a woman who was due for the break-up of her marriage and the cybernetic function of her mind went to work to make it so.

The trouble is that we often find ourselves feeling oddly fulfilled when a script comes true. There seems to be a kind of masochistic joy when we go down with yet another sniffly cold. Perhaps it's because we still need to please mummy or teacher or older sibling or whoever it was that unwittingly set us up for future unhappiness.

Janette Rainwater calls the working out of such scripts, 'trips' and describes what she calls 'self-torture trips' — for instance, that enjoyed by Californians who have fantasies about earthquakes, with some pretty horrific visualizations accompanying them.

We all go on such trips as these, or have scripts in which we visualize ourselves in some situation where disaster may strike. They, too, are all uncontrolled visualizations and should, wherever possible, be brought to full consciousness and replaced with 'good-fortune scripts', as I suggest later. If an earthquake was to strike your home, a visualization of possible escape strategies could be more than useful.

Recollective visualizing

We've all had the experience of getting into an argument with someone, getting the worst of it and re-living the situation in our imagination afterwards. In such visualizing we generally come off best, with a wealth of witty and destructive repartee springing to our lips that didn't occur to us at the time. Such visualizations might seem to us to be useful as rehearsals for future encounters, but the trouble with this is that life does not repeat itself and so really the visualizations can only be means of applying balm to bruised egos. Recollective visualizing is a form of daydream.

Daydreams

A daydreamer is a very different person to a visualizer. The latter exercises thought, judgement and perseverance. Daydreams, on the other hand, are a kind of mental activity in which we indulge as a sort of wish-fulfilment. They are fantasies in which we dream — without much thought or judgement — of making life more exciting and fulfilling. In them our wishes are granted: the girl or boy on the bus smiles at you, the sun shines and you both suddenly discover that you have the day off. Again, daydreams may seem to have some characteristics of rehearsals for real-life situations, but we know they are not.

Such a realization needn't mean putting an end to daydreams, but again, such a natural propensity of the mind is one that can be used more profitably and constructively. For instance, a visualization of how to realistically engineer striking up an acquaintance with the person on the bus is no longer a daydream, but a controlled visualization.

Controlled visualizing

The girl or boy on the bus smiles. What do you do? Get off at the next stop, covered in confusion and cross with yourself or have you prepared for this heavenly moment by some judicious *controlled* visualization?

If you have prepared the ground through imagining just such a scenario and your reaction to it, a happy day may result for both of you. Do you wish to be positive yet relaxed, joyful but not obviously over the top? Then visualize in advance.

Such planning is called by the Japanese, 'looking back from the point of victory', for it is easier to trace the path back from a destination than to discern it from the first step.

Piero Ferrucci summarizes how such a looking back may be put into effect in *What We May Be* (Turnstone Press, 1982):

> ... imagine yourself as already having that [desired] quality in the highest degree of purity and intensity. Allow the image to take shape in detail. See the look in the eyes expressing the quality; the physical posture; the facial expression. (The image may not be very stable in the beginning; it may be fuzzy, or appear and disappear in flashes. Even so, it will exercise a powerful influence on your subconsicous.) Hold this image in your mind for a few moments, encouraging it to increasingly express the quality you have chosen ... Imagine *walking into* this image and becoming one with it — something like putting on new clothes.

Everything that we do, except for innate (unconditional) reflex actions, is born first in the imagination. Lifting a cup to the lips is first run through in the imagination — or rather the end product is first seen in the imagination. Then the cybernetic system takes over — energizing the muscles, estimating and comparing weights and distances, co-ordinating hand and eye — but it was *imagination* that set the ball rolling. It is therefore the imagination that provides the target at which the psycho-cybernetic process aims.

Slimming

As Roberto Assagioli enlightened us earlier, '... images and mental pictures tend to produce the physical conditions and the external acts corresponding to them', so here goes.

Do you need to slim? If so, sit or lie down in a comfortable position. Take a few breaths and relax your body, your mind, your entire being. Then, simply imagine your body as you would like it to be. Imagine your ideal body, strong and young and beautiful, however you wish to see it. Imagine that you are drawing that body to you and that you are merging with it, becoming it. Imagine your body conforming to your newly created, slim body, so that your physical body is actually changing, becoming slimmer and more beautiful.

Focus your mind's eye on any particular area of your body where you want special change, special attention. Create the body you wish in your mind's eye and know that you are on your way to creating it physically.

Say to yourself, as you finish the exercise, 'I am young and slim' or 'My body is becoming younger, slimmer and more beautiful every day.' Then get up, stretch and *feel* younger, slimmer, healthier and more beautiful.

José Silva in *The Silva Mind Control Method* (Souvenir Press, 1978) describes another method by which someone could slim. He recommends the use of all five senses, for while the visual sense is used primarily, we have seen that other senses (the kinaesthetic, for instance) may also be used.

> *Sight*: find a photograph of yourself when you were as thin as you would like to be now.
> *Touch*: imagine, when you are thin again, how smooth your arms and thighs and stomach will feel to your touch.
> *Taste*: imagine the flavors of the foods you will emphasize in your new diet.
> *Smell*: imagine the odor of the foods you will be eating.
> *Hearing*: imagine what those who are important to you will say about your success at losing weight!

Sports performance

Again, the mind and imagination are directed solely at the target to be achieved and this allows the body to use the cybernetic powers it possesses freely. As an example, John Reid, a cricketer from New Zealand, is quoted as saying,

> At the start of my Test career I used to lie in bed and watch the bowlers bowl at me. I could see, say, Abdul Qadir bowling at me and the gaps in his field. I could see him bowling his leg spinner and I'd work it wide of mid-on or his wrong' un and I'd steer it behind point . . . When you're out in the middle, there's an uncanny feeling when a ball you have rehearsed comes along. I knew then I was hyped up and things were going right.
>
> Scyld Berry, *The Observer*, 1988

Herbert Benson in *Your Maximum Mind* (Aquarian Press, 1988) cites a similar instance of a woman tennis player who never quite achieved her potential, always losing just when victory was in sight, who tried visualizing her games in her mind's eye and instantly improved after just one session. Donald Wilson in *Total Mind Power* (Camaro Publishing, 1976) describes the sort of thing she would have done.

> You see yourself watching the tennis ball approach your backhand side.
> As it crosses the net, you see yourself bring your racquet back with its head dropping below your waist.
> You now see your right foot step over and point to the left side of the court.
> You feel the weight of your body shift to your right foot as you make contact with the outside undersurface of the ball.
> Your stroke moves smoothly forward.
> You see your racquet meeting the ball out in front of you, just before it reaches your right hip.
> You see yourself watching the ball intently.
> You can even see it sink into the taut racquet strings, compress, then travel back towards the top of the net as you complete the stroke.
> You feel the head of the racquet move around your body and stop at your right side.
> When the racquet contacts the ball, you visualize the muscles in your forearm.
> The muscles of your wrist and fingers hold the racquet very firmly, and perpendicular to the court surface.

This sort of visualization sets up a positive psycho-cybernetic process. Maltz describes the process succinctly:

> This Creative Mechanism within you is impersonal. It will work automatically and impersonally to achieve goals of success and happiness, or unhappiness and failure, depending upon the goals which you yourself set for it. Present it with 'success goals' and it functions as a 'Success Mechanism'. Present it with negative goals, and it operates just as impersonally, and just as faithfully as a 'Failure Mechanism'.
>
> *Psycho-cybernetics*

Such techniques of controlled visualization owe something to people like Maltz and much to the impact of Zen Buddhism on the West through writers such as D T Suzuki and Eugen Herrigel.

Zen approaches such self-improvement from the other end of the continuum, from its concern with human *spiritual* development.

With the kind of devotion a World Masters Champion or

Wimbledon Singles Champion or any Test player displays, Eugen Herrigel spent six years of his life subjecting himself to the rigours and rewards of learning the art of archery the Zen way. Early on he was greatly concerned with the question that any golfer asks: how to hit the target?

> This prompted me to ask the Master why he had never yet explained to us how to take aim. There must . . . be . . . an approved method of sighting which makes hitting possible.
> 'Of course there is,' answered the Master, 'and you can easily find the required aim yourself. But if you hit the target with nearly every shot you are nothing more than a trick archer who likes to show off . . . the "Great Doctrine" holds this to be sheer devilry . . . It only knows of the goal, which cannot be aimed at technically . . .'
>
> *Zen in the Art of Archery* (Routledge & Kegan Paul, 1953)

Herrigel progressed, until he became a Master himself and reached a state of detachment in archery in which he could say, 'Bow, arrow, goal and ego, all melt into one another, so that I can no longer separate them.'

This reminds me of the story, recounted by Chuang Tzu, of Khing, a master furniture-maker. He produced a piece so perfect that his Prince asked him his secret.

> 'There's no secret,' was his reply, 'I quieted my mind, and avoided having it disturbed by trifles. I forgot all thought of being famous, forgot about my body, forgot all about you, your Highness, waiting for your furniture. *I emptied my mind of everything but the vision of the furniture.* After that I went into the forest and searched for the right tree. At last, inside one tree, I could see the furniture waiting to be made. Then I set to work, and here you see the result.' (My italics.)

Clearly, the better your powers of concentration, the more likely you are to succeed in the endeavour. Later, I shall outline some ways in which concentration may be improved.

Chuang Tzu, Herrigel and his Japanese masters all would say of John Reid that he could never become a Master, for he was merely concerned with success and failure and was thus living for mere subsidiary aims. Nevertheless, it is through the achievement of such subsidiary aims that many people find themselves embarking on a path towards greater, more transcendental targets, indeed, the Ultimate, the Great Doctrine. This is, in fact, what Herrigel himself did.

The footballer who passes to a team-mate sees in his mind's eye, the ball travelling towards his colleague a split second before his foot kicks it. His body does the rest, while his imagination then sets about picturing the likely course of subsequent events and sends his body off in the appropriate direction. So, too, with the swordsman who as Herrigel says, '. . . sees and feels what is going to happen, and at the same moment he has already avoided its effect without there being "a hair's breadth" between perceiving and avoiding.'

Compare this with what happens to an experienced footballer — a hard-pressed goalkeeper, for instance. He, too, in his imagination has seen the ball on its way to the back of the net and his body responds accordingly. No long periods of ratiocination are possible, yet the power of his imagination has set in motion an incredibly complicated cybernetic train of bodily reactions in the 'hair's breadth' between perceiving the ball at the opponent's foot and his own response.

Imagination, then, is the means by which you can set your targets. In the main, these are everyday situations, but how does this model stand up to situations that are unusual?

Emergencies

Regarding the unusual, let us take the example of a sudden emergency. A car on the other carriageway of a motorway loses control and crosses the central reservation. You are likely to be killed. Your imagination sees the impending crash, transmits a goal to the cybernetic system and you avoid the oncoming car. Unfortunately, your imagination has not been able in the time to also picture the effect this will have on the traffic that shares your carriageway, nor the likely reactions of the other drivers. You are seriously injured.

You could have prepared yourself, however, for this horrendous happening in the same way that John Reid prepared himself for the wiles of Abdul Qadir: by preparing for it mentally, much as an anxious salesman will go through the likely outcome of a meeting with a prospective customer, covering all the possible eventualities in his imagination. You can prepare a good-fortune script. As you drive, imagine what would happen if that approaching lorry was suddenly to swerve towards you. Visualize yourself calmly surveying the verge on your side. Is it clear and wide, does it give you room to avoid the lorry? Visualize yourself turning onto it safely and calmly. Or, how about the other carriageway? Is it clear for you to aim to pass the lorry on that side? If so, visualize yourself doing that, calmly and effectively. It is possible that such an exercise can save your life.

Successful visualization

Controlled visualization is something that has to be worked at, but what is needed?

First, relaxation. I shall go into this in more detail later, but for the moment, it is enough to remember that John Reid prepared himself for the rigours of the cricket field while lying in bed. The exercises described in this chapter indicate the need for such relaxation as a prerequisite for successful visualization. As you have no doubt found, anxious over-concentration on a goal of any kind is likely to be counterproductive and so you will have learned that there is a state of relaxed balance that is likely to lead to success. Most of us, when we achieve that state of relaxed confidence, do so in a split second that embraces the action and the hit and dismiss it as a halo effect of the success, but this relaxed confident balance can be learned. Darts masters apparently do it through the effects of drinking large amounts of lager, emulating, perhaps, certain Taoist poets, but most of us find that we have to use inner aids.

We can get a hint of how to turn unprofitable uncontrolled visualizing into its opposite if we note the kind of mental state we are in when we find ourselves daydreaming. We will find, if we observe ourselves, that we are very often in an abstracted state, as though we've taken five minutes off from the real world. If we see ourselves in a mirror, we see we have a faraway look, are generally still and relaxed, our bodies comfortable. Our eyes will be moving as they follow the events that are being unfolded before our mental eyes. Perhaps we frown or smile, but generally we are happy and tranquil as we sit and create our perfect world. As I shall show later, the first step towards controlled visualization is being able to get into that happy relaxed state.

At its most effective, successful controlled visualization comes about by means of a relaxed approach and by utilizing the will, emotions and 'affirming', that is, verbal suggestion.

Will

In relation to visualization, this does not mean beetle-browed, jaw-jutting, sweating effort, which would, in fact, just get in the way, but perseverance.

Assagioli stresses the need for a strengthening of the underlying will and he describes a visualization exercise to do just this. In it he recommends the visualization of what he believes to be symbols of the will, such as a flaming torch, fire, a lance, a sceptre, a crown, a man at the helm of a boat or the conductor of an orchestra. Visualizing oneself merging with such symbols, he believes, will bring about the corresponding characteristic.

Emotion

Every bit as important is the use of the emotions. It is, after all, the emotions that provide much of the motivational power in everyday living. So, in the words of Rebecca Clark in *Macro-Mind Power* (A Thomas, 1980), 'Let all the feelings you expect to experience upon attainment of your desire flow forth. Feel the joy it will bring you. Feel the meaning your desire will bring into your life . . .'

Assagioli's symbols of the will clearly aim at recruiting the emotions and, indeed, he goes further and suggests the use of auditory symbolism as well, such as the playing of a record of Wagner's 'Siegfried's Motive'.

Affirming

The auditory sense is, in most people, second only to the visual. It is therefore, as I've shown, important in changing one's self-concept. The mother who repeatedly tells her little boy that he is naughty, for example, will reap what she sows — or her boy will.

It was a Frenchman, Emile Coué, who reminded the modern world of the power of the word over the body and one's circumstances. In doing so, he was merely saying what every shaman, every witchdoctor and every exponent of voodoo has known since the dawn of human history. For example, he tells the story of the sick nun who heard her doctor say carelessly of her, 'She won't outlive April.' In spite of getting better for a while, when April came along, her appetite disappeared and by the end of April she was dead. This story could have come straight from Haiti.

Words are powerful. What significant others say of us will translate into reality. Equally, what we affirm as true of ourselves — good or bad — will likewise come true.

Coué studied psychology and hypnosis and realized that there was no need always to go to a doctor or a hypnotist for a cure — that power lay within everyone. People can cure *themselves* of many of their illnesses.

He said to his patients, 'Say every morning and evening, "Every day in every way, I am getting better and better".' He also added, 'Don't think what you are saying; say it as you do the litany in church.' In other words he recommended the blanking out of the critical mind — a point I shall return to.

Another of his principles was that there should be no negatives, no naming of the illness, no future tenses. For example, the patient should say, 'My back is easier,' and not, 'My back will get easier,' or 'My back is not hurting so much.'

Fundamentally, he believed that there is an important psychological truth, which has been confirmed by later workers such as Assagioli, which is that if will and imagination are in conflict, the imagination wins.

This power of auto-suggestion is an important accompaniment to the tool of visualization. Baudoin wrote a classical treatise on the subject of suggestion and divided it into three categories: hetero-suggestion (suggestion by others, such as the careless doctor mentioned above and by hypnotists in general), and two forms of auto-suggestion, which he called 'spontaneous suggestion' and 'reflective suggestion' (corresponding to my uncontrolled and controlled visualization). Nowadays, when auto-suggestion is employed by an individual in his or her own treatment, it is no longer called auto-suggestion, but affirming — a very much more positive term.

Affirming is reflective suggestion, and is distinguished from spontaneous suggestion in that the latter takes place without any volition on the part of the person. Spontaneous suggestion is seen in those messages our mind is constantly passing to our bodies in that state of unmindfulness we often find ourselves in, such as 'I feel terrible today,' or 'I suffer really badly from colds every winter.' Tell such things to yourself often enough and your wish will indeed come true.

Summary

The use of the term visualization gives an impression of directed purposiveness and this is certainly a characteristic of the practice, a practice which is in use from the training of golfers and salesmen to the practice of meditation by roshis and lamas.

It sounds simple. The practice demands first that you use your imagination to create a clear image of something wished for. Second, it is necessary to focus on the idea or picture regularly by use of the will, giving it positive emotional energy and affirmation until it becomes an actuality. Once it has become a reality, you spontaneously achieve what some have called a 'flow state' of effortless achievement or what Maslow has described as a peak experience.

Maltz's book is often quoted as a breakthrough in helping people to take more control of their personal destinies, but it remains just that — a book that is to do with personal achievement, success and fulfilment. In all his discussion of the self-concept, there is no mention of anything beyond, no discussion of such a concept as the superconscious, the collective unconscious, archetypes, and so on. However, this may be a strength of his book for people who are beginning to wake up to the undoubted fact that they can do something about their destinies. For his book is, in fact, more along the lines of books such as *How to Win Friends and Influence People*, Dale Carnegie's famous best-seller that did so much to open people's eyes to the possibility and rewards of self-improvement. Such books are rather typical products of the New World, with its belief in the material possibilities open to all men (and some women) regardless of creed and (sometimes) colour. Although there were moral overtones of the kind, 'Mommy'll give you a cookie, but be sure now to be a good child and love your mommy', improvement in the spiritual sense — beyond getting God on your side — was seen as the province of the professional religious and not something to be attempted by the layman or woman — feet were to be kept firmly on the ladder of material success. Nevertheless, such books sowed seeds for people to nurture.

We can, however, use the power of our imaginations to alter our behaviour and to create a better world for ourselves and others.

I shall leave until later deeper questions of thought energy becoming so concentrated that concrete objects are created — as is claimed, for instance, by observers of Tibetan practices. For the moment, we limit ourselves to asserting that imagination can change us and that by changing ourselves we can change our environment.

Imagination is a capacity that all humans have (we do not know if higher animals have it), but it is a capacity that, like so many others we possess, we seriously underuse and misuse. Our imaginations, however, are fundamental to the shaping of our everyday lives and, consequently, our life-histories.

In the next chapter I shall begin to examine the implications of this statement in the field of health.

2.
To Heal Ourselves

All our bodily systems work towards the maintenance of dynamic balance and disease is an imbalance in one or more of our systems. Our bodies are always curing themselves and will continue to do so as long as we don't block the cure. In this chapter I shall concentrate on medical procedures that use visualization as part (or the whole) of the process of cure.

Modern medicine tends to forget the fact that the body can cure itself. It is too technological in its outlook, preferring to tell people that allopathy is the only way of maintaining balance, that individuals are not able to take control of their own destinies, and that only fully-qualified medical professionals can help. Yet, as Penny Brohn says in *The Bristol Programme* (Century, 1987), 'The most famous and widely used way of using the mind to enhance tolerance of, and recovery from, heavy medical procedure is to visualize the process as having a healing and therapeutic effect.'

There are alternatives, too, and, as writers like Andrew Stanway point out, more and more doctors are beginning to help patients to use their minds in alleviating disease. Recommended methods include hypnosis, meditation, relaxation procedures, biofeedback, yoga and visualization. Hypnosis, dream therapy and visualization have been used since ancient times, for the mind has long been recognized as a vital component in curing disease.

In healing ourselves, it is important that we take a correct view of the curative powers possessed by the body. Meir Schneider, for instance, in *Self Healing* (Routledge, 1987), says 'Our power of healing exists in every muscle of our bodies, in every brain cell, every nerve fibre, every blood vessel,' and this is a view shared by most of the workers I shall introduce in this chapter. Visualizing such agents will affect cure.

Thought as energy

In considering the power of mind over body and its diseases, it is, as I pointed out in the previous chapter, a fundamental belief among therapists from Coué to Assagioli that cell structure can be changed by the power of thought. We shall see this to be so in this chapter when we look at self-healing and Autogenic Training and in a later chapter that deals with psychic healing and group healing. Thought is a form of subtle energy, of the same nature as its gross material forms. As Penny Brohn says, 'You may need to keep reminding yourself that thoughts and feelings in your mind transmit themselves into physical bio-chemical changes in the body . . .'

There is emphatic theoretical support for this mind/body unity in the words of David Bohm in *Unfolding Meaning* (Ark, 1987). In the book, he makes a direct connection between body and mind, highlighting his belief that the separation we are accustomed to make between the two may not exist: 'The aspect of soma cannot be divided from the aspect of significance. Whatever meanings there may be "in our minds", these are, as we have seen, inseparable from the totality of our somatic structures and therefore from what we *are*. So what we are depends crucially on the total set of meanings that operate "within us".'

If we are able to alter a 'set of meaning' within us, we may thus, it would seem to follow, alter our soma, our body. In other words, if we can control our thoughts about our bodies, we can control the physical state of our bodies and, indeed, complex changes seem to be possible through the use of the mind (see below). However, before I look at the treatment of ailments, I shall consider the maintenance of everyday health.

General health

Reported cures of disease using visualization

Relief of tension headaches (1)
Alleviating allergies (1)
Control of heart arythmias (1)
Control of migraine headaches (1)
Decrease of epileptic seizures (1)
Change of concentration of stomach acid in ulcers (1)
Controlling acne and other skin disorders (1)

Control of insomnia and other sleep disturbances (1)
Control of blood pressure (1)
Obesity (1)
Improving eyesight (1) (2)
Blindness (2)
Control of cancers and tumours (4)
Decreasing possibility of heart attack (1)
Cure of addictions: smoking, alcohol and drugs (Many)
AIDS (Autogenic Training)
Furunculosis (5)
Prostate conditions (3)
Arthritis (2) (3)
Warts (1) (3)
Sugar diabetes (1) (3)
Removal of calcified tissue (3)
Frozen shoulder (3)
Removal of polyps (3)
Polio (2)
Back problems (2)
Multiple sclerosis (2)
Anaemia (2)
Hernia (2)

Key
1 = Donald Wilson, *Total Mind Power* (Camaro, 1976) 2 = Meir Schneider, *Self Healing* (Routledge, 1987) 3 = EH Shattock, *A Manual of Self-Healing* (Turnstone Press, 1982) 4 = Penny Brohn, *The Bristol Programme* (Century, 1987) 5 = KAS Sage, *Live to be 100* (WH Allen, 1975)

Peripheral medical advantages using visualization (according to Donald Wilson)

Prevention of muscle spasms
Controlling skin temperature
Increased command over bowel functions
Influence on galvanic skin response
Decreasing the body's response to stress
Contraction and dilation of blood vessels

I have shown previously, and shall continue to do so throughout this book, that what we believe to be facts about ourselves have strange ways of being confirmed in practice.

We may tend to ignore minor ailments or, if elderly, shrug them off as inevitable accompaniments to growing old and *see* ourselves at this time of life as nearing death. However, it has often been suggested that the optimum life span of a human being ought to be at least 120 years and there are examples of many who have lived to that age and beyond. Almost all authorities agree that the way to maintain health in old age — indeed, at any age — is to remain physically and mentally alert.

Such alertness, of course, is the natural reflection of a positive self-image. In turn, part of a positive self-image is the ability to allow the body's natural healing processes to occur, to accept the fact that these processes include rest (that's what illness is often telling us to do) and to try to sort out what emotional problems may be causing any discomfort. Above all, it is wise to picture yourself as strong and well and as having overcome the problems.

At the basic level, we saw how visualizing a successful tennis stroke brought about dramatic improvements in performance. Similarly, boosting a feeling of confidence about an exam, seeing ourselves succeeding and remembering past feelings of success can also have a marked effect upon the outcome. *How* this happens is due to the powerful effect of thought energy on the physical world through visualization.

So, as regards maintaining health and being aware of possible problems, it is a good idea to carry out a stock-check of your health from time to time. You can of course ask your doctor, have body scans, general medical check-ups — these are sensible — but, equally sensible is to be aware of the strong possibility that your body — its each and every cell — also has an awareness of its general state. Many people ignore this possibility and are less healthy for it. There is no reason why a general visualized check-up might not be a daily or weekly procedure, providing an awareness of problems perhaps before they have the chance to develop.

There are a variety of ways of doing this. Joel Levey describes one such in *The Fine Arts of Relaxation, Concentration and Meditation* (Wisdom Publications, 1987) when he advises carrying out a mental bodyscan. He recommends deep relaxation, followed by marking on a sketched outline of the human body the intensity of sensations in any region of the body on a scale of -5 to $+5$ — 0 being neutral, -5 extreme discomfort and $+5$ extreme pleasure. He suggests one doodles in a representation of the *feelings* of tingling, vibration, density, numbness, and so on. He advises against drawing conceptualized anatomical structures, such as bones or organs, etc, but instead, suggests that you graphically represent feelings in any region of the body in which they occur.

Another method — less objective and more fun — is to lie relaxed upon waking and take a stroll around your body, visualizing the state of the head, for instance, and speaking to the inner managers in charge of the brain, the lungs, the stomach and so on, generally acting as an efficient general manager of your entire body. In this game, too, awareness of subliminal clues from the body can also be developed.

Causes of disease

Quite obviously, some causes of disease are, or appear to be, completely somatic. Extreme proponents of the psychosomatic school, however, would tend to say that *all* disease is mind-born. If we were to go along with Freud in his *Psychopathology of Everyday Life*, even a broken leg might be seen to be the product of the mind. Such a consideration might lead one to suggest that the fracture enables the sufferer to avoid some feared situation.

Guiding every personality is a dim mental picture of the individual and it is in conforming to this dim visualization that we find ourselves behaving as we do. It is clear, therefore, that this self-concept may be the cause of inappropriate and/or false beliefs about one's health. Shakti Gawain, for instance, says in *Creative Visualization* (Whatever Publishing, 1978), 'If the mind's belief system (on a conscious or unconscious level) says that it is appropriate or inevitable to get sick in a certain situation, it will signal the body accordingly and the body will obligingly manifest symptoms of illness; it will in fact become ill.' The beliefs that affect the self-image, and which are therefore the foundations of illness have no clear boundaries, but for the sake of clarity may be categorized under three headings: familial, social and emotional.

- **Familial**

  A person who models him or herself on his parents who have suffered in the past from a disease may adopt a parent's state of health as appropriate to themselves. We have met with this idea already when we looked at the idea of life scripts (see page 17).

  A belief that illness can arise from exposure to the illness of another person (even though contagion may not be a factor) can

result in that person becoming ill. Indeed, it is not uncommon for such a person to visualize bacteria floating in the air towards them.

- **Social**
  These causes can include a need to avoid certain situations in which a negative experience gave rise to a negative self-image — 'I'm no good at school' leading to inexplicable illnesses in term-time, for instance. Parents and teachers should be aware of this and be aware, too, that they may visualize a child in their care in ways that cause them to exhibit behaviour towards the child that will cause such illness.

- **Emotional**
  Much research has shown that emotions such as anger, fear, grief and worry can alter the physical body. Such alterations may range from permanent facial expressions to cancerous growths. We have no difficulty in accepting the first of these, so why do we have difficulty with the second?

  We seldom use our awareness of these emotions rationally or constructively, tending to label them as 'negative' emotions because we have been conditioned to think that we must always be happy (as if that were possible), therefore discounting and ignoring them as far as possible. We are not accustomed to trusting our feelings and the result is that we fail to acknowledge them, much less act upon them. Such repressed emotions nevertheless form a part of our self-image and thus may have a direct effect upon the health of our bodies, leading in some cases to stress, hypertension and severe dysfunctions such as cancer and severe depression of the immune system (see below).

The effects of emotion on health

Chronic tension	arteriosclerosis, high blood pressure, thrombosis, coronaries, migraine, ulcers
Resentment	jaundice, hepatitis, liver problems, cancer, tumours, arthritis, rheumatism, boils, abcesses, sinusitis, ulcers, throat infections
Anxiety	asthma, chest problems, bladder problems, digestive disorders, shingles, cataracts

Grief	acute depression, cancer, heart ailments, throat problems
Guilt	acute depression, alcoholism, stroke, venereal disease, prostate problems, menstrual or menopausal problems, warts, skin problems

From Samarpan, *The Feeling Good Book* (Turnstone Press, 1983).

Fear in itself need not be destructive to health, though. Indeed, it can improve and maintain health by giving advance warning of threats to one's well-being. In emergencies, of course, the so-called 'negative' emotions can mobilize our defences. Anger, in particular, can be transformed into much positive energy.

As I said, familial, social and emotional causes of ill-health overlap. I have paid most attention to the emotional causes, for we have seen, and shall see again, that emotions are powerful in reinforcing visualizations in the cure of disease.

Controlling pain

The body sends out many warning signals, the most effective and unpleasant of these being pain and fever. Pain, though unpleasant, is necessary to our health. Those few people who are born without the capacity to experience pain suffer terrible injuries and often do not survive infancy as a result.

It is now generally widely agreed that much suffering from pain is made worse by inappropriate mental interpretation and response to the situation. Emotions such as fear, helplessness, frustration, anger, guilt and blame — all mind-born — often serve to intensify the pain and constrict the body and mind so as to cut off part of oneself from natural self-healing. Rational behaviour, on the other hand, should lead to an investigation of the cause of the pain, to taking steps to cure the cause and finally to dealing with the pain itself.

The ability to control pain has a long history. Whereas now we use anaesthetics, in the past trance-like states were induced by means of suggestion by early physicians to distract sufferers from the fact of their pain. Perhaps this is a safer method, if reports of full consciousness but the inability to say so under anaesthetic are to be believed.

Having received the warning signal, it is thus possible to alleviate the pain while waiting for medication or while taking the pills.

Traditionally, meditative visualization has often been used so as to *mask* pain. One of the simplest modern methods, described by Donald Wilson in *Total Mind Power*, involves deep relaxation, followed by the visualization of a simple on/off switch in the strongly pictured bundle of nerves leading from the affected part to the central nervous system.

Though such masking techniques can be effective, the latest emphasis is on applying the mind to *working with* pain and directly investigating and understanding it. The first step to mastering pain in this way is in fact to be open to it, to almost welcome it, to consciously investigate it and allow it to change, to *see* it flowing and floating freely in the body. When this is possible, pain is no longer related to as the enemy or as an emergency and so the sufferer is better able to accept it, even eventually to love the part that is in pain. Being open to pain in this way enables the sufferer to learn to recognize patterns of mind that intensify suffering and those that bring greater harmony and lessen the pain.

Careful examination of the field of sensation we label 'pain' leads us to the discovery that it is not an unchanging entity. It is a dynamic field of sensations and feelings that can change with each minute and state of mind.

One way to investigate pain is to visualize it in some form: perhaps to 'see' it as a red mass, to 'watch' it expanding and contracting and to enter fully into its life. It is sometimes possible to visualize it slowly shrinking and finally disappearing. Whether or not this happens, pain can become an even more positive aid to health and equanimity. There have been 12 studies into the effects of such meditative techniques on the alleviation of pain. As Joel Levey reports in *The Fine Arts of Relaxation, Concentration and Meditation*, all confirmed their usefulness.

Self-healing

Normally, the body works to cure itself, as when lesions close — in itself a minor miracle, surely. Normally, too, the body works to maintain homeostasis, which can be seen very clearly in the way it maintains body temperature. When the body is ill, however, its recuperative powers are out of balance. Curing a disease is thus a matter of regaining this balance through drugs or surgery or through more traditional methods.

Consider Chinese medicine, particularly, but not solely, the art of acupuncture. The Chinese, especially Taoists, see the body as reflecting the cosmos in that it is also maintained in a state of dynamic balance between negative and positive tendencies — *yin* and *yang*.

Energy flows, they believe, through channels in the body (as yet undiscovered to the senses) and good health is the maintenance of a balance of this energy. Acupuncture is a means by which the positive and negative forces flowing in those channels may be controlled in ways that help the body to regain its lost balance. It is interesting that Chinese self-massage advises visualization of those channels and of the energy flow within them. Similarly, in physical exercises (such as the slow motion dances of *T'ai Chi Ch'uan* so often seen being performed *en masse* in Chinese cities and towns) the advice is the same — visualize the flow of *ch'i*.

Allopathic medicine, with which Westerners are more familiar, has as its basis the same aim of redressing imbalance. Unfortunately, however, few patients are yet encouraged to take part in their own cure by means of visualization.

Some examples of visualization in the cure of disease

As we have begun to see, all visualization, if it is to be effective, requires that a period of deep relaxation be undergone as a preliminary stage. The following examples take that as read.

Blindness
Meir Schneider, born blind, had a self-taught therapist who cured him and who, in the early stages, '. . . told me to imagine something in motion . . . I found it difficult to visualize something I'd never seen. He also instructed me to visualize total blackness. I had a hard time with that, too.'

Lowering blood pressure
Visualize the heart as a pump and then visualize blood vessels. At first, see the latter as very narrow and the pump as working very hard — a pressure gauge registering a high reading. Then direct the mind to relax the blood vessels and visualize them as opening up. See the pump as slowing, and the pressure gauge as going down. As much detail as possible should be visualized: 'Whether or not the concepts are medically correct is not relevant. The important thing is that your mind is directed towards accomplishing the end result you want. If

you are under medical treatment for the condition, get as much information about your condition as possible from your doctor and add it to the (visualization), so your mind and his treatment can work together.' (Donald Wilson, *Total Mind Power*)

Arthritis

José Silva in his book *The Silva Mind Control Method* gives an example of the sort of visualizing that can be done by someone suffering from arthritis. He recommends that a fine sieve be visualized, filtering impurities from the blood, followed by the visualization of a delicate brush that sweeps away the white powder (calcium) '. . . that can be seen psychically . . .'

Controlling a cancerous tumour

Visualize the tumour with a nerve supplying it with what it needs that can be switched off, so that when this is done the tumour shrivels.

Alternatively, visualize an antibody machine in your body. Activate this, and direct the antibodies to fight the tumour cells.

A method made famous by the Simontons is to see the white cells as sharks eating up a cauliflower — the tumour.

Penny Brohn gives a number of examples in her book *The Bristol Programme* of the sort of visualizations she has recommended or that patients devised for themselves. For example, '. . . one patient used to tell me she used to picture the chemotherapy as a champagne of white light that smothered out all traces of unwanted cells'. Other examples include picturing the cancer cells as ice cubes on a plate that is put in the full glare of sunshine in a beautiful garden, visualizing '. . . beautiful, clean white goats . . . gentle and benign creatures . . quick on their feet, agile and fast moving . . . moving throughout the body, eating up all the rubbish' and a golden vacuum cleaner buzzing all round the body, sucking up all the dirt and rubbish and unwanted debris from every possible nook and cranny, the person using this last image saying, 'Oh, I don't keep it anywhere, I leave it running all the time, so I actually have to go and find it before I begin.'

When visualizing cancer-cures, Penny Brohn advises, 'Don't leave the job half-finished. Each time you embark on a session of visualization, always end it with the cancer completely overcome and swept away . . . finish up with a mental picture of being clear and free of disease . . . [it is] important for the body for us to conceptualize the possibility of perfection.' This concept crops up continually. If the internal model is to be effective, it must be consistent, that is, no negative input should be allowed if at all possible. Difficult though this may be in the face of painful fact, it is an ideal to be aimed at. The end result must always be visualized in positive and glowing pictures, ones in which the emotions are also involved.

Emotional programming

Maxwell Maltz wrote in *Psycho-cybernetics*, 'We do know this much: mental attitudes can influence the body's healing mechanism.' The AIDS victim *imagines* himself dying, *sees* this uninterruptedly and has a heavy emotional investment of energy in it. In healing, however, the opposite must become the case. The sufferer must be led to *see* himself as able to live, to concentrate on this throughout the time given to the healing programme and thus become increasingly emotionally positive towards the programme.

Silva suggests that there is a three-pronged curative process in emotional re-programming methods. This will be apparent in Autogenic Training, which I consider below. The three prongs are:

- *imagination*: the sufferer imagines that he or she *is* in the desired state of health.
- *concentration*: the sufferer *wants* this state uninterruptedly.
- *emotion*: the sufferer *feels* in imagination how it is to be in the desired state.

Mindfulness

A great deal of our waking life is spent in a trance-like state. This means that we are open to an immense amount of influences from outside. A typical instance of this may be seen in any supermarket in the way in which we shop. Much of the time we are quite clearly in a trance, responding not to our own considered judgements in making purchases, but to shop layout, colours and TV advertisements, which we also view in a state of trance. It is almost mass hypnosis and it is well known that the layout of supermarkets is designed to profit from this lack of mindfulness.

We have a similar 'unawareness' of the state of our bodies. Only very noticeable symptoms drag us from the usual trance — hideous headaches, grumbling appendices, sore tendons, angina. This unawareness leads us to wear ourselves out day by day in unwanted stress and other results of the repression of the signals our bodies give us until the day comes when we meet a crisis of pain or illness or emotional problem.

As will be stressed in Chapter 6, a necessary habit to acquire if a person wishes to take more control of his or her own life, including that person's health, is that of mindfulness. In the case of health, mindfulness means to become much more aware of the signals that the body is sending out, as well as being aware of the vision we have of ourselves, that is, what it is we are visualizing in relation to the ever-changing states of our body. On the other hand, knowledge of the effects of trance can be helpful in self-healing. Since this trance state affects behaviour and the self-concept in important ways, it can be consciously used, and used in ways that need not be negative in its effects. It can be used positively through visualization and deep relaxation places the subject in a state approaching that of trance. An example of this approach is provided by KAS Sage in *Live to be 100*, where he describes a method of using a form of auto-suggestion — mainly affirmatory — in the small hours when it could be employed on a drowsy mind. He claims to have cured himself of chronic furunculosis (a disease that causes boils to appear) by these means and describes a form of visualization. However, most of his method relies upon the constant repetition of healing phrases.

This latter aspect of Sage's approach seems to be directly descended from the work of the pharmacist Emile Coué, best immortalized, as we saw earlier, in his own recommended words: 'Every day in every way I am getting better and better.' The disadvantage of such methods of repetition is that the imagination gets in the way — bare repetition tending to get the imagination busy in perversely picturing the opposite of what is being willed. As Coué himself said, 'When the will and the imagination are in conflict, the imagination invariably wins the day', and it is this that Maltz emphasized when he wrote in *Psychocybernetics*, 'We act, or fail to act, not because of "will", as is so commonly believed, but because of imagination.' One of the ways in which visualization is found to be successful is in its employment of the imagination in harness with the will, for example in the notoriously difficult business of giving up smoking.

Self-hypnosis

I discuss hypnotism more fully in Chapter 4, but at this point it is worth taking a brief look at it as a technique that can be applied by the patient to himself. Sage, for example, was half-asleep and most of the examples I have cited so far rely on the subject being placed or placing him or herself in a state of deep relaxation. This may be achieved by having the subject imagine a peaceful, perhaps nostalgically favourite scene or floating peacefully in a balloon above the tranquil Earth (for methods of inducing deep relaxation, see Chapter 6).

This approach is used on the growing number of tapes, both audio and video, commercially available that can be used by people keen to effect self-cure. That they are effective, I can personally attest to, having given up a lifetime of 40-a-day smoking within a couple of weeks when using one. This is the sort of thing that I found on my tape.

After having achieved a state of deep, tranquil relaxation by being asked to visualize myself in a peaceful country scene, with blue skies and birds singing, without a care in the world, gently dozing off and being spoken to by this friendly, positive, confident voice, I was recommended to visualize my lungs when they were pink and healthy, as when I was a child. I was to see them expanding and contracting efficiently and see myself running free in a field like the child I once was. I was then to desire to get back to that situation. Then I had to visualize my lungs as they *now* were, black and labouring, choked with carbon and sticky tar and had to see myself running in the same field, but soon out of breath and needing to lie down to recover. I was then persuaded to decide in my semi-trance-like state to change my lungs and visualize myself as feeling joyous at having given up and in situations in which I was turning down proferred cigarettes. I pictured special blood cells circulating in my lungs, attacking and dissolving the black tar. Finally, I saw myself as having completely given up the habit, noting how much easier my breathing was, how much more I appreciated food and aromas, walking up a steep hill effortlessly. This programme was repeated daily for a week, and then decreased as it took effect.

Similar tapes are available for a range of addictions and allergies, such as obesity and stress, and for generally improved healing.

Autogenic Training

Autogenic Training is a form of self-hypnosis that consists of practising, two or three times a day, a short set of mental exercises that turn off the stressful 'fight or flight' mechanism in the body and turn on its capacity for deep relaxation.

Lying down with eyes closed the patient affirms and visualizes:

- I'm calm, I'm at peace
- my right arm is heavy

- my right arm is warm
- my pulse is calm and strong
- my breath is peaceful and regular, it breathes me
- my solar plexus is warm
- my forehead is pleasantly cool.

Such a relaxation method is being used in the treatment of AIDS and is followed by an 'intentional formula' designed to counteract symptoms. Autogenic Training is seen as part of a holistic programme that might also include advice on nutrition, exercise and the use of mineral supplements and vitamins. In addition, suggestions may be made about psychotherapy, meditation, yoga, biofeedback, homoeopathy, acupuncture, art, music and dance.

The rationale is familiar. If a sufferer is told that death is likely within 12 months, then death will follow within that time. Tell him that he will survive, that he has inner resources to fight the illness, and the chances are that he will survive. In other words, the concept of the sufferer as a dying man or woman is replaced by an image of a living, energetic, positively-motivated person.

Direct visualization by the sufferer of himself as a survivor of terror can help. The efforts of the medics and, more importantly, of the sufferer him or herself has this effect of revising the self-image. An experimental session in 1985 with five patients at St Stephen's Hospital involved seven two-hour sessions. At the end, as Anne Gati reports in *The Guardian*, 1 March 1988, '. . . they were actually believing they could live, that they could go on living and that they didn't just have to lie back and wait for the 13 months to be up'. The therapist, Dr Kai Kermani, a GP from Essex, England, believes '. . . that the most valuable contribution we can make as carers is to give our patients hope and confidence in their fight, not only for survival, but for a fuller, richer, life. If you destroy hope, you destroy their chance of survival.'

The article goes on to describe how a patient died within a few days of his doctor greeting him with the words 'I see your 20 months is almost up', 20 months being the average survival period for his particular illness. In this case, the patient's will was undermined, his self-concept as a survivor reversed and he died, just like Coué's nun did.

Think-see

I shall turn now to the work of a lone pioneer in the field of self-cure, an original thinker whose work demands more notice than it in fact receives. As might be expected, the method is quirky, but well within the parameters we see being set in other approaches.

EH Shattock comes from an unlikely background for a healer, rising as he did to be an Admiral in the Royal Navy, a hard-headed enough position. Untypically for a man in that situation he became interested in Buddhism, entered a Burmese monastery and there practised the mindfulness exercises in which Theravada Buddhism excels. He wrote a book, which he called *An Experiment in Mindfulness* (Rider, 1958).

It is interesting that during his stay in the monastery he found that a method of dealing with the pain and discomfort he experienced in the early stages of his mindfulness meditations was to direct mental energy towards it. Stemming further from his mindfulness experiments, in a way that I am not sure he has ever made clear, he developed a method of self-healing that, while idiosyncratic and quite amusingly revealing about his naval training, illustrates the practical value of visualization and affirmation techniques in looking after one's own health. As a result, he wrote a further book — *A Manual of Self-Healing* (Turnstone Press, 1982).

In it he starts from the premise that the entire body is a 'totality of consciousness', made up from the individual consciousness of the atoms and cells that make up the body. He calls them 'little minds' and considers that each of them is amenable to orders from the autonomic mind, a 'subsidiary of the conscious mind' (that part of the subconscious that controls basic life actions). As I have suggested before, it does not seem far-fetched to attribute some form of rudimentary awareness to individual cells: after all, some life force animates the lowliest of independent life forms (if any life form can be said to be truly independent). Andrew Stanway, for example, in *Alternative Medicine* (Pelican, 1979) describes Lakhowski's theory that every living cell possesses a fundamental energy; that when the cell malfunctions, its energy field changes and that this change can be detected. Shattock, however, was apparently not aware of this kind of research. He acknowledges instead a debt to Coué, but uses his method, as he says, '. . . with a more precise expression'. Apart from this, it seems that Shattock was something of an original thinker, ploughing a lonely furrow.

He uses both visualization and affirmation in *A Manual of Self-Healing*. Visualization he calls 'Mind-Picturing' or 'Think-see' and tries to make his mind-pictures conform to reality as accurately as possible. For instance, when he concentrates on his prostate gland, he has an accurate picture of the gland to work on. Having prepared the ground in this way, he then proceeds to affirm and give the agents precise instructions, for example, 'Think-speak "Attention phagocyte cells . . . clear away harmful calcified tissue"', while picturing the process as clearly as he is able: 'Think-see: see the white cells engulfing bits of the calcified tissue, i.e. little bits of bone-like substance, and carrying them away.'

As we saw previously, most healing visualizers believe that precise representation of the affected parts and curative agents is not necessary for healing. Of course, there is every reason to enlist the aid of your doctor in getting a picture of the disease and its physical manifestations, but precise picturing is not vital. What is important, however, is that the mind is directed to achieving the desired result in ways in which vivid visualization is possible. Indeed, Shattock himself admits that precise picturing may have been the cause of problems that he encountered. For instance, he says that the contracting of all the arteries supplying blood to the affected part '. . . resulted in a severe infection of that organ, which I had, so to speak, to go to "action stations" to put right.' Nevertheless, by using these methods, in which it must be admitted he tends to issue instructions to his body cells as though addressing the quarterdeck, he cured himself of a prostate condition and an arthritic hip.

His writings give a very clear illustration of a disciplined mind using visualization in curing disease and in the treatment of wounds. It is worth emphasizing at this point that his Buddhist mind-training exercises led him to hold the firm belief that the mind has unrecognized powers and the confidence to work on this belief. No doubt his naval training gave him the necessary self-discipline to continue his experiment in faith, for, as we shall see, it is necessary to exercise discipline if success is to be achieved in visualization, as in any other pursuit.

Dolores Ashcroft-Nowicki, however, uses a less-disciplined form of visualization in healing, as in so much else. I have already mentioned an interesting exercise that she recommends, that of taking a stroll around the body in your mind's eye, visiting each limb and each organ and taking stock of them, seeing if there are any complaints. She says in *Highways of the Mind* (Aquarian Press, 1987), 'There are many ways in which we can use the power of inner journeys to help our bodies as well as our minds. They can help us to start out each morning feeling ready to cope with the day. They can heal cuts and bruises very quickly . . . The first lesson to learn is this: *you are not your body*' (my italics). By this she means that you are much more than *merely* your body — you are a mind, you have emotions and you have a will. All of these, she is saying, can be enlisted in curing yourself of many, if not all, your ailments.

With a deep cut or wound of any kind, she recommends a practice remarkably similar, even in its terminology, to that evolved quite separately by Admiral Shattock: 'Imagine yourself in the brain control room and send out the Red Alert signal requiring antibodies and rebuilding cells to report to the scene of the accident.' Even broken limbs may be led to heal more rapidly: remember Penny Brohn's words at the beginning of this chapter to the effect that recovery from heavy medical procedures can be enhanced by visualizing a healing and therapeutic effect at work.

In this chapter I have concentrated in the main on self-treatment. In Chapter 4, I shall look at how visualization can be used in the healing of *others*, but first it is time to look at how visualization actually *works*.

3.
How it Works

There are two models: one looks at the phenomenon from the *inside* — and there is no better term to describe it than Maltz's psycho-cybernetics — the other looks at it from the *outside* and I have called this the mystico-religious model.

Psycho-cybernetics

I noted earlier that Roberto Assagioli said that every image has a motor-drive and that, consequently, mental picturing tends to produce '. . . physical conditions and external acts corresponding to them'. No one, however, has yet produced a formal scientific theory that would explain how visualization 'works', that is, how it is that mental images *do* produce physical changes (nor, for that matter, how the physical world comes to be represented in mental images). That there *is* a connection is clear enough and we have mentioned David Bohm's thoughts on the connection earlier, but the mechanics of the process can be glimpsed only vaguely.

I mentioned earlier, too, that the (reasonably non-problematic) act of lifting a cup of tea to one's lips is first performed mentally. Assagioli says in *The Act of Will* (Turnstone Press, 1974), '. . . every external act requires that it be first imagined or visualized, even if unconsciously.' He then goes on to say, 'But then during its performance the self-observation that accompanies it creates an image that, in its turn, produces a reinforcing effect, a positive feedback process' and thus leads to an internalized image, a mental model. In *Psychosynthesis* (Turnstone Press, 1965) he says that '. . . every movement requires a previous image of the movement to be executed.' Visualization may thus be seen as the construction or modification of mental models.

It is worth noting that problem-solving is often carried on by processes of visualization. Give the average human being a formal problem in logic and the chances are overwhelmingly likely that he or she will *picture* the situation and will contrive to make a mental model of its parameters. The use of the principles of formal logic is more often than not quite hopeless, but it has been shown that picturing the problem produces correct results very quickly. So, finding a short cut through town, for instance, depends upon our having a model of the town in our mind and of being able to problem-solve by visualizing the possibility of previously unknown connections in it.

Hofstadter and Dennett in *The Mind's Eye* (Harvester Press, 1981) provide some insight into the mechanics of this. They ask, 'Hey, let me think how it would feel to be a bat' and go on to say that this '. . . sets up a mental context. Translated into less mentalistic and more physical terms, the act of trying to project yourself into a bat's point of view activates some symbols in your brain. These symbols, so long as they remain activated, will contribute to the triggering patterns of all the other symbols that are activated.'

RL Gregory in *Concepts and Mechanisms of Perception* (Duckworth, 1974) provides more insight. 'In general, the eye's images are . . . merely patches of light [which] serve as symbols for selecting internal models . . .' He goes on to say that visual perception is not directly of sensory information, but rather of the internal models selected by sensory information. The special feature of perception is that it does not mediate behaviour directly from current sensory information, but always via internal models of reality. A cup of tea is thus a blob of light and results in behaviour (lifting it to the lips) on the basis of previously constructed models that that blob of light activates. So, in the case of the cricketer, John Reid, lying in bed and watching the bowlers bowling at him, we have the development of internalized models from which he can choose as he sees the blob of light he calls the ball growing larger on his retina. As we drive along the motorway, we can have at our disposal a repertory of models to choose from in an emergency that can issue in appropriate behaviour and save lives. Having dealt with a situation in the privacy and peace of our own minds, we are better able to deal with the situation as it emerges in real life because we deal with it more calmly.

This process of imagining or planning the future is dependent upon the human brain's frontal lobes. This area of the brain has nothing directly to do with the sensory areas, nor with those associated with memory, nor with the motor centres, but is solely concerned with the integration of inputs from these other centres and with planning, anticipating, judging, with choosing future-oriented ideas and with problem-solving. It is the front lobes that provide yet another distinction between humans and their animal companions on earth. Where animals are confined to the present moment and its facts, humans are capable of visualizing hypothetical, non-factual situations that may then become actual behaviour. This provides the human being with a freedom that is not possible for animals whose mental models are more rigid, innate and instinctive and this characteristic is as much a characteristic of being human as possessing language.

The images that we are able to create, then, stay around and may produce actions that tend to confirm them. More than that, they may produce physical changes in the brain, in the body and, in a wider sense, in the environment. The energy of thought is translated into the energy of matter, for both are identical. So suggests science and once more science is seen to be approaching older, pre-scientific, explanations. I explore the leading edge of science further in Chapter 10. For now, I turn to my second category of explanation.

Mystico-religious explanations

We saw previously how Maltz described the situation when he wrote in *Psycho-cybernetics*:

> This Creative Mechanism within you is impersonal. It will work automatically and impersonally to achieve goals of success and happiness, or unhappiness and failure, depending upon the goals which you yourself have set for it. Present it with 'success goals' and it functions as a 'Success Mechanism'. Present it with negative goals, and it operates just as impersonally, and just as faithfully as a 'Failure Mechanism'.

His use of upper-case letters indicates to me that he was relying on a non-scientific explanation of the sort that I call mystico-religious.

This type of explanation depends on the idea that we are all a part of a greater whole, a concept that is met with under a variety of names, such as the *Tao*, Macrocosmic Mind, Universal Consciousness, the Word, the *Logos*. This greater whole is seen as the source of all phenomena in the universe, a constant field of creation. Such creative energy streams forth through *ch'i*, God, Yahweh, Infinite One, or a host of other names for it. The consequent theory is that men and women — as distinct from all other living creatures on earth — are able, if they will, consciously to latch on to this source of creativity. Visualizing is a means of tapping and manipulating that source.

How, though? By prayer, meditation, visualizing the source, affirming the connection — by faith, in other words.

Increasingly through the book, there will be these two aspects: opposite sides of the same coin (though it is we humans who make them opposite). On the one hand there are individual men and women busy exercising their minds and spirits in efforts at self-improvement and fulfilment, on the other there is the field of creation, constantly flowing to, in and through human beings.

The trouble with us human beings is that we think we are more clever than we are, believe ourselves to be capable of fulfilment independently of the source of fulfilment. We have free will and we prize this, are unwilling to give it up, to say 'Thy will be done, O Lord, not mine' or, as Assagioli says, 'Let the Will of the SELF guide and direct my life.' The difficulty here lies in knowing what the Lord's will is because the stream of creativity does not reveal itself often if at all in words. Scientists point to this as evidence that a preverbal state of infantile being is being activated, in which subjective and objective worlds are not easily distinguishable one from the other and it was Freud who coined the term 'Oceanic experience' to describe the feeling of being a part of such a unified field. But was Herrigel in a preverbal state of infantilism?

What sort of self-concept had Herrigel got at the end of his six years, at any rate in relation to archery? What sort of self-concept has a *samurai* swordsman or a flower-arranger? Herrigel, for one, says he lost the last traces of any preoccupation with himself and his moods (like Peter Pavel), yet he was still Eugen Herrigel and identified himself as such. The swordsman, even though he is taught to be detached not only from himself but from his opponent, remains a named flesh and blood warrior. His sense of self is of a being who is purposeless and not thinking of himself. A flower-master ends his lesson as though he had '. . . guessed what Nature had glimpsed in dark dreams'. A good driver flows with the traffic, free of self-preoccupation and fluctuation of emotion. A master batsman becomes one with the wiles of the bowler. The self-concept, which is the aim of the psycho-cybernetic mechanism, is one of egoless awareness.

We are reminded of the word Maltz uses to describe the cybernetic creative mechanism — it is the word 'impersonal'. It is impersonal in the sense that it appears no longer to need any conscious control from the individual, and is, instead, an automatic effect of a cause and the Master flows into appropriate action. Is it, in fact, a mechanism, a mere matter of synapses, or is there another cause, a Mechanism (of the Tao or Universal Consciousness)?

Eugen Herrigel became a Master, for, like all Masters in all fields of activity, he was no longer concerned with personal, ego-centred success, was untroubled by subsidiary aims, was concerned only to become one with his bow, at which point '. . . art becomes artless'.

While Masters are thus no longer concerned with the question of success or failure, mere champions are halfway there because they have the greatest difficulty (while they are, in John Reid's words, 'hyped up') in seeing themselves as failing. Ordinary mortals, alas, see themselves quite definitely as subject to frequent failure.

What Herrigel's Master was saying when he said, 'It only knows of the goal, which cannot be aimed at technically . . .' was that the psycho-cybernetic process must be allowed to operate. It is an unconscious process and its source is in the brain. However, as the brain, in the last analysis, is energy, mind-stuff, the question of whether there is a further, egoless source must be left open, for the moment at least.

Summary

So how does it work, this tool we can learn to use for our own fulfilment and the betterment of others?
There are two models.

A psycho-cybernetic model
The process appears to be this:

- there is a need
- the need is filled in imagination
- the imaginative visualization may be strengthened by affirmation
- the emotions expected upon satisfaction of the need are also generated
- the visualization, affirmation and emotions cause a regenerating loop to be set up in the brain
- an internalized image or mental model is created
- further external stimuli, the need, activates the process and the second, third and fourth stages may be repeated.
- this results in additional feedback and a strengthening of the process: the mental model becomes open to more sensory cues, becomes more detailed and generalized and a part of everyday repertoire
- as the process is repeated, the repertoire becomes fixed.

A master darts player is constantly monitoring the flight of his darts.

A shot misses the treble 20. The 'feel' of the shot is still stored in the muscles and the mental image is open to modification. By visualizing the next shot, the mental image is adjusted and nerve impulses are sent to the appropriate muscles. As Assagioli says in a different context, '. . . during its performance, the self-observation that accompanies it creates an image that in its turn produces a reinforcing effect, a positive feedback process'.

A mystico-religious model (after Assagioli)
- The individual's conscious self is surrounded by ever-widening consciousnesses, all of which are at one's disposal, as it were, for increasing personal mastery of one's life through tapping a universal network of energy. (Various means of getting in touch with such a network will be discussed further later on in this book,

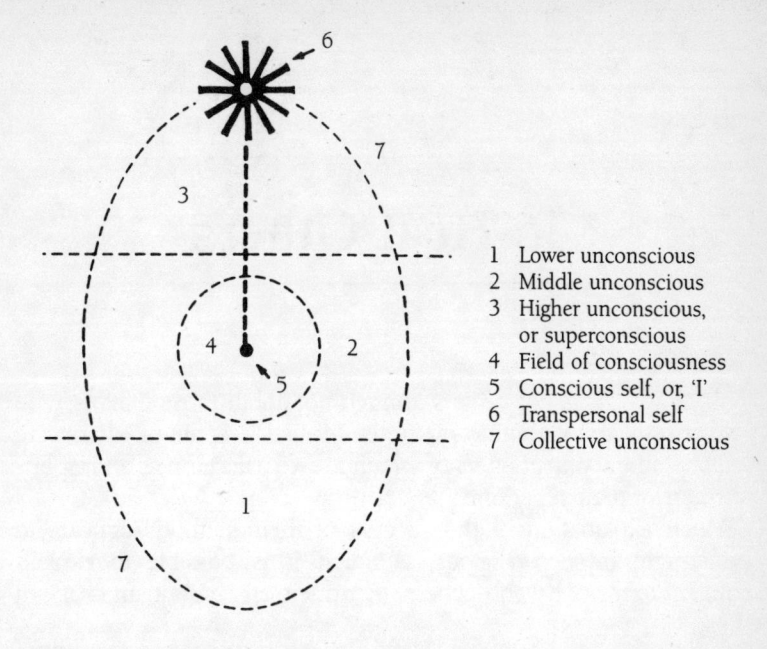

1 Lower unconscious
2 Middle unconscious
3 Higher unconscious, or superconscious
4 Field of consciousness
5 Conscious self, or, 'I'
6 Transpersonal self
7 Collective unconscious

and some preliminaries are to be found in the next chapter. However, such preliminaries are also necessary in effective psycho-cybernetics, so that and the mystico-religious model are just that, models.)

Both models are products of the human brain examining itself and each is a different model of the same phenomenon, for a common belief unites the two. This is that anything we imagine issues forth as fact. The reverse of that coin is the belief that everything we do and are, we do and are *first* in our imagination. A severe weakness of the psycho-cybernetic model, however, is that it fails to address questions that will be raised increasingly from here on in, namely, how visualization can change the environment. More and more, we shall be thrown back on to mystico-religious explanations and my next chapter begins to illustrate this.

4.
To Heal Others

This chapter is about healers, though not about those doctors who rely mostly on allopathic methods. Instead it is about 'alternative healing', many practitioners of which use visualization as an important part of their repertoire.

Much explanation of the success of their methods appears to be strictly mystico-religious, although it is possible to explain some in terms of psycho-cybernetic principles. Hypnotism is one of these.

Hypnosis

Healers who use hypnosis evoke mental images in their patient. As we know, the effective evocation of images, or visualization, depends upon relaxation. The aim of a hypnotist's relaxation procedure is for the subject to descend (or should we say ascend?) to a dream-like state of suggestibility, so that the hypnotist can focus the drowsy mind in such a way as to effect the reorganization of mental images.

What else happens when the patient relaxes? It may be that relaxation leads to the left hemisphere of the brain — the dominant, rational, coolly logical, scientific half — being reduced in influence as against the intuitive, dreamy, creative right hemisphere. If this is what happens in hypnotism, then the waking, watchful consciousness is set aside and the patient is thus made more open to suggestion.

While I go into this important topic more fully in later chapters, especially Chapter 9, I mention it now because some such process as this is almost certainly at work in other forms of alternative healing, for example in faith or psychic healing.

Pyschic healers

David Foot, a faith healer, writes in *The Healing Word* (WH Walter, 1979):

> I therefore anointed my wife with a little olive oil, and putting my hands on her asked the Lord to heal her sinus trouble. This was during a weekend at Broadstairs in 1960. Since 1940 she had suffered from chronic septic sinus and infections which recurred constantly in summer and winter: and with children often bringing colds back from school, life was a nightmare trying to avoid infection. She spent many days in her room, kept at a temperature of 60°, and was only able to avoid operation through a specialist who frequently had to pierce through the bone and flush out the septic sinus.
>
> In the 19 years from the day my wife was anointed she has had no more sinus trouble and was immediately able to breathe freely as she had seldom done before.

Such descriptions are not rare. That the body itself possesses powers of recuperation and healing is undeniable. That it is possible for the individual to mobilize these powers for himself or herself and make them more efficient has already been indicated in Chapter 2. It is also possible for similar methods to be utilized by healers curing others of a wide variety of ailments by psychic healing (see overleaf).

Books such as Foot's are rich in examples like the one just quoted. Foot firmly bases such cures within the realm of Christian faith and practice.

Such faith healing can often be a case of 'Your faith has made you whole' and there seems often to be no need for intervention by another person, although there may be a 'laying on of hands' or an anointing perhaps. An important factor in this is that faith encourages strong visualization of oneself as being, for example, in the arms of a loving, healing, god. We know, however, that it is also possible for people without strong faith to be healed, but, for such people, it is the reputation of the healer as a healer that is a most important part of the healing process and replaces faith in a supernatural being.

In all psychic healing, there is a visualization of the end-product: it may be that with the Christian, cured by faith, there will have been some sort of visualized image of being 'free from sin'. Equally a non-religious person will be cured by a visualization of being free from disease or injury.

How do psychic healers mobilize their power? Alexis Carrel, involved with cancer patients, is quoted by Maltz as believing that the body's own natural healing powers were 'speeded up' by the influence

> ### Faith healing — one practitioner's record of cures
>
> Arthritis
> Bleeding
> Broken bones: fibula*
>   femur*
> Bronchitis
> Cancer: pelvis*
>   unspecified
>   unspecified blood condition*
> Chicken pox*
> Compaction of the bowel*
> Conjunctivitis
> Cystitis*
> Heart: coronary attack*
>   weakness in an octogenarian*
>   stroke*
> Influenza
> Measles*
> Migraine
> Mumps
> Scalding
> Shingles
> Sinusitis
> Skin disease — unspecified*
>
> * are acknowledged by qualified doctor.
> (From *The Healing Word* by David Foot, WH Walter, 1979)

of intense faith, but he begs the question, which Maltz attempts to answer by referring, almost unwillingly, to a growing (mystico-religious) belief he had of a Life Force with many channels of expression and many manifestations. (As an aside, one can only admire the way in which a hard-headed medical doctor, a product of the twentieth century, was led through openness of mind and experiential evidence to a belief in a religious, supernatural power.) This power, whatever it may be, manifests itself in some form of mobilization of energy fields and may just be explicable in terms of psycho-cybernetics. The healer induces in the patient a reconstruction of mental models.

Whether such explanations are tenable in all cases, however, is doubtful, particularly in cases of the sort of healing that is reputedly carried out, for instance, by psychic surgeons in the Phillipines. Observers have said that such healers visibly draw clots and tumours through the skin without recourse to knife, using only their bare hands. The surgeons, if such they may be called, believe that they have the ability to manipulate some sort of energy field and in this belief they are joined by native doctors in Africa, lamas in Tibet, witch-doctors in Africa, aborigines in Australia, as well as our own faith healers. More importantly, their belief is shared by their patients.

Psychic healing

The preparation for all healing involves inducing in both the patient *and the healer* a state of deep relaxation as a preliminary, leading to deep mental quietude and suggestibility.

That achieved, there is often then a visualization *by the healer* of being a channel through which the energy field can flow, whether it is called healing cosmic energy, Life Energy, *ch'i, prana* or whatever is culturally or psychologically appropriate in the circumstances. Such healing energy is then directed to the patient.

In Shattock's terminology in *A Manual of Self-Healing*, for instance, the procedure is seen thus:

> Think-see energy [from the sun] that is all around [is] being drawn in at a spot between the shoulder blades and concentrated in the area of the spleen: see the energy as a golden stream proceeding from the spleen to the spine and hence to the area that requires it, along pathways that run parallel to the nervous system.

When such a visualization is established in the healer, it is said to be possible to detect abnormalities by mentally 'asking' the patient if there are any special requests. Alternatively, the healer can see if he or she can detect within themselves any impulse to work on any part of the patient's body or mind. The flow of energy should be directed to that part until the person is *seen* as deeply immersed in the energy in the form of a golden light, looking radiantly healthy. The subject should be spoken to in the healer's mind and should be told (or reminded) that he is actually a perfect being and a part of the perfection of the cosmos or Godhead or *Tao* — whatever is culturally appropriate and acceptable to the healer and the patient.

After the session, meditation or service, the subject should be thought of as being perfectly healthy. As I pointed out previously, each visualization session must always finish with the subject being seen to be whole, complete and perfectly cured. The same should be the aim of all future psychic healing sessions also: no more energy should be allowed to empower the negative aspects of illness as the mental image formed in the mind by the visualization should contain only positive aspects.

There seems little possibility of explaining such healing in psycho-cybernetic terms and even less of healing that takes place at a distance.

Distant healing

Manipulation of healing energy is possible without physical contact between healer and sufferer. In other words, healing can be carried out at a distance, as in intercessionary prayer.

An example of a procedure suitable for distant healing is provided by José Silva in *The Silva Mind Control Method*. He recommends using a visualized screen upon which the picture of the sick person is projected. He recommends placing alongside the visualized sick person a further visualization of whatever needs to be done to cure him and, next to that, a picture of the person as radiantly fit. As he says, 'Just as we detect abnormalities by visualizing them, we visualize conditions as we want them to be — without the abnormalities. This is psychic healing. It's as simple as that.'

'Simple' is hardly the word — it is skilled work — and a necessary note of caution is expressed by Admiral Shattock, who writes the following about his own experience in distant healing in *A Manual of Self-Healing*:

> I felt a very definite lack in that I was working in the dark; I had no ability (psychic sense?) that would enable me to diagnose the trouble or to receive feedback on the progress or lack of it, that the treatment was resulting in. This lack could be dangerous because one *might* be trying to do something that could harm the body and one must know this at once. In the case of self-healing, one is very quickly aware of harmful results and can take the necessary action before real harm is done. In distant healing this is not the case and one cannot always rely on the person one is working on having the same degree of perception into physical reaction that one has oneself. This is a very important defect of this method, unless the healer has the necessary psychic perception to be able to 'see' for himself.

Whether the sufferer is told that such distant healing is being carried out or not, depends to a great extent on how far they are prepared to accept (on faith) that this is happening and how far they accept that it is possible to be helped. The wonder (and the worry) is that healing can take place at all in the face of ignorance on the part of the patient.

Group healing

If what appear to be miracles can be effected through the power of thought by individuals, then it is not unreasonable to suppose that the combined thoughts of a group of people will exercise at least as much power. Shakti Gawain says in *Creative Visualization* that 'Creative visualization is particularly good when used by a group, because the group energy automatically gives it a lot of power. Each person's energy tends to support the others and in this case the whole becomes more than the sum of its parts.'

The power of a mob is well known and stems from the advantage the mob has of a relatively clearly defined emotional target — the immense power generated by a house painter of renown at Nuremburg rallies, for example. Similarly the battle cries and chants of football hooligans and traditional armies of all kinds, best exemplified by television pictures of such as traditional Zulu warriors have tremendous force. This is the other side of the coin: the energy engendered by a group is neutral, but the motives of the group are not.

Two purposes may be met by group healing. One is the cure of a problem shared by a number of individuals, while the other is for a group healing of a single individual. Slimming groups are an example of the former that might use the power of group visualization for their mututal benefit. Other examples include groups formed to overcome additions, such as smoking and alcoholism.

As for the cure of a single individual, the group proceeds as if it were a single therapist, focusing its combined effort upon the sufferer. There is much power here and members of a group meeting for healing are able to use certain techniques, and need to take certain precautions.

Techniques

Chanting, music, singing (for example hymns) at meetings are long-recognized means of raising the emotional temperature. They may be used at any type of meeting, from gatherings for battle to love-feasts.

In addition to creating mood, a means of focusing is necessary. In healing groups, if the sufferer is not present, a photograph of the person may be used instead. In this way, all members of the group are not only reminded of the object of the meeting, but are helped to visualize its subject. Methods such as that advocated by Silva, described above, can be used or the more common one of visualizing healing light enveloping the diseased part or whole person of the sufferer. Each member undertakes a silent visualization of that kind and this may be followed by a period of affirmation of the good health of the subject, either singly, in pairs, or as a whole group.

Precautions

The process can be draining and a period of what would nowadays be called in other circles 'debriefing' should follow. Tea and biscuits, prosaically enough, will provide a pause for a return to normality — after all, what could be more emotionally neutral than a digestive biscuit? Only after such a pause should members of the group return home.

Ethical questions

At least two ethical questions arise from all this. One of these is whether healing at a distance, by individual or group, that uses methods that are as capable of doing harm as well as good are to be encouraged. The other, more serious, is whether healing should be imposed on a sick person without their knowledge and permission.

At this point, and it is a topic I shall return to, it does seem to me that Shakti Gawain is over-optimistic when she repeatedly says that the power of creative visualization works *only* for good, to quote one of her chapter headings. It may be true that misused visualization, that is for a destructive or harmful end, is storing up karmic retribution, as she says, but on the face of it it seems completely within the realms of possibility for the technique to be misused.

The problem of proof

Sceptics will claim that many of the cures and alleviations of misery I have cited in this chapter and in Chapter 2 may be put down to coincidence or will certainly claim that natural remission could account for them.

We live in a scientific age, but as Louis Kronenberger has written in *Company Manners* (Bobs Merrill, 1962), 'Nominally a great age of scientific enquiry, ours has actually become an age of superstition about the infallibility of science, of almost mystical faith in its non-mystical methods . . .' and, we might add, an age that still exhibits closed minds to many other recognized means of understanding the chaotic diversity around us. Science demands replication, strict measurement, control groups and the like, regardless of the fact that some of the softer sciences themselves are not amenable to such rigorous proof.

The fact is that, at the moment, there is no scientific way of proving that visualization does cure and no way of proving that it can even aid conventional methods, though, as I have shown, science, after all, may be providing the beginnings of an answer. The fact that a good many people acquire a greater sense of control over their lives and bodies does not take us one step nearer to proof. Such people, those who have actually experienced it, would say that they need no proof, that proof would add nothing to their experience or sense of satisfaction.

Conclusion

In my two chapters on healing, I have shown that in sickness and in health, it appears that we can, if we choose, be masters and mistresses of our own health and the health of others to a far greater extent than is normally recognized.

The power of visualization is seen as affecting our all-important self-concepts and in these chapters we have seen how this can affect our bodily circumstances, even our life-span.

Similarly, day-to-day health problems can be affected, not only by our long-standing self-concepts, but by the way in which we see ourselves reacting to circumstances as they arise. No one will readily deny that a physical illness will have mental effects, such as depression. That being accepted, it is equally valid to say that mental causes result in bodily effects. Our mental pictures of ourselves are all-important and affect our daily behaviour.

Do we rush for the paracetamol when a headache strikes or do we explore the pain, let it flow and thus help our self-diagnosis? Do we recover quickly from indisposition, or not? Whichever it is, our own self-image is basic to the answer we give. Similarly, if we are struck down with a life-threatening illness, such as cancer or AIDS, it is becoming quite clear that our chances of survival are very much influenced by how we, quite literally, see or are led to see ourselves in the situation.

As I have shown, and shall continue to show, basic to the power of visualization is the belief that all phenomena are a form of energy and that all energy is one. Nowhere is this more apparent than in the maintenance of health. Thought, mental energy, is only a more subtle energy than that which manifests itself in grosser form such as our bodies and it does seem that we are able to influence the forms of gross energy by utilizing the subtle, just as it is obvious that the gross can affect the subtle — it must be so, for they are, in fact, one.

Even so serious a wound as a broken leg can be hastened in its cure by taking appropriate thought — by the sufferer or by others. As for St Peter's ear, perhaps there is an explanation to hand of that particular miracle.

As we have seen in previous chapters, visualization methods are varied and range from the highly disciplined of such as EH Shattock to the relatively low key, dreamy methods of such as Donald Wilson or Dolores Ashcroft-Nowicki. While visualization techniques will never be a substitute for traditional methods, they can do no harm when used in conjunction with them. It is highly unlikely that an individual will come to harm when carrying them out, and in this connection I venture to remind readers of Penny Brohn's opinion, already quoted, that '. . . the most famous and widely used way of using the mind to enhance tolerance of, and recovery from, heavy medical procedure is to visualize the process as having a healing and therapeutic effect.'

This chapter ended by considering the effect that our visualization can have on others, sometimes at a distance. It is apparent that such powers can be used selfishly or altruistically and we shall return to this prickly subject later, particularly in the chapters on the paranormal and the occult.

Of course, the ability to imagine events and play them out in the mind is the basis of every success book ever written, but it is all very well to describe such methods, the difficulty is to get the show on the road. People who are attracted to such techniques are often subjecting themselves to negative self-images and have neither the confidence nor the energy to want health 'with every atom of their being, to the exclusion of all else'.

A journey of a thousand miles may indeed begin with the first step, but in the case of this particular journey, it is the first step that is the most demanding and difficult. That is why expert help, as in Autogenic Training, is so much more likely to succeed, because the initial effort is not self-imposed — the motivation comes from an outside authority. However, in Chapter 6 I do discuss ways in which an individual can get their own show on the road through their own efforts.

In the meantime, it will be profitable to look first at the power of visualization in the creation, maintenance and dissolution of human relationships.

5.
To Love Another

There is a commonly used phrase — 'a meaningful relationship'. In it lies an admission that some relationships have meaning at a deeper level than others, probably in terms of bodily or mental or spiritual satisfactions. It is sad when such a relationship changes for the worse, when it may have outlived its usefulness to one or both parties. Or has it?

Behind the chemistry

What is meant by a 'relationship'? There is a clear implication in the word that communication is involved, but then not all chance encounters in the street or on a bus qualify as relationships — though a smile or a frown are not lost in the scheme of things even there. In addition to communication, there is the notion of a contract, unwritten, it is true, but nevertheless existing.

When does a chance meeting become a relationship, then? It is surely when an agreement, a contract, is implicitly recognized between the parties. All relationships are taken up for their utility, for recognized or unrecognized short-term or long-term gains. In fact, it is possible to see all relationships as having a purpose and, if that sounds like a cold-blooded suggestion, you are invited to analyse just what you gain from a relationship. Of course, there is no doubt that you are contributing to that relationship for the benefit of the other, but the relationship is maintained by both of you, just as in any business contract, for its value to both of you.

When we 'strike up a relationship' there is mutual choice, with expectations and reservations on both sides and the progress of the relationship may be seen as the process of development of these. Marcus Allen, among many others, suggests in *Tantra for the West* that our relationships have been created by ourselves not on accidental grounds, but, at some level of our psyche, quite deliberately. He says, 'Every relationship is a tantric relationship: a deep sharing we have created in order to learn and grow.' According to Allen, Tantra is a path, a means, to personal freedom, but such a definition is partial and superficial. I'm not sure, then, that 'tantric' is the right word: I prefer to say that every relationship is a *karmic* one.

I believe that *karma* is a better term to be used in our context, because it implies that in relationships, as in so much else, we find ourselves working out long-standing problems throughout our lives with varying degrees of success.

Karma is a word often met with these days, now that Eastern philosophies and religions are becoming more widely accepted. Of course, a full acceptance of the idea involves one in questions to do with that other Eastern concept, reincarnation, and this I shall leave to one side until later.

We don't need to go as far as accepting either karma or reincarnation, however, to understand that we may not have as much choice as we think in forming new relationships. Computer dating does not always work, for the simple reason that the ingredients that go to make up a successful relationship are not easily analysed and integrated. Indeed, some friendships — the best — are struck up so easily that it really does seem that a couple were destined to meet, their friendship made in heaven. Similarly, some relationships seem to be so bad, so lacking in hope, and apparently formed in hell, that it is incomprehensible to everyone, not excluding the unfortunate victims involved, how the relationship can continue, yet it does. Often, indeed, it is quite clear that in some perverse way the partners do actually *need* each other.

Jung has made us aware that we are all of us subject to the influence of innate archetypes. These psychological constructs, which represent deep-seated urges and impulses that we all share, according to Jung, with everyone else in the world, can exercise a powerful force in attracting people together. In Jean Bolen's words in *The Tao of Psychology* (Wildwood House, 1980), '. . . whenever a person is either magnetically drawn to someone who carries a positive archetype or overly condemns someone who is intensely felt to be a completely negative person, an archetype probably has been activated in the environment.' The world, according to Jungians, is full of karmic meetings.

Beginnings

We are born, male or female, into a particular family in a particular social and class setting. This fundamental relationship in everyone's life, the one that affects all succeeding ones, is the first one, that which exists between the child and its mother or mother substitute — enough work has been done by Freud and his followers to persuade us of that.

When the body receives an injury it may form scar-tissue that is often tougher than the flesh it replaces and which is often less beautiful. Physical scarring is easy to see and any resulting deformities are easily understood. Emotional scarring, on the other hand, is neither easy to see, nor are its resulting deformities that emerge in behaviour so easy to understand. However, it is easy to understand *how* these emotional scars come to be formed.

Anyone who is hurt by another and who wishes to avoid future hurt, will form a 'spiritual callus', to use Maltz's term, which not only protects that person from the person who originally injured, but also from people in general. As an example, sexual rejection by someone in adolescence may cause corresponding suspicion and rejection of the opposite sex throughout life, with consequent scarring and unhappy relationships. Similarly, parental rejection in infancy can cause lifelong withdrawal from close emotional ties, as Dr Bowlby among many others has pointed out, and this is a topic I shall pursue in later chapters.

So, the psyche is full of unresolved hangups. These may surface in many ways: for example, we may have the habit of seeing in other people those of our own characteristics that we would like to disown. 'Projection' is the technical word for this defensive psychological process. If I find myself consistently noticing and condemning certain behaviours in other people, I can be quite (if unwillingly) certain that I possess those very self-same traits of character, even if (or because) I have managed to repress or suppress them. It is an ego-defence system, a way in which I protect myself from disagreeable feelings about myself that are often born of guilt experienced in infancy. Such defences ensure that I remain in a one-up position in my social environment, which includes, of course, my relationships. How often do we notice that we are accused by another of the very thing that we believe to be a trait of their own behaviour? Such projections reflect a deep need for affection and approval, expectations of how to maximize comfort and much unfinished childhood business with 'significant others'.

How to recognize and cure oneself by visualization techniques of the sort of emotional scarring that can ruin relationships throughout life is dealt with in this chapter, which finishes with a short passage on the subject of forgiveness, for it is forgiveness that can best perform emotional plastic surgery, removing emotional scar tissue.

It is not, of course, only forgiveness of *others* that must be achieved — very often, it is forgiveness of *yourself* that is needed. To have behaved badly, even just once, and even by other people's warped standards, can cause self-hatred, so that you see yourself as utterly beyond the pale of ordinary decent people. As Maltz says in *Psychocybernetics*, '. . . one of the biggest mistakes we can make is to confuse our behaviour with our "self" . . . to conclude that because we *did* a certain act it characterizes us as a certain kind of person.'

Fully adult relationships are not possible until a man or a woman has thrown off the leading strings acquired in infancy that tie him or her to mother (or mother-substitute). Babes are helplessly dependent in every respect on the mother for their very survival and become increasingly aware of this threatening fact, rebelling unconsciously then and throughout life against it. This is doubly significant in these latter days of nuclear families, where the lack of dynamic balance between weakness and strength in this fundamental relationship is not alleviated by the extended family of grandmothers and aunts, nor by the tribe of neighbours. Increasingly in developed societies, individuals — particularly the weak — are threatened both physically and psychically by others of their kind and there is less protection.

Even when a mutually beneficial contract is freely entered into by two adults, it may often turn out to be one-sided and sometimes life-threatening. Yet often the contract was set up even though there were pretty clear karmic signals of what was to come. Unfortunately, it is often the children of such ill-fated contracts that are the victims.

In a valued relationship, there may be a tendency to act in ways that were successful once in this and other relationships and there is an element of self-visualization in this. The visualization, however, may be based on past experience that may no longer have any bearing on the present circumstances. The other may have changed. As Joseph Needham writes in *Science and Civilization in China* (CUP, 1954), 'Can you go on loving when someone you intensely love rejects you? . . . Can you go on loving when he or she is sunk in neurotic depression, or some other situation, when either for social or neuro-chemical reasons he or she can no longer feel love to love you back?'

Repairing relationships

Our important relationships do not happen by chance. Energy resonates with energy: we meet the people we need to meet. These are not necessarily those whom we would *want* to meet, but are those that, at some level, we believe have the capacity for improving the quality of our lives. If this is true, it may be helpful, hard though it may be to imagine it, to tell ourselves that even those relationships that cause nothing but pain are nevertheless there for our benefit, to be used in order to allow us to move towards fulfilment.

It takes two to tango and it takes two to make a relationship. It is worthwhile examining the choices we make in sustaining a relationship. As I have said, there is always a reward for us in whatever we do, otherwise we wouldn't be doing it. Marcus Allen puts it in the following terms in *Tantra for the West*:

> That other person isn't 'doing it to you' . . . you are doing it to yourself, you are making yourself angry. That other person is doing you a favour, by providing you with someone who makes you aware of your areas of unconscious and points out where you need to change in order to be truly free.

So it is useful to examine our reasons for maintaining a relationship, even when it would appear that the best possible thing to do would be to end it. Having discovered what it is that makes us tick in a relationship, it is then possible to use visualization methods in order to change things for the better — to deal with attitudes, for instance, that are limiting our development and growth.

An example of how *not* to repair relationships is to be found in the book *How to Fall Out of Love* by Deborah Phillips and Robert Judd (Futura, 1981). Parts of it are fairly unexceptional, such as 'So being in love with someone and not being loved back, being rejected and being criticized all change the way you see yourself in specific, hurtful ways . . . How do you repair and improve that damaged picture of yourself? Ans: write down every day at least two positive things about yourself.' That's fine and much of the book is largely to do with revising a self-image through action, acting as though you are the person you wish to be in that particular aspect — a sound principle endorsed by Roberto Assagioli.

Reward is used a great deal — you are encouraged to buy yourself chocolates or bask for an hour in a warm bath when you have done something positive and therapeutic for yourself — but, on the other hand, less positive methods are also advocated, including the arousal in oneself of revulsion towards the one who is to be fallen out of love with. This involves the visualization of unpleasant things about the other person's character, personal habits and physical features. In this the book illustrates an extreme and is a typcially aggressive Western way of dealing with negative feelings. The feelings are seen as originating 'out there', not within the psyche. In fact, of course, *all* our feelings exist within us, latent, though their manifest expression may be due to some external cause.

There are, fundamentally, two positive approaches — inward and outward — to do with repairing failed relationships. The two approaches share a common belief, which is that in our relationships, as in every aspect of our life, we are, in fact, free to create whatever we desire. They are distinguished by the fact that the outward approach uses the negativities in the *situation*, whereas the inward approach seeks to eradicate the negativities in the *self*.

The outward approach

Roberto Assagioli describes the therapeutic use of 'Imaginative Evocation' and specifically recommends its use in '... the realization of harmonious interpersonal relationships'. As a therapist, he encourages guided visualization. However, some of his followers — notably Piero Ferrucci — have freed themselves from the necessity of professional shepherding and recommend a do-it-yourself approach.

General method

If a relationship seems to be going sour, going off the boil, it is a good idea to appraise the situation. A simple visualization exercise that uses simple psycho-cybernetic processes is to:

- sit comfortably and observe your breath, that is, deeply relax
- visualize the other in front of you, visualize their posture, clothing, expression and so on
- talk to the person, say what you appreciate about them in full — search your heart to complete the list
- now tell them what you resent about them, in full, especially those things you have difficulty in talking about face to face
- talk about how you see the relationship in two years' time, stressing positive results.

This is a step towards making things better and it works, quite simply, by means of altering your perceptions of yourself, of the other and of the dyad formed by your two selves. Apart from any other way in which visualization might work, this must in itself alter the dynamics of the relationship. Such picturing of the other person will bring its own insights, some understanding of what makes them tick and, most importantly, ways in which you yourself collude in their ticking. It may lead to the adoption of the inward approach.

Battered women
Situations may develop in which, in place of harmony and balance, there remains only empty form and ritual and in which develop extremes of physical and/or mental cruelty (for who but an erstwhile lover can know better how to hurt?) Direct confrontation with the negativities in the situation can be threatening, paralysing and sometimes physically dangerous. Theoretically, a woman in a violent relationship could walk away. However, circumstances may bind her economically and in many other ways to the situation. To be coolly objective, it is true to say that she *chooses* to carry on the relationship. From the point of view of a belief in karma, it can be said that she chooses to remain in the relationship for reasons best known to her inner self — it is a karmic relationship.

Whether she gets out or stays, visualization can help her. An exercise such as the one above or similar to the one below can be used by her to deal first with the negative feelings in herself and in the situation and then in replacing those with new and positive feelings and actions.

Jealousy
Nowhere is the fact that upsets in relationships are created by the individuals concerned more clearly illustrated than in jealousy as jealousy is almost entirely produced by the suffering individual. There may be real reasons for anger at a situation a partner has set up, but the way in which that anger is expressed is entirely a matter for the sufferer.

An outward approach to its alleviation that is often recommended is that you start by throwing a tantrum or beating a cushion. This is largely cathartic, in that it allows the bodily tensions that preclude relaxed visualization to be dissolved in violent action. Your feelings will change and you should flow with those feelings, allowing your attitude to the cushion to change accordingly. Imagine the person you are jealous of as the cushion. Give yourself permission to hurt, strangle, kiss it or whatever. Then sit down and have a dialogue with the cushion. First you do the talking, then the cushion talks to you. Then put the cushion aside and visualize your partner in the way recommended at the beginning of this section. (A bonus attached to this kind of exercise is that you may realize that if you can get just as mad with a cushion as with your partner, perhaps the problem really is not in either the cushion or your partner, but in yourself. This again can lead to an inward approach.)

A combination exercise is this:

- visualize that you are sitting down with the other and there is a period of silence while you look at one another

- after a while, you can tell the other how you are feeling now about them, how you are afraid that your feelings may not be understood or accepted by them, how you are frightened of them and so on

- then sit silent again and wait for a reply, which will come

- check it out with the other: is it what they really meant? Tell them how you felt when you heard it

- repeat the process — you may feel that things are getting worse: if so, don't be afraid to shout and scream at them and express your feelings as strongly as you would never dare to do in real life — how do they respond? (You may need to take out your aggression in some physical way now, like beating up a pillow — which is similar to the Japanese experiment of providing rubber models of bosses for the workers to beat up in order to get rid of their aggression towards authority), but be sure to return to the visualization, then express your feelings about how you feel now and ask them how they feel

- remember, it is essential that you finish constructively, in dialogue with the other — agree on a way that you will behave differently and agree on how this may possibly affect their behaviour.

It is crucially important that the ending of a visualization session ends positively. Roberto Assagioli recommends that a patient be encouraged under relaxation to relive in 'imaginative evocation' traumatic events in relationships and then to evoke imaginatively future behaviour in the relationship, but he is careful to say that only after re-experiencing rage and hatred and other negative feelings is it possible to move to the '... next stage of visualizing the possible "love" attitude', which is sometimes said to just flow from the evocation. So don't dodge the cushion exercise or an equivalent.

In repairing relationships through visualization in such an exercise, we come up against an interesting phenomenon (see the third point above), which we shall develop further in Chapter 8 in the section

'Best Therapist'. This phenomenon is that whatever questions you may ask in imagination, an answer always appears. Just as the body, left to itself, more often than not knows what it needs in order to be cured of an illness, so too the mind has hidden curative resources. The quieter and more focused you are on one thing, the better the answer is likely to be since, if you are to mobilize those hidden resources, you need to be free of emotional self-centred clutter.

In this outward approach, anger is seen as a natural energy that should not be restrained. To divert it, as in the exercises mentioned, is one way of dealing with it. Indeed, an interesting spin-off is that it may provide a good 'head of steam' to apply to mundane matters, such as dusting the house or to less mundane affairs, such as tackling starvation in Ethiopia. As Piero Ferrucci writes in *What We May Be*,

> Now realize that these feelings are energy at your disposal, energy that is precious and can *do* things. It can hurt, but it can also become the propelling power for the project or activity you have chosen.

Such a diversion of the anger does not really deal with the 'negative' energy that remains, is excused and may in fact be consciously fostered in order to provide the necessary head of steam for such other purposes.

Inward approaches

Following on from this, Kathleen McDonald asks in *How to Meditate* (Wisdom Publications, 1984) why such feelings are regarded as being 'negative'. She says they are neutral and self-created and that there is a need to work on the self in their eradication.

> It is not that anger or desire are inherently evil or that we should feel ashamed when they arise. It is a matter of seeing them as the delusions that they are, distorted conceptions that paint a false picture of reality.

They are negative when they lead to unhappiness and confusion.

One of the ways in which we cause an immense amount of suffering for ourselves is the way we have of blaming everything and everyone for our own feelings. It's a good idea to ask how this can happen. Is it by magic or is the truth really that we create our own feelings, that our reactions to others are often in response to some predisposition latent in our own psyches? If the latter is the case, then it is inside ourselves and not in some outside agency that we need to seek a remedy.

Some people have difficulties in their relationships generally. It is probably a good idea to explore the nature of these relationships and Piero Ferrucci gives an example of a drawing technique that set out to do this in *What We May Be*. Choosing five people there are difficulties with, the idea is to place yourself in the centre of a sheet of paper, with those relationships around you. In the space intervening, you draw freehand the nature of each relationship. This clarifies them. Afterwards a visualization exercise — like one outlined above — may help to clarify insights about yourself.

Kathleen McDonald gives a number of methods that can be used to overcome 'negativity' in *How to Meditate*. For example, to deal with anger in a relationship she recommends that you have a conversation like the one above, but do it almost entirely from the side of the other person. In this way you can seek to understand their humanity, their unhappiness and miseries and generate compassion in yourself for that person. Again, typical of the Buddhist faith she espouses, is to see that, as was said above, we have ourselves chosen that relationship and that any misfortunes that come to us through it are the result of previous actions of our own (in this or a previous life). We need to sort this out, to change direction within ourselves and regard the situation as an opportunity that has arisen to enable us to learn from it. Falling out of love, for instance, can be tackled differently by focusing on your own characteristics rather than the other's and on exploring the bodily sensations that go with your feelings. By concentrating on these, as in dealing with pain, the cause of the discomfort will be understood and decline.

In sum, the inward approach is used to work directly and immediately on the negativities within the self, which is, of course, where they truly lie.

Sexual relationships

For a good part of almost all people's lives, sex is important to them — unless cultural peculiarities interfere, as, for example, in the practice of female circumcision, after which the sex act, at any rate, is associated only with physical pain. Nor are we in the West blameless. Although it has only recently become generally known in the United Kingdom, there is widespread interference in children's normal sexual development in the form of sexual abuse of them by adults. It may be peculiar to the United Kingdom or to developing nations or it may be universal and so widespread that we may need to revise our notions of 'normality'. Normal or not, the result of what I'm sure is rightly called sexual *abuse* is pain for the children at the time, both physical and mental, and regarding the formation of their relationships. Whatever the truth of the matter, it is clear that we have here another baleful influence on the potential for sexual happiness of men and women. Indeed, it may be only another manifestation of the modern tendency to depersonalization, so that the phrase 'making love', is largely replaced by the phrase 'having sex', which turns the other person into an object for our gratification. Nor is it only men who have this manner of behaviour. The results of such shallowness of relationships need little emphasis.

While it is generally accepted that sexual abuse in childhood leads to warped sex in adulthood, it is by no means the only cause. Parents do not have to abuse their children physically to give them warped sexual responses when they grow up. The need to placate a parent in order to be granted warmth and love may lead to all sorts of adult behaviour that to an outsider will seem inappropriate and indeed counterproductive.

We've most of us met the man or woman who will sleep with anyone, it seems. They are promiscuous, it is true, but this may not be their true nature — they may be seeking the one person who can make them happy and fulfilled human beings. What they do not realize is that that one person is unattainable, being a fantasized version of a loving parent, perhaps, who once in fact harshly rejected them. The worst of it is that the *way* they are going about finding this ideal person results in each new partner rejecting them. It is a part of their life-script and so they go on in a hellish state that is only occasionally relieved by rapturous hope.

Another inappropriate way of behaving is to make sex not a vehicle of love, but a comforter or a weapon. It is used in all sorts of ways to keep danger at bay and to placate the powerful, as Janette Rainwater points out in *You're in Charge*. The use of sex as an antidote to loneliness, as a means of starting a relationship, as a duty, as a means of obtaining security, as reassurance and so on — all are uses of sex that are very far removed from its functions either as a means of procreation or as an expression of love, pure and simple.

These misapplications combined with what appear to be consumer-oriented goals, such as the pursuit of perfect and perfectly-timed orgasms and similar needs to match some externally imposed standards of performance, lead to too many people persisting in either living out sexual relationships of quiet or not-so-quiet desperation or just giving it all up and separating to try again with someone else, too often with the same dismal result, because the underlying neurotic needs remain unchanged. Hence the Kinsey Report, the advent of sex therapy, of Masters and Johnson and the whole sex-problem trade that does little to alter the fundamental emotional scarring.

What sort of self-concepts are possessed by us today in the area of sex? The dutiful wife, the horny he-man, the gentle lover, the parent? Or are we lucky enough to see sex as only one among many means of expressing our love?

If your sex-life is a mess or if it is just not as good as your inner sense tells you it should be, then you can do something about it for yourselves. The use of visualization techniques to improve love-making or to normalize it is a viable adjunct to the Johnson and Masters type of sex therapy. The latter aims to demystify the sex act, to make it more matter-of-fact and to abolish neurotic fantasy. This, of course, can be all to the good as the sort of uncontrolled visualization that neurosis brings with it may in some cases need to be replaced by a more realistic visualization of yourself and your partner being made more nearly perfect. Controlled visualization has its part to play in this aspect of our lives, not least in successful love-making, otherwise we may find ourselves slaves to some mental creation that imposes unattainable standards of beauty or performance upon us or our partner. Fantasy and mystery, however, have an important part to play in human love-making and Masters and Johnson may have got rid of an important baby with the proverbial bath water. They may have improved performance, but there is little doubt that they have reduced the all-important magic.

Controlled visualization

Therapy is often needed for sexual performance and visualization can help here. For instance, a man may suffer from premature ejaculation.

The problem here is that the male sufferer (his partner also suffers because of his difficulty) is visualizing his energy as centred in his sexual organs, so his whole attention is centred there either in anticipation or anxiety. The result is that he visualizes the sexual fluids rising irresistibly and the body follows the mind, as it always will, with the inevitable result.

A visualization that will help in this situation is to imagine the energy circulating elsewhere — throughout the body, for instance or rising up the spine, even circulating around the *partner's* body. Again, the body will follow the mind and love-making will last longer.

Let us look at another example. Here is a visualization that could be used when the magic is going. It can be used by one of the partners or both, but separately:

- sit or lie, relax and watch your breath
- picture yourself meeting your lover
- picture yourself as having all the qualities of a lover that you and your lover desire
- visualize yourself touching and caressing the other, making love, easily and effortlessly
- visualize the after-glow.

As in all visualization exercises, the results may not be dramatic or immediately apparent. Apart from the time generally needed to be aware of desired changes taking place, in this delicate field there may also be much forgiving to be done before scar-tissue is transformed or transmuted.

Forgiveness

If you are finding it difficult to forget and forgive, the proper way to go about the latter is to begin by forgiving yourself — the inward approach again. As is the case with many visualizations or other exercises to do with self-improvement, particularly with regard to improving your relationships with others, it is no good trying to do anything about it until you have begun to get things right with yourself. At one level, this is simple common sense — a person who is screwed up inside is in no position to be doing much unscrewing of relationships.

The practical advice in this situation is also simple. After relaxing and observing your breath or doing whatever you find makes your mind receptive and still, affirm forgiveness, saying, 'I forgive myself for whatever I have done in the past, intentionally or unintentionally, my actions, my words and my deeds.' Then visualize in front of you a person you want to forgive or from whom you need forgiveness and say, 'With all my heart I forgive you for (what has been done or said) intentionally or unintentionally, by your action, your words or your deeds. I ask that you forgive me for anything I may have done to you that has hurt you, intentionally or unintentionally.' Visualize the other person as receiving and accepting your words, visualize the happiness and feel the joy and love between you. Let the images fade away into empty space. (Note the use of affirmations and the generation of feeling.)

Even if the person is one you feel great antipathy towards, the procedure remains the same, but this time, precede your effort by forgiving yourself and follow it by forgiving someone to whom you have friendly feelings, then finish by visualizing and affirming the hard one, trying to keep the feelings of love and joy, the picture of friendliness that were easier to engender in the first part of the exercise.

Improving normal relationships

Not all relationships are going bad, but even the good ones can be improved. One of the joys of visualization, even when it involves another person, is that it is something that can be done solo. Just as your health or tennis can be improved using visualization techniques, so too, can the quality of your relationships. Of course, in some relationships, it is possible for each member to work with the other in exploring the inwardness of their relationship. In too many, however, it is not possible and it is then that the methods outlined on page 67 may be utilized — first of all to get the negativities out of the way and then to work on the positive, creating beautiful, loving and fulfilling relationships.

It is in improving relationships that a variation of Roberto Assagioli's 'acting as if' technique might be peculiarly useful. Instead of acting on yourself alone, act as if the entire relationship had a desired quality, then act as if both of you in the relationship knew what to do to improve matters. Remember, as I have hinted before, that the mind has inner resources and often appears to know precisely what to do in order to produce a desired end once a target has been introduced.

If you wish a relationship to be a happy one, then it does not seem impossible to achieve this through visualizing yourself and your partner as being happy and smiling and also acting as if a happier state of affairs actually existed. It's easier to change a facial expression than an emotion. I'm reminded here of Roberto Assagioli's second operative law, as expressed in *The Act of Will*: 'Attitudes, movement and actions tend to evoke corresponding images and ideas; these in turn . . . evoke or intensify corresponding emotions and feelings.' All that Assagioli is saying is what is generally conceded, that in relation to improving skills in relationships, the way to go is to *do* positive things.

We go one step further. As much of what we choose to do first crystallizes within the mind before emerging into action, this implies that the way to improve a relationship — as in acquiring a positive self-image — is to visualize yourself and your partner doing positive things and the cybernetic system will do the rest. However, no one would say that relationships are easy to maintain or to repair: a good deal of self-knowledge and self-control is involved. Indeed, the pursuit of effective visualization in any field is not all that easy — a fair amount of preparation is needed and it is to the latter that I now turn.

6.

Preparation

This chapter is about how to prepare yourself for serious visualization. It is also about how visualization itself can help you do just that — an actual and joyous example of pulling yourself up by your own bootstraps!

To succeed in changing through controlled visualization seems easy because it sounds as if you just imagine it and it will happen. If that were indeed the case we'd all be millionaires. Perhaps it hasn't helped that all the examples I've used so far emphasize relaxation, but, paradoxically, it is by no means easy to maintain relaxation. This is a skill that has to be learned, unless you are lucky enough to be like John Reid who apparently discovered the secret of controlled visualization by accident while lying in bed. Having said this, neither does it need to be as hard as Eugen Herrigel made it for himself.

We have seen that we are what we are through the internal mental models we construct, reinforce and use to interpret the information we get through our senses. It is changing these models that is the difficult thing and that demands hard work. Successful controlled visualization is not easy and is a skill that is generally underrated. If we are to use our powers of imagination and harness our wills and emotions to the task of shaping our lives at whatever level we choose, we need to practice fundamental skills. Fortunately, as I've said, they can be practised as a part of the visualization process itself.

Obstacles to success

The monkey mind
With so many of our mental pictures prepared and presented ready-made to us via the TV, we are perhaps fast losing the power — never very strong — to consciously construct our own pictures. Similarly,

the pictures we have in our minds are in general very fleeting. There is a constant input of stimuli via our senses and, as a consequence, our minds flit unceasingly from one image to another, never concentrating for very long on any one of them — rather like the telly-addict flicking unceasingly from channel to channel in search of the ideal programme.

At least the TV channels are limited in number. Not so the welter of fleeting 'programmes' at our disposal within our skulls, or wherever the mind may be situated. There are various ways of describing this welter: Janette Rainwater refers in *You're in Charge* to 'Head Chatter'; Kathleen McDonald in *How to Meditate* compares mind to an ocean and '. . . momentary mental events such as happiness, irritation, fantasies and boredom to the waves that rise and fall on its surface'. I, however, prefer to call it the monkey mind, for to get a monkey to rest for any length of time on any particular branch can be very difficult if not impossible. We have the electronic chatter outside and the neuron chatter inside, both conspiring to weaken our control of our mind and its power, but this need not be so.

Cultural spectacles

Another obstacle is a cultural barrier, one that is gradually being dismantled, but one that is still there nevertheless.

Through our culturally-distorting 'spectacles', any talk of stilling the mind is something that is seen as being the province of the mystic and the mystic is seen as an ineffective dreamer, a drop-out from the 'real' world. Yet no one thinks it strange if a neighbour goes off to the local gym once or twice a week and trains there in a disciplined manner in order to improve his *physical* fitness. Just as most people's *bodies* are relatively unco-ordinated and less efficient than they need be, so, too, are their *minds*. At the very least, then, greater everyday efficiency will result from disciplined mind-training, whether or not it is undertaken in order to increase effective visualization.

It is hard work, yes, but if a person goes to play squash twice a week in order to maintain fitness and lessen stress, he or she is surely able to devote the same sort of time and energy to getting their mind in shape.

The mental gymnasium

A squash player is motivated to beat his or her opponent. A gymnast knows exactly what he or she intends to achieve by way of particular exercises. Just as gymnasts and squash players are hyped up to succeed for *themselves*, so, too, should anyone intent on taming their monkey mind be doing it because *they* want to and not because of pressures from outside, such as those from a wife, husband, coach, boss or bank manager.

A coach or a guru is able to succeed only in so far as they cause their pupil to generate self-motivation. No amount of shouting from the sidelines will be very effective.

Just as a gymnast needs a gym, or at least some minimal apparatus, and a squash player needs a court, so, a person preparing their mind for greater efficiency has some minimal requirements. Since relaxation is a prime need, these can indeed be very minimal — a bed, an easy chair, a room free from distractions is all that need be recommended.

For visualization sessions, then, relax in a quiet place at a time that is likely to be free from interruptions. The spot chosen should feel good, and have pleasant or at least neutral associations. Kathleen McDonald in *How to Meditate* recommends reserving a comfortable and pleasing room or corner for your sessions, having a particular seat and a table with inspiring books and so on. In crowded accommodation such words are often counsels of perfection, but it is, when all is said and done, the attitude of mind that is of prime importance.

You may already find yourself at this point yawning, thinking of having another coffee, flicking through the pages of the book. What has happened, of course, is that the monkey mind is trying it on again! People need to find their own way and one of the things to try to do is to lull that monkey mind into a false sense of security. The essence when beginning is to make this as easy as possible for yourself. We carry a lot of cultural baggage around with us that will make us ready to laugh at ourselves and give the whole thing up as too ridiculous, too time consuming. We will also find the monkey mind has lots of tricks up its velvet sleeve that it will use in order to avoid being tamed. Just keep the person you want to be at the forefront of your mind, find that quiet corner and peaceful time and begin — begin by breathing.

Breathing

Breathing is something we do all the time. Relaxing is not, yet proper breathing can lead to relaxation and is, in any case, important and worth cultivating for its own sake in these noisy, stressful days in which we live.

All relaxation exercises, as I shall shortly show, have as a prerequisite the attainment of regular, unforced, easy breathing and all breathing exercises in their turn have as their *raison d'être* not only relaxation but greater control of the mind and body.

How we breathe shows the state of our internal being. Perturbations of body, mind or feeling are always accompanied by characteristic breathing. Healthy breathing is breathing that benefits the whole person, not just the physical body: it benefits the mind, the emotions and the spirit.

As I have shown previously, the belief that matter and spirit are opposite extremes of a dimension of energy is a common one, especially in the East. The breath, too, is often seen as a form of that energy. Chinese Taoists, for instance, from time immemorial have placed much emphasis on the breath. They regard it as a relatively coarse form of cosmic energy uniting men and women with the ground of being that they call the *Tao*. In martial arts, Taoists are encouraged to visualize the flow of breath, which they call *ch'i*, and to direct its energy to parts of the body as appropriate. Most Eastern religions, indeed, share this basic belief and Hindus, for instance, say 'Whenever inbreath and outbreath fuse, at this instant touch the energyless energy-filled *centre*' (Paul Reps, *Zen Flesh, Zen Bones*, Pelican, 1971).

Zen Buddhists, too, use consciousness of the breath in their various forms of meditation. As Alan Watts in his *The Way of Zen* (Pelican, 1970) says,

> Whether Zen is practised through *za-zen* [sitting meditation] or *cha-no-yu* [Tea Ceremony] or *kendo* [swordsmanship], great importance is attached to the way of breathing. Not only is breathing one of the two fundamental rhythms of the body, it is also the process in which control and spontaneity, voluntary and involuntary action, find their most obvious identity. Long before the origins of the Zen School, both Indian *yoga* and Chinese Taoism practised 'watching the breath', with a view to *letting* — not forcing — it to become as slow and silent as possible. Physiologically and psychologically, the relationship between breathing and 'insight' is not yet altogether clear. But if we look at man as process rather than entity, rhythm rather than structure, it is obvious that breathing is something that he does — and thus *is* — constantly.

All that having been said, it will surely do us in the West no harm to become more conscious of the flow of our breath and to try to use it to help control our tensions and restlessness.

Can visualization help with this? Well, yes it can because, as Alan Watts just mentioned, a widely used method of using the breath in encouraging relaxation is called 'watching the breath'. The phrase instantly brings to mind the act of visualization. In watching the breath, you may choose to follow it as a thin mist as it enters the nostrils, flows deep down into the body and out again or you may choose to concentrate on the tip of your nose and just observe the breath as it flows in and out. Kathleen McDonald in *How to Meditate* advises us to 'Keep your attention on this subtle perception and observe the full duration of each inhalation and exhalation.' Some people prefer to count the breaths, seeing a visualized numeral drop down into their body as each breath is counted. Some Zen practitioners see a heavy ball of lead descending through the centre of the body on each outbreath, the heavy ball squeezing out stale air from the lungs as it falls slowly and deeply.

Joel Levey in *The Fine Arts of Relaxation, Concentration and Meditation* suggests going further. He suggests that you think of a word that reflects the quality you wish to be filled with, such as relaxation, harmony or balance, then 'See that particular quality as luminous energy that, as you inhale, rises within you, fills you and flows through you, completely permeating your bodymind. Allow this light energy to dissolve all your negative states of mind, tension or pain . . .' As you exhale, he suggests you see the tensions and so on flowing out of you and melting away.

Effective breathing is not just important for effective visualization, it is equally important to effective living, being the basis of good health, mindfulness, calmness and good humour. Janette Rainwater in *You're in Charge* suggests that it is, therefore, a good idea to stop whatever you are doing from time to time and to ask yourself four questions:

- 'What am I doing?'
- 'What am I feeling?'
- 'What am I thinking?'
- 'How am I breathing?'

By the time the first three questions have been answered, the breath will generally have become easy and deep, so close is the relationship between body, mind, feelings and breath.

Mindfulness

To concentrate thus on watching the breath is an exercise in mindfulness. The practice of mindfulness, in other words concentration on what is happening here and now, is the most basic and can be the most difficult of the exercises it is necessary to master to achieve any task at any level, whether or not you are practising visualization. It is clarity of mind that is to be practised, by which I mean the achievement of what has been called one-pointedness, in order to rid the mind of the stream of irrelevant lumber that pollutes its clarity. By doing this one gains the ability to empty the mind of all except that which you *choose* to have in it, which is obviously of immense benefit in visualizing when the clearer the thought, the more pointed the energy and the more likely the transformation of mental images. It is also of immense benefit to your tranquility.

Mindfulness needs to be practised — there are no short cuts to taming the monkey. As with weight training, becoming a scratch golfer or learning a language, persistence is needed and none more so than in the practice of what is basic to all of these — control of the monkey mind. If readers balk at my inclusion of weight training as an occupation needing control of the mind, I reply that even in so physical a pursuit, for best results, the mind must be enlisted in order that it may lead the body to improvement. Visualization of blood flowing to the muscles, for instance, will actually have an effect on the flow. Indeed, we can learn from weight trainers. None of them would try a method for a couple of minutes, or even a single session and then leave it and flit to something else. In the same way, it is clearly necessary to recommend at least two weeks of practice at any one of the exercises I describe in this chapter for 20 minutes a day before trying another.

Techniques for inducing mindfulness

Watching the breath, as we've seen, is a suitable means.

A gentler introduction to the practice than this, which can be quite difficult in the early stages, is suggested by Joel Levey in *The Fine Arts of Relaxation, Concentration and Meditation*. He suggests you choose an activity you enjoy and then determine to bring prolonged and full attention to it for increasingly lengthy periods of time, gently bringing the attention back when it wanders, as it surely will. He suggests that at the end of such a session, you reflect on 'the new richness you have discovered' in the chosen activity.

Joel Levey and others also suggest that mindfulness can be practised in the midst of mundane, everyday household activities. All such activities, from peeling potatoes to vacuuming the carpet, can be transformed into exercises in mindfulness. It is in the paying of really close attention to the activity, and to whatever is happening in this present moment, that is found the key to this transformation. A quality of mental aliveness is engendered by such exercises and this quality does not emerge from the activity, but from the depth of mindfulness that is brought to bear.

Thich Nhat Hahn, in his book *The Miracle of Mindfulness* (Beacon Press, 1975) says,

> If while washing dishes, we think only of the cup of tea that awaits us, thus hurrying to get the dishes out of the way as if they were a nuisance . . . we are not alive during the time we are washing the dishes. In fact, we are completely incapable of realizing the miracle of life while standing at the sink. If we can't wash the dishes [with awareness], the chances are we won't be able to drink our tea [with awareness] either. While drinking the cup of tea, we will only be thinking of other things, barely aware of the cup in our hands. Thus we are sucked away into the future — and we are incapable of actually living one minute of life.

This insight is not new. Theravada Buddhists in particular have long practised mindfulness of those two everyday activities: breathing and walking. An excellent insight into their practices may be obtained by reading EH Shattock's book *An Experiment in Mindfulness* in which he describes his own experiences at a Burmese Buddhist meditation centre. When he wrote of his experiences in the 1950s, his account was thought of as being truly unusual, but nowadays such meditation centres are fairly common and the practice of mindfulness of breathing is not unusual.

Mindfulness of walking is rarer. We in the West have not yet slowed down sufficiently to do this, necessitating as it does a mindful concentration on the three phases of walking. These are lifting the foot, swinging it forward and placing the foot on the ground. The meditator is instructed to mentally name each movement 'up', 'forward', 'down', together with mindfulness of 'stopping' and 'turning'. Try it, for, if time can be found for it, this mindfulness exercise is of true value. Indeed, anything that can slow down the frenetic pace of many people's lives must be of benefit.

Levey, making allowances, suggests a less arduous 'mindfulness of walking' exercise in which he suggests counting five paces, then six paces and so on up to ten, before repeating the procedure. This can be practised in a busy Western street without embarrassment, but is of less value than the Burmese practice.

Eating, too, is an everyday activity that can be practised mindfully. In this you try to become aware of seeing the food, then of your intention to eat it, reaching for it, touching it, lifting it, opening your mouth, putting the food in, lowering your arm, feeling the texture of the food, chewing, tasting and swallowing. This can be followed by mindfulness of the desire for more food and so on. It is best done alone, and not in the local fast food eatery.

Another method of getting the mind into the way of one-pointedness is to use a 'mantra'. This is a method that has been used by all religions in enabling their followers to become rapt in contemplation of the divinity, but God or a god need not be involved for the practice to be beneficial. What is done is to repeat a phrase over and over again, so that you become aware only of the chanting and of nothing else. Religious examples include *Om* and *Hare Krishna* from the East generally, *Om Mane Padme Hum* from Tibetan Buddhism, *Deus in adjutoriam meum intende* from Christianity, *Nam myoho renge kyo* from Nichiren Shoshu Buddhism (the latter being the religion that uses the mantra almost to the exclusion of everything else and which has a growing number of adherents in the West). There is no harm done if the phrase appears to be meaningless, indeed, many, including Lawrence LeShan, prefer meaningless phrases.

The method is also used by those who practice Transcendental Meditation in which each member is given a personal mantra to aid concentration in meditation.

Relaxation

And so we come to relaxation, without which no visualization can begin to be successful.

Relaxation is not a limp ineffective passivity, it is a contrived letting go of tension, often associated with that awareness of breathing that leads to non-stressed, easy mental alertness that so many practitioners of self-improvement recommend. Herbert Benson in *Your Maximum Mind* (Aquarian Press, 1988), for instance, speaks of the 'Relaxation Response' and Donald Wilson in *Total Mind Power* of 'Focused Awareness'. It is a skill the acquisition of which is not merely useful in preparation for mindfulness exercises, but useful in all of life's activities. It is a skill that is often thought to refer only to the body, but it can be applied to emotional well-being and mental activity too. While the three go together, it is useful to be able to concentrate on one or another, depending on where the stress is most strongly manifesting itself. As skill is acquired, you will know more often when it is your body that is over-stressed, and what part of the body can be let go of, whether your emotions are the seat of the problem or whether it is the monkey mind that is needing to rest.

Techniques of relaxation

Physical relaxation
Advice as to physical relaxation abounds. Here are some typical methods.

- Sweep the body with your attention, starting at the top of the head and passing down the body, concentrating on each part of the body and allowing it to relax.

- Tense your body as hard as you can, clenching your fists, curling your toes, expanding your biceps, screwing up your face. Hold the maximum tension possible for a few minutes, experiencing how it feels. Then relax completely, exhaling all of your breath, letting go into gravity. Repeat a couple of times.

- Make a note of which parts of your body are touching the chair or floor or bed. Every place that is touching you is also supporting you, so let yourself go a little more into that support and imagine the chair or bed or floor rising a little to support you better. Relax any muscles you are using to hold yourself up.

- Begin by getting comfortable, keeping the body still. Take five slow full breaths, then breathe slowly and smoothly with no breaks between breaths. Visualize and feel the flow of relaxation as you repeat or listen to such phrases as 'I feel quiet', 'I am beginning to feel quite relaxed', 'My feet, my ankles, my knees and my hips feel heavy, relaxed and comfortable', 'The whole central region of my body feels relaxed and quiet', 'My hands feel warm, heavy and relaxed' and so on up to the head. Then say, 'My jaw and my forehead are deeply relaxed. They feel comfortable and smooth, my whole body feels quiet, comfortable and deeply relaxed.'

- Yet another method of physical relaxation mentioned by Kathleen McDonald in *How to Meditate* is to visualize your body as hollow.

    Starting at the centre of your chest, imagine that all the internal, solid parts of your body dissolve into light, and then into empty space. Everything within your chest, head, arms and legs gradually dissolves and becomes empty. Your skin transforms into a very thin membrane of light to enclose this empty space. Concentrate for a while on this experience of your body being hollow, like a balloon.

Most relaxation techniques do in fact concentrate on relaxing the body, leaving the mind to follow, which is, of course, perfectly valid, but since the general tenor of this book is that the mind more often leads the body, I now introduce some techniques that aim to relax the mind.

Mental relaxation

- One method — indeed, a fundamental method — of easing mental tension and excitement is to concentrate firmly on the breath and let the mind become as calm and even as the natural rhythm of the breathing. Observe whatever thoughts arise without getting involved in them, imagine them as waves of the mind, rising and falling.

- Another typical method is, after taking five deep, slow, full breaths, to breathe slowly and smoothly with no breaks and at the same time visualize and feel the following: 'I feel quiet now, my mind is very quiet, calm and clear as I withdraw my thoughts from the surroundings and I feel serene, still and at ease. Deep within myself I can visualize and experience myself as relaxed, comfortable, open, flowing and still.'

Emotional relaxation

Emotional agitation may be eased by visualizing the following: 'My hands are heavy and warm, I feel quiet, very quiet, warmth is flowing into my hands, they are warm. As I breathe in I am filled with warmth and well-being, exhaling, I am able to let my heart and mind open to allow my feelings to come and flow.'

A combination of physical, mental and emotional relaxation is to be found in what Levey and others call Rainbow Light Relaxation in which you imagine you are surrounded by a luminous red-coloured mist of relaxation and well-being. Breathing in, you imagine the mist filling your head, neck and shoulders, sinking into and permeating every pore and fibre. Breathing out, you visualize exhaling all physical tensions, thoughts, cares or mental dullness that is around in this part of the body. Repeat with the torso, the genitals, buttocks, legs and feet and finally the whole body. Direct the mist to any part of the body or mind that seems out of balance. With practice, it is possible to experiment with different colours to see which suits you best.

Getting and giving help

All of these techniques can be carried out solo, or with a partner and there are pros and cons associated with each.

Solo
When going it alone, many people may think that they have to remember the exact words and get worried about this. The feeling is clearly interfering with complete mindfulness and the person ends up as tense and stressed as when they started. Some try to get round this by recording the words on a tape-recorder. The disadvantage of this is that the timing is never right. The pauses are either too short or too long, generally the former, and the words themselves may be quite intrusive. The solution is to get the *general idea* in the mind and let the psycho-cybernetic process take over.

Many find themselves reaching the end of the planned meditation in a very short time, when a longer time would have been more effective. It is one of the curses of our age that we do everything in a rush and beginners — and, indeed, experienced people too — may find the habit creeping into their practice sessions as they sit trying to concentrate with the monkey mind forever reminding them of train timetables, shopping lists, appointments and all the other minutiae of modern living. It is here that some sort of opening and ending ritual is useful. A meditation is going well when time is felt to be of no importance.

Paired
If you meditate with a partner, take turns to talk the other through the visualization. Some sensitivity and closeness is needed for this to be effective and it is a good idea to spend some time in feeding back to the talker the effect they are having, whether it is the speed they are going at, the quality of their voice or whatever.

At its best, such paired practice is good. Provided there is trust and empathy between the partners and sufficient awareness and sensitivity in the guide, this can be a highly effective method. It is effective because the time scale can be better controlled.

Distractions
The world is a noisy place and sound from the outside world and the kids downstairs can be a problem. Donald Wilson in *Total Mind Power* goes so far as to suggest tuning into a television station that is not transmitting programmes as the sound of its carrier wave can be, he suggests, a highly effective way to blot out outside noises.

Meditation tapes are available on which soft melodious music, the sound of running water, bird song and other such gentle sounds are played. I personally find these more distracting than helpful, but clearly there is a market for them. If you own a personal stereo, you could do some experimenting.

As regards visual distractions, Donald Wilson suggests that these can be screened out by setting up weak strobe lights. He recommends that these be set to 12 beats a second, the rhythm of alpha brain waves. He warns against their use by epileptic patients and I would say that such apparatus is, in any case, too elaborate for use by many people. A much more effective thing to do is to darken the room. The presence of a lighted candle in a dimly-lit room can be soothing, as can the aroma of a stick of burning incense.

Most important of all, however, is to feel comfortable. Any of the aids I've mentioned can detract from the desired effect if they cause embarrassment. As the mind becomes tuned and feels the benefit of training, such feelings will pass. You doubtless had similar feelings when going out of the door the first time you went jogging and it may have been some time before you gave up the old trousers and plimsolls in favour of a tracksuit and trainers.

So far as internal distractions are concerned, it is necessary to distance yourself from everyday worries. The setting helps to do this, providing as it does an environment that is different from the normal. Eugene Gendlin in his book *Focusing* (Bantam, 1981) suggests mentally 'standing back' a little from everyday problems. As a problem or other preoccupation emerges from the recesses of the mind, he suggests you acknowledge it and then put it to one side. Do the same with succeeding ones, making a mental promise to look at them some other time, and then dismiss them. Visualize them being lined up to one side.

Above all, it's important to show the monkey mind who's boss. Decide firmly to leave behind all problems, worries and involvements, immerse yourself in the silence of your special place and inner world and relax — but not too much.

Posture

Posture is important. John Reid lay in bed to do his visualizing, almost daydreaming, but most people in such a posture would just go to sleep. Instead, position your body in such a way that you stay alert as that monkey is as ready to introduce the idea of muscle pain and bodily itches as it is mental blocks and other resistances. Of course, itches and aches do occur. They can be dealt with in the same way as pain can be controlled, that is by making them a part of mindfulness of the present. They go quite quickly.

Almost everyone who is into such mind-training agrees that what is fundamental to comfort and concentration is for the spine to be straight. Beyond that, advice varies considerably, with recommendations varying from lying down, to sitting in an upright chair, to sitting in the full lotus position. There is room here for experimentation as nothing is barred if it results in effective monkey taming. My own method suits my no-longer-young body. I kneel, having a small cushion beneath my ankles and a larger one between my heels and my buttocks. Anything goes!

In addition, I've found that as I get into meditation my body very often makes necessary corrections of its own volition. Certainly, to visualize an ideal position and then to allow the body to follow its cybernetic tendency is very effective.

Meditation

So far, I've been carefully avoiding over-use of this word, because it is an activity that a good many people shy away from. This is certainly due to some misconceptions.

Mental pictures of bearded, half-naked swamis sitting cross-legged in lotus postures, of trance states in which sharp spears are driven into naked flesh, of claims for levitation, all made possible through the achievement of some other-worldly higher state of mind, through union with Cosmic Consciousness or with God, are part of the considerable prejudice that gets in the way for many people when the word 'meditation' comes up. It is, they think, the field of mysticism and this, too, is a word that they shy away from.

There is no doubt that the practice of meditation is a path by which many people attain union with their gods and it is equally true that most meditational techniques have been developed by mystics, but many *more* people, who may have no pretensions to religion or mysticism are finding the practice of benefit. As Joel Levey says in *The Fine Arts of Relaxation, Concentration and Meditation,*

> Today, meditation techniques are undergoing a secular revival as our state oracle of science discovers and proclaims the benefits of meditation as a remedy to the epidemic stress of modern life . . . many people are being introduced to powerful and highly effective mental technologies of personal transformation that have been the cherished and often secret practices of many ancient traditions.

So, it seems clear that the practice of meditation has found (or regained) its place in the art or science of psychotherapy, the subject of succeeding chapters. At the very least, it can lead to inner peace and increased powers of confidence, concentration and, indeed, of visualization, which it can both foster and utilize. It is in these increased powers, particularly of confidence and concentration, that the common idea of mystics as dreamy people divorced from the concerns of the world is very far from the mark. On the contrary, their mental gymnastics make them both intellectually and emotionally highly efficient. Indeed, it was Alan Watts who indicated earlier that many Eastern meditational traditions such as Buddhism or Taoism are akin to Western psychotherapy in their effects. It is in the respect of increased concentrative powers that this present chapter has been concerned.

So what is meditation? A dictionary definition is that it is '... to consider thoughtfully'.

Lawrence LeShan writes in *How to Meditate* (Turnstone Press, 1983) that the '... real goal of meditation was to "come home" to parts of ourselves that we had lost, to become fuller human beings.' Janette Rainwater writes in *You're in Charge* that '... it is a discipline that enables you to take responsibility for the contents of your awareness.'

Meditation has, it seems, become respectable again. It is used by business people and by sports people, it is practised privately at home and publicly in locker rooms, it forms part of the preparation for examinations and football matches. It is worth remembering, however, that all these heavily utilitarian applications are the growing preoccupation of only a fraction of the people on this planet. The older, less overtly utilitarian uses, such as reaching towards wholeness and striving for self-realization, are maintained more widely as men and women wrestle with the problem of marrying together the dualities of their being — the earthly and the transcendental, the individual and the social, the human and the environmental. A wider definition that embraces these concerns is that proposed by Joel Levey who defines it in *The Fine Arts of Relaxation, Concentration and Meditation* '... as a skilful means of moving from the pain of our personal and planetary fragmentation towards the direct intuitive understanding of our wholeness and potential as human beings.'

So far, I have concentrated attention on one particular type of meditational technique. This is the type of meditation with which most people in the West are concerned, namely, the development of one-pointed concentration, of mindfulness, of getting in touch with now. Kathleen McDonald calls it *stabilizing meditation*. There is another type, which she calls *analytical meditation* and which Roberto

Assagioli calls 'Creative Meditation'. This is like a kind of 'intensive study session' and is made possible through the development of the powers of concentration brought about by stabilizing meditation. It is a kind of meditation that I shall return to in a later chapter where I shall show that it is through this kind of meditation that techniques of visualization have been developed to a high point by members of some religious traditions.

On a lighter note and to end this Chapter with a bit of fun, next time you have a knotty problem, try this exercise, described more fully by Janette Rainwater in her Chinese Temple Exercise in *You're in Charge*.

First, get in a meditative position and observe your breathing. Next, imagine that you are climbing many stone steps up a steep hill. At the top of the hill there is a Chinese temple with a pagoda roof. There are doors in the centre of each of the four sides. On each door is carved a golden dragon. Push open one of the doors and enter the temple.

There is no furniture inside, just many scrolls in racks like the stacks in your public library. Select one of the scrolls. Take it to the centre of the room where there is a bright light coming down from the raised skylight. Unroll the scroll. Read it and find the answer to your question.

7.
To Love Ourselves (Part I)

At the beginning of this book, I suggested that neurosis arose as a result of a conflict between our ego ideal and our present being, but what is the ego ideal? I suggest that it is based on our own inner potential for growth and fulfilment rather than on any external model.

We have seen how the self-concept is fundamental to our success or failure in life because of the fact that if our self-concept leaves us dissatisfied, leaves us aware that there is more to us and to our life than is presently apparent, we feel that we have failed, we cannot love ourselves.

We have seen too, how visualization is a means of directing the flow and form of energy and reshaping the self-concept. Psychotherapy often uses visualization techniques and is good when it is leading us to realize that ideal that we feel lies within us. Not all therapy does this, though, much of it being concerned only with adjustment.

I have already shown that our working model of the world and ourselves in it is formed early in life. If we are regarded by our peers and others as reasonably mentally healthy, it is too often because our working model conforms fairly closely to the view of the world that is accepted as valid by those other members of our culture, not excluding our parents. That we may therefore be acting inauthentically is neither here nor there. Pressure to conform is great, reaching its nadir in pre-Gorbachev Russia but potentially present in all groups, in which anyone deviating from the consensus is seen as weird and perhaps psychiatrically ill and so in need of cure. The object of a cure in such cases is to return the patient to 'normality' (whatever that may be), in other words to rearrange his or her perceptions of 'reality'.

It would seem that psychotherapy, then, is central to the concerns with which we are faced in this book (it is no accident that this chapter arises near its midpoint). In this chapter and the next, I shall largely, but not entirely, confine myself to a consideration of those therapeutic methods that use visualization as a part of their procedures. I shall seek to show that the further East one gets from specifically Western therapies, the more we find visualization is an important weapon in the therapist's armoury.

In this chapter, I have divided my chosen therapies into two basic categories: the traditional one-to-one situation, which I call the 'guru model', and the group situation, which I call the 'ashram model', and in the next chapter, I shall look at some do-it-yourself methods of therapy. In both chapters, I shall be concerned to show how therapies seek to rejig reality and to repair the emotional scars that result from a conflict of realities. As I've suggested, the conflict may be interpreted in two ways, broadly conforming to two master models, the one leading to adjustment, the other to transcendence. On the one hand, for example, there is Sigmund Freud, with his structural scheme of the mind as being composed of parts he called the id, the ego and the super ego and his notion of the individual's basic drives, the id, coming to terms with the real world. On the other hand, opposing, or complementing, this is the view that therapy is concerned with the soul, with self-realization and in this it may be seen to be replacing or complementing traditional religion. Carl Jung's name will probably spring to mind at this point and it is noteworthy that he is the therapist who explored the East the most thoroughly of all Western therapists.

Guru therapies

The first several of these aim at adjustment. It is worth noting that few of them make much use of visualization, but I describe them so as to present a balanced picture and to illustrate the prevalence of the limited and traditional view of therapy as a means of adjustment.

Existential Therapy

Many people thinking of seeking psychotherapy are of the West, Western and may no longer have the fall back on religion that their forebears had. Nor, too often, do they have the protection that used to be found in the extended family and the local community. The picture of the nuclear family separated from old friends and relatives in a distant, sanitized suburb leads to a realization of how large numbers of people feel isolated and subject to that inner emptiness dignified by such terms as 'existential angst'.

Binswanger and Laing are two therapists who represent the Existentialist approach to therapy. Although Joel Kovel in *A Complete*

Guide to Therapy (Pelican, 1978) says that such approaches are engaged in 'Salvaging faith in a godless world', their methods are present-moment oriented, working not from the larger perspective of ancient philosophies that see the present as coexistent with past and future, but from the limited, empty present moment that characterizes the existential despair of modern, Western men and women. Like Jung, they are critical of the alienation characteristic of the scientific age ('. . . no one can begin to think, feel or act now except from the starting point of his or her own alienation' — Laing). Unlike Jung, they completely eschew any mystical picture of the universe.

Directive Therapy
I have looked at this kind of therapy in my chapters on healing, in which physical cures, cures of allergies and so on, might be effected, for example, by hypnosis and a consequent surrender of the patient's will to that of the therapist (with a consequent reliance on the authority of the latter). It is a pragmatic approach, taking things to be as they appear to be on the surface and dealing with those symptoms.

As we have seen, hypnosis sets out to induce an altered, passive state of consciousness that then becomes fertile ground for visualization and counter-suggestion. While it is very effective in terms of helping patients to give up smoking cigarettes, for example, it is likely to be less so in curing deep-seated neuroses or even in curing the deep-seated neuroses that led in the first place to smoking cigarettes. Nevertheless, a sufferer may be content to live with an improved self-image and improved health and to let the deeper problems go hang.

Behaviour Therapy
Similarly, Behaviour Therapists use operant (Skinnerian) conditioning to modify surface behaviour. Just as pigeons may be taught to read — or rather to go through the *motions* of reading by a system of food rewards — so similar methods of reinforcement are used to modify aberrant (that is, socially unacceptable) behaviour in humans. It is much used for ridding people of phobias by means of progressive desensitization. For instance, to a person suffering from a phobia of snakes, it introduces rewards for tolerating tiny worms before moving on to larger and larger and finally to huge snakes. It is also used in the treatment of school phobia and juvenile delinquency.

Transactional Analysis
This starts from a thesis that we've met before, namely that each person has a life-script that is written, as it were, in early childhood

that shapes relations with others throughout life. The human personality is seen as consisting of three parts: the adult, the parent and the child and all human interactions are seen as interactions between these. A woman, for instance, may consistently act as a compliant child in her relationships with men, and consequently draw out of her men the strict, perhaps punishing, parent. By looking at such interactions, Transactional Analysis gives the opportunity to 're-write' the life-script by rejigging the self-concept.

Joel Kovel makes the point in *A Complete Guide to Therapy* that Transactional Analysts mimic the parameters of modern life (with its emphasis on tapes, scripts, games and so on) and that the 'adult' that participants are urged to develop is the ideal principle of the bourgeois order. 'TA appeals precisely by staying away from the extremes of experience and so unifying people . . . with the compact majority in the middle.'

Reality Therapy

So-called Reality Therapy goes further and takes as basic the belief that if we behave more responsibly, conform to the mores of society, then neurosis will go away. This is another form of reliance on authority and there is an implicit belief that society offers the best of worlds. Such a view reached its nadir, as I have said, in Russia in the classification of political deviants as mentally deranged.

Before moving on to those therapies that are the main concern of this chapter in that they utilize visualization as a basic tool, it is inevitably necessary to look at the ideas of the founding father of scientific psychotherapy.

Freud and the Neo-Freudians

The best-known of all guru therapies is, of course, Freudian Psychoanalysis. The underlying theory presents a view of how a neurotic self-image may be formed. The characteristic of this very lengthy and expensive therapy is that it is concerned with the repression of infantile sexuality, such repression causing a fundamental and often lifelong blockage of its expression. In this we see how the preoccupation of Freud's culture situated in Europe in the latter part of the nineteenth century came out in his view of what was an acceptable model of reality. Indeed, it is interesting that it is now becoming acceptable to show how Freud changed tack when it became apparent that his suspicion of prevalent child sexual abuse did not fit in with the culture's *Weltanschaung*.

It may, of course, now be the case that sex is no longer the main aspect of our lives to be repressed, but neurosis still occurs, indicating that its cause may lie deeper. Leaving that for the moment, it has become generally accepted that the developing infant's difficulties in adjusting its own intense and unbounded feelings to the hard reality of even the most loving family is a root cause of neurosis. After all, a lifelong working model of the world as being unpredictable, inconsistent and inimical to one's perceived best interests is easily developed.

An illustration of the strength of this repression of intense feelings in young children — intense because it is boundless — may be seen in Arthur Janov's Primal Therapy, in which neurosis is seen as stemming from deeply buried, painful, negative childhood experiences that, in Joel Kovel's words in *A Complete Guide to Therapy*, '. . . sit like a lump in the breast through all later days'. A chronic state of tension results. The 'Primal Trauma' of Janov's theory is the emotional scar that formed like a callus when the child realized that his parents did not love him. All his patients end up by screaming out this very real, if subjective, fact, therapist-led though the dramatic therapeutic climax may be. Something similar seems to happen in Turning Point group sessions, where what appears to be a nice example of uncontrolled visualization occurs: 'During the weekend, I had a rebirth . . . I screamed . . . I rolled up on the floor . . . they helped me . . . I got this phlegm in my throat — it happens to newborn babies . . .' and so it continues.

Such theatrical excesses are avoided by traditional Freudian analysts who pursue the gentle way of the Analytic Basic Rule. This Rule is that the patient is to say (or try to say) to the shadowy therapist beyond the couch whatever comes spontaneously to mind. Free-flowing spontaneous expression is the aim. Such analysts follow the Basic Rule not because there is any curative property in any of the knowledge so acquired, but because the cure comes, if it comes at all, through the struggle to overcome repressed barriers to saying what comes to mind to another person who may — indeed, must — take on the characteristics of that person who was the original cause of the neurosis. Whatever more effective working model of reality emerges, if it ever does, one thing is certain. This is that the self-concept of the analysand is invariably altered in the direction of dependency on the analyst — that shadowy figure behind the couch. It is no longer such a Woody Allen-type joke to claim that people really do avoid making often quite insignificant decisions before consulting their analyst and this is hardly a result that would appear to be leading to autonomy or emotional independence.

As is well known, Freud's followers departed from him on many points. Alfred Adler, Karen Horney, Eric Fromm and other neo-Freudians rejected his libido theory as the main cause of emotional scarring. Instead, while accepting it as a prime causative agent, they placed more emphasis on the two other important influences with which I opened this chapter. First there was the influence of the wider culture in which the child grows up. In our own day this is more and more consumer-led and competitive, encouraging greed, and at odds with the highest of which men and women are capable. Second there were the interpersonal relations of which the child was a part. Although both of these influences were coloured by the initial trauma and were to do with the feeling of isolation of individuals, with their feeling of being cut off from a community that they believe is rejecting them, there was a concern less with re-living or rediscovering the trauma and more with self-realization, assertiveness, self-evaluation and so on. An example of the sort of therapy that emerges from such a view is that of Gestalt Therapy.

Gestalt Therapy

'*Gestalt*' has no exact equivalent in English, but its closest approximation is 'configuration' or 'pattern'. Its founder, Fritz Perls, based his work on the fact that individuals do live within an environment and that the nature of the relationship between them and their environment determines their behaviour. He felt that much of the neurotic confusion suffered by an individual was due to a lack of flexibility in the individual's self-concept. He or she was too often constrained by having to adopt one single role in society, with a consequent inability for spontaneous growth in other directions.

Perls' therapeutic approach lays emphasis on what is happening right *now*, rather than on what happened in the past or what will happen in the future. In its use of non-verbal experience and methods (by putting bodily movements and sensations on the same level as verbalizations), it is clearly trying to develop the use of the right hemisphere by moving away from the intellectualizations so beloved of the left and open up a pathway between the two. As Perls himself says, '. . . real communication is beyond words'.

It is a far cry from the couch-oriented therapy of Freud, making use as it does of an active form of therapy that may include much movement, such as talking to chairs, beating up cushions, visualization and so forth that I described in Chapter 5.

Carl Jung

Perhaps the most famous deserter of the Freudian fold was Carl Jung. His therapy is known as Analytical Psychology and, instead of regarding psychotherapy as a science, he was more inclined to see it as a present day continuation of an age-old quest by men and women for their highest good. While concerned with adjustment, Jung saw this as occurring only when the patient was put in touch with his higher self. Carl Jung has much to say that is recognizable to people in non-Western cultures and to followers of Eastern philosophies in particular. His basic organizing assumption is that the mind is more than that which is given by individual experience and includes the transpersonal 'collective unconscious'. Just as the skeleton and the genetic make-up of each of us is a function of our history as a species, so, too, is the basis of our psyche.

Apart from reflecting the history of the human race and containing submerged archetypes that emerge in the mental life of the individual, Carl Jung says it is the collective unconscious that provides the motivational power of everyday life and thus we are able to say that it is comparable to such Eastern concepts as *ch'i* and *prana*. Jungian Therapy is to do with allowing the free flow of the influence of the collective unconscious and its archetypes. Any blockage will cause neurosis, but freedom of flow, on the other hand, leads, in Jung's view, to a realization and union with the self (see diagram on page 51). He encouraged this flow by allowing patients to express themselves through free-drawing, thus objectifying and controlling uncontrolled visualizations.

His basic theory was an optimistic one. He believed that man's intrinsic good nature was there waiting to be released. Like Sigmund Freud, he believed that what was preventing this flowering was a fear of hubris, of accepting the possibility of improvement, creativity and greatness. Unlike Freud, he believed that this fear of knowledge of oneself was to be cured by present- and future-oriented self-discovery rather than a backward-looking search for causes.

In this, he was echoed by such people as Abraham Maslow, who, in his investigation into the best of which man is capable in his research into peak experiences and the movement of individuals towards autonomy, believed that any generalization of findings derived from studies of mentally ill people was a waste of effort. To find how fast athletes could run, he said, you studied fit athletes, not unfit plodders. Studying 'self-realizers', he came to a conclusion that echoes that of Jung — that man's intrinsic good nature is essentially a biological feature, innate in the human species. Psychotherapy he saw to be transitional and a preparation for a still higher psychology — as he put it in *Towards a Psychology of Being* (Viking, 1971) '... transpersonal, transhuman, centred in the cosmos rather than in human needs and interest, going beyond humanness, identity, self-actualization, and the like'.

With the exception of Gestalt Therapy, all the therapies so far discussed have relied largely on verbal interaction between therapist and patient. We turn now to those that take as fundamental the assumption that we live essentially through the body and so minimize verbalization and social intervention. We shall see now that we are continuing to leave Europe behind and exploring not only the New World but the East. As I have hinted before, it is in the East that the ultimate in visualization techniques are to be found.

Reichian Therapy

Probably the best-known proponent of such bio-functional therapy was Wilhelm Reich, who took as a fundamental tenet the belief that anxiety is the emotional outcome of incomplete sexual release, which can often be observed not merely in behaviour, but in acute physical symptoms. In addition, he eased characterological blocks by paying attention to breathing, the creation of muscular tension and to movement patterns. These involved the therapist putting the patient's body (sometimes quite violently) into stress positions and pressing on muscles. The basic idea was to get the energy moving, for that was fundamental to his therapy. He applied this principle to mental problems such as schizophrenia (in which he believed the energy blockage was behind the eyes) and to physical diseases, such as cancer (which was caused, he believed, by a total bodily depletion of energy).

Reich's concept of energy, or life force, which he called 'orgone energy' is very close indeed to Indian *prana* and Chinese *ch'i*. Manipulation of the body by a therapist (as in Japanese massage (*Shiatsu*)) and by the patient him or herself (as in *T'ai Chi Ch'uan*) is common, but gentler, in Eastern remedies. He was thus moving away from the individual unconsciousness and towards the collective.

Psychosynthesis

We come now to a therapy that owes much to Jung, and is unashamedly concerned with the ego ideal, the superconscious, the self.

It is interesting that Psychosynthesis relies to a much greater extent than the other therapies we have looked at upon the patient practising visualization and, for that reason, I shall go further into it in my next chapter.

Its founder, Roberto Assagioli, took the Gestalt method a stage further. As we see in so much therapy, for example that of Carl Jung, Fritz Perls and Carl Rogers (below), a basic belief is that we already possess all that we need for our life-task. Quite overtly, Psychosynthesis brings in concepts such as self and superconscious. Roberto Assagioli and his school have devised an amalgam of various methods aiming at wholeness. As his disciple, Piero Ferrucci, says in *What We May Be*, this is '... the emergence of will and self-determination; the sharpening of the mind; the enjoyment of beauty; the enrichment of the imagination; the awakening of the intuition; the realization of love and the discovery of the Self and its purpose.'

One of Roberto Assagioli's most important tools is visualization, using concepts with which we are growing familiar. Here is his description of the creation of the 'Ideal Model'.

> The purpose is clear: that of utilizing the plastic, creative, dynamic power of images, particularly of visual images ... Here we emphasize the creative aspect of imagination in the sense that imagination creates mentally and emotionally, and then that which has been imagined and visualized is expressed outwardly through the use of natural means.
>
> In therapy it is a process of substituting a realistic, attainable model for those already existing in the subject which do not have such qualities.

He further takes as fact what Fritz Perls and our intuition persuades us is true — that we are not one personality, fit for all purposes and situations. Instead, we are a multiplicity of sub-personalities. We have public sub-personalities, switching them in accord with the social demands of the moment. We also have private sub-personalities and, as the Portuguese poet Fernando Pessoa wrote (*Una Sola Moltitudine*, Milan, 1980), 'In every corner of my soul there is an altar to a different god.' Each of us is a crowd of sub-personalities, continually scuffling in unceasing struggle.

Roberto Assagioli's methods involve a great deal of free-drawing, visualization and affirmation exercises. The visualization exercises, at their best, tend towards the non-verbal (right brain), using emotional images as well as visual. Affirming, on the other hand, clearly uses the verbal left brain. Between them they aim for an integration of the two.

Ashram therapy

So far we have concerned ourselves with therapies that set out to eradicate neuroses on a traditional one-to-one basis, with analyst and analysand closeted together. Two of these set out to enable us to scale the heights of which humans are capable, therapies that are as much for the soul as for the psyche. Others set their sights lower, more pragmatically, and aim either at adjustment of the neurotic individual within society or culture or with the eradication of symptoms. This brings me now to what I have called Ashram models of therapy.

In these, not an individual, but a group meets at the feet of a leader. In such groups, it is possible to play at alternative modes of acting in the world and to do so all the more confidently in being sheltered for a time from that world. Much experimentation may go on, since there is a relative absence of dogma.

Such therapies generally stem from the New World. For the moment we turn our backs on Europe and the East and immediately see important differences. Where the gurus of the East and the therapists of the Old World are not afraid to work with negative psychic forces, those of the New World largely ignore them. In addition, New World therapies, as a rule, are less concerned with cure than with progress towards worldly success, less concerned with the cure of the neurosis and psychosis and more with progress towards greater happiness and *communitas*. They are less concerned, too, with the past than with the future. Almost all ashram therapies, it is true, do found themselves on a basic belief in humanity's perfectibility, but they are less aware of the brilliance of the heights and more content with the dappled sunshine of the valley. They are a part of the New World's general genial optimism, a part of the 'How to Win Friends and Influence People' syndrome.

This kind of therapy uses visualizations, affirmations and role playing, games, group processes and so on. It seeks to enable the patient to become more assertive in relationships and to realize positive, sensible plans for getting ahead in life and having more fun. It relies on a commonsense exposure of self-defeating behaviour patterns, the participant being led to believe that it is his or her own belief system that leads to defeat or success.

Such groups seldom exceed 15 or so people, and may indeed be as small as two, as in co-counselling, in which two, often untrained, individuals take turns to listen uninterruptedly to the other.

Sex Therapy

As we saw in the last chapter, sex therapy is concerned with adjustment to neurosis or to relationship problems.

In sex therapy, the recognition of the fact that sexual dysfunction is the cause of much current unhappiness is accepted. The therapy generally takes a group of two as its subjects and often uses a couple as therapists (you have only to think of Masters and Johnson) and, in Joel Kovel's words in *A Complete Guide to Therapy*, '. . . aims at creating an emotional climate whose first and foremost role is to demystify sex, to make it more matter-of-fact'. As he goes on to remark, and as I emphasized above, this has the unfortunate effect of down-grading the fantasy side of sex. It is surface adjustment rather than inner change and the effects of this we have already noted, together with an example of a way this undesirable result can be counteracted.

Family Therapy

Neurosis is born in the family and, as we saw at the start of this chapter, the change in family patterns and, indeed, the virtual disappearance of the extended family as an institution is one of the two reasons for the appearance of therapy as a force in modern society. Children still start out in life as a member of a rudimentary family and the neuroses that can result from early childhood experiences are none the less real and the more serious if the family is failing or is inadequate. There is, therefore, a concern to prop up the family and Family Therapy is a result. In this, the whole of the family's relationships are observed and advised upon. The present state of the art uses a 'systems approach' that focuses on communication patterns within the immediate family as well as the larger family and neighbourhood.

Encounter Groups

These are very characteristic of ashram therapy, and were invented by Carl Rogers. In these, people come together not primarily to be cured of neuroses, but to encounter the possibility of more joy and spontaneity in their lives. This is achieved not least by physical encounter, physical and emotional group support, as well as by methods such as guided visualizations. Such groups are rarely larger than 15 members.

Their *raison d'être* is typified in such Rogerian words as,

> One of the most revolutionary concepts to grow out of our clinical experience is the growing recognition that the innermost core of a man's nature, the deepest layers of his personality, the base of his 'animal nature' is positive in nature — is basically socialized, forward-moving, rational and realistic.
>
> *On Becoming a Person* (Constable, 1974)

Many games are played, in which, for instance, individuals' abilities to trust others are explored. There will be guided meditation, in which members are encouraged to visualize ideal scenes or are guided in imagination through a landscape in which obstacles are overcome. There will be much touching and talking.

Group Therapy

By contrast, *est* (Erhard Seminars Training), Insight and similar methods use really large groups of 200 or so people, isolated from everyday life for a weekend in order to explore the possibility of self-development through the visualization of alternatives and resources such as the Best Therapist, ideal scenes, and above all by the exercise of choice. People are too often unaware of how much choice they can, in fact, exercise in their lives and of how many times they can see that what appears to be a necessity is, in fact, an opportunity to exercise choice, the chance to say 'No'.

Such group therapy can be extremely draining emotionally, as we saw above, for example, in discussing the 'Turning Point' groups. It is characteristic of group methods that way-out approaches may sometimes be tried. Clearly, unscrupulous group leaders as well as psychotic group members may take this opportunity to exercise control over people and severely neurotic people become over-stressed. However, many groups are a lot of fun, many of their procedures being joyous and light-hearted, and who is to say that they are any the less beneficial for that? It is a part of our puritan culture to believe that medicine is only effective if it is nasty and we must beware of taking the same stance in respect of psychotherapy. In general, it may be seen that what Group Therapy is about is giving members an idea of greater choice, as much by seeing the experience of others as by self-exploration. In addition they have the advantage of enabling people to be with others in such a way that those others are seen as non-threatening and the possibility of solidarity is encountered as well as a chance to open up new skills of relating with others.

It seems that all group therapies are concerned with the adjustment of the individual to, and their development within, society. Unlike religious ashrams, they are narrowly society-focused, not transcendence-focused. This observation returns me to a starting point.

This was that another reason for the growth of the therapy industry was the death of religion.

Among its many functions, religion had within its purlieu the mental health of its followers. Therefore, it may be that what Joel Kovel calls the 'mysticotranscendant' approach to therapy may be the most helpful to us latter-day neurotics. Jung and, from the point of view of our present concern, Roberto Assagioli, typify such approaches — the latter with his use of visualization as a means of channelling the flow of psychic energy within us.

We have noted how many therapists, having reached the limits of an objective approach to cure, find themselves looking East for inspiration and guidance.

As Joel Kovel says in *A Complete Guide to Therapy*,

> ... much Eastern doctrine is equivalent to a Western psychology as seen by a mind that gives greater weight — hence 'reality' — to its subjective forms. From another angle, this amounts to asserting the greater interrelatedness of all things — man-nature, male-female, knower-known, nation-nation — as against their separateness and opposition.

The basis of these approaches is that a different, more integrated and healthy state of consciousness is within us, waiting to be achieved. Abraham Maslow's peak experience or Freud's 'Oceanic Experience' may be the first (and for too many of us the only?) taste of the transcendent that lies within.

I hope I have shown that visualization techniques are not a New World invention, but are universally used and, most importantly, are not concerned solely with short-term advantages but with the individual's 'life task'. I'm encouraged to find that it is in those therapies most concerned with the latter that we find visualization to be a primary tool.

How a person sees his or her life task is very much a matter of how they see themselves in the world. Thus, from the point of view of this book, I feel it is those therapies that reorganize the self-image by means of visualization that are to be recommended, particularly Jungian Analysis and Psychosynthesis.

We shall see in a later chapter how visualization techniques are employed in spiritual development so that the Oceanic Experience may be deliberately fostered in an individual's thrust towards fulfilment.

8.
To Love Ourselves (Part II)

Macbeth	Canst thou not minister to a mind distress'd
	Pluck from the memory a rooted sorrow,
	Raze out the written troubles of the brain,
	And with some sweet oblivious antidote
	Cleanse the stuff'd bosom of that perilous stuff
	Which weighs upon the heart?
Doctor	Therein the patient
	Must minister to himself.

Shakespeare, Macbeth, Act V, Scene 4

Many people minister to themselves by ignoring therapy and adopting Yoga, Sufism, Zen, Nichiren Shoshu or Tibetan Mahayana Buddhism, Judaeo-Christian mysticism and meditation and the like, without overmuch (or any) recourse to a guru or to ashram. Others bypass even such traditional approaches as these and go for modernity, exploring biofeedback, audio and video tapes, psychedelic drugs and other such avenues.

I shall leave truly religious approaches to integration to a later chapter and confine myself here to therapies that are of the twentieth century, that make claims to scientific validity, to being mainly non-mystical, which use visualization techniques to some extent and that can be used 'in the privacy of one's own home' at one's own pace.

I start with two that are strictly of this age, using some of the latest modern technology: biofeedback and magnetic tapes.

Biofeedback

This is achieved through the use of machines that feed back tones or visual signals of body processes like heart-rate, skin temperature, brain waves and so on. Using such signals, you can learn to control these processes that were once believed to be beyond voluntary control.

Using the machine induces an increasing ability to acquire the relaxed and alert state required for meditation and visualization. More importantly, it leads you to have confidence in yourself and your ability to control these so-called involuntary responses. As a result, your self-concept is altered and, as we know, changing your expectations or fundamental assumptions about yourself can have far-reaching and profound effects on your physical and mental health.

Tapes

We saw in a previous chapter that audio tapes playing suitable music can be very useful as preparation for visualizing and meditation generally. As an advertisement for one of a series of such tapes has it, they provide 'A gentle stream of music that floats upon one's consciousness with scarcely a ripple'. This sums up their approach to calming the mind and body. Other audio tapes use hypnosis as a means of curing allergies and addictions, as I noted earlier.

Video tapes, too, offer a powerful means of hypnosis, using as they do the visual and auditory sensory modes. They may be used in improving sports performance and self-healing and make possible a more direct approach to self-psychotherapy.

Both audio and video tapes may use subliminal programming as well as hypnosis. Subliminal suggestions are made verbally and/or visually and consist of very brief, scarcely noticeable messages. Such messages are able to slip past the sentry of our normal rational wary consciousness (for that reason they are banned in advertising) and get their message across very effectively.

Most tapes of this kind are concerned with psychological matters, such as self-confidence, creativity, chakra balance (a subject I will look at in Chapter 12), positive thinking, stress and so on. They are effective twentieth-century remedies that rely on twentieth-century technology and appeal to twentieth-century people.

I shall turn now to self-administered therapies that stem directly from the guru and ashram therapies discussed in the previous chapter.

Focusing

There is an American psychotherapist, Eugene Gendlin, who has developed a method of self-therapy that he calls Focusing. While visualizing does not feature to any great extent in his therapy, I'm including it because it uses some concepts that have already appeared and which will be met with more frequently later in the book. In addition, it gives hope that self-therapy is possible, since it is specifically designed for self-administration.

The method was developed by him because he was exasperated when he saw that not all people got any better through traditional psychotherapy. Those that did improve, it seemed to him, did so by tapping into some internal process by which means they were, in fact, their own therapists. He then set out to explore that internal process and this led him to find two elusive phenomena that he called 'felt sense' and 'shift', which successful therapees appeared to use. This discovery resulted in a procedure that encouraged patients to focus on the *feeling* associated with a problem and to ignore the words that the monkey mind threw at it in efforts to dodge the painful issue.

'Felt sense' refers to the feeling that a problem has to it, shorn of conventional, top-of-the-head, responses. By focusing on this, getting a clear feel of it, non-verbally and only *afterwards* trying to fit words or phrases that best describe it, there occurs the 'shift'. This he describes as a click of recognition accompanied by a feeling of a breakthrough to a new intuitive understanding of the problem. This breakthrough to intuitive, non-verbal responses is to do with the concept mentioned above, namely the balance desirable between the two hemispheres of the brain.

It seems to me that there is a problem with any form of self-therapy, but particularly with psychotherapy. This is the difficulty of achieving any sort of objective view of the problem, which is why many people give up and seek out professionals. It is extremely difficult, for instance, to see oneself, in the middle of a relational crisis, in any way other than self-justifying. The strength of Gendlin's method is that it encourages the sufferer to ignore the internal chatter and argumentation, to get behind the clutter and to centre down onto the non-verbal emotions and feelings that are around. After all, as most of our neurotic problems were formed at the pre-verbal stage of our development, it follows that the neurosis will be best 'expressed' in non-verbal terms, using only that which we had at the time of the formation of the neurosis — in other words, using our feelings.

Wholeness in health of any kind is, as we have seen, a matter of balance. In the sphere of the mental, that balancing act is required between the logical and verbal on the one hand and the intuitive and pre-verbal on the other.

Man as a species is *what* he is because of language and his mastery of this has caused him to rely more and more on the logic made possible through language, neglecting the other, intuitive, older, side of his nature, that side which in animals enables them to live harmoniously with nature. When priest and grandmother were an intrinsic part of culture, they kept the intuitive, the mysterious and numinous alive for humans in fairy-tale, myth and miracle. Now that they are largely ignored and technology is on the ascendant, we are forgetting that that balance is essential to us.

Marilyn Ferguson in her introduction to Eugene Gendlin's book *Focusing*, puts forward the idea that the act of focusing brings into mesh the right and left hemispheres:

> . . . the brain's analytical left hemisphere, dominant for language, names that which heretofore was inarticulate and diffuse, known only to the holistic, mute, right brain. New information seems to be mediated primarily by the right brain, which is also more richly connected to the evolutionary older limbic brain.

One of Gendlin's stages demands the bringing together of the felt sensation with a realistic verbal handle, thus providing a link across the hemisphere gap between emotion and logic. Once this has been done and a realistic label applied to it, then it may be that self-therapy by means of visualization can profitably take place, perhaps on the basis of images evoked in the procedure of contacting the intuitive side of the brain. Much psycho-therapeutic work does, in fact, involve the free drawing of non-verbal images and it is the non-verbal side of the brain that needs to be mobilized in much therapy.

Non-mystical and intensely practical, Eugene Gendlin's 'focusing' is a kind of meditation. As he says, the first step is to '. . . find a time and place to sit quietly for a while'. Then, instead of watching the breath or a candle or visualizing an object of devotion, we are invited to simply watch the feelings that are troubling us, to avoid naming them, to avoid being side-tracked and simply watch them until they crystallize. Then we cross the bridge to the other hemisphere and see what the verbal side can do now that the hurly-burly has died down. A sense of relief generally signals successful focusing, as I and others have found.

Psychosynthesis

You will remember that this, too, aims at inducing the intuitive, non-verbal side of the brain to be actively and consciously employed by the patient. It was included in the previous chapter because it is often administered by a professional therapist, but it is particularly suitable for self-administration and relies heavily on self-administered visualization, so I have also included it here.

The therapy was named Psychosynthesis by its founder, Roberto Assagioli, who sees that people — in general, not just sick ones — need to move towards a higher state of being, to experience an unfolding development and synthesis of their psyche. One of the charms of Assagioli's work is his insistence on providing as strict a theoretical and experimental basis to all his recommendations as is possible in the circumstances. Another is the way in which non-verbal symbolization is extensively used.

As an example, one of the exercises he recommends, which is excellently described in Piero Ferrucci's *What We May Be*, is to visualize a rosebud, initially closed and enveloped by its green sepals, gradually opening. We are invited to experience a similar opening going on inside ourselves and to 'see' in the centre of the rose an image emerging. He suggests that image, whatever it may be, is of particular significance to us here and now. Of this, Robert Assagioli writes in *The Act of Will* in a brilliantly descriptive passage,

> Such a dynamic symbol, conveying the idea of development, corresponds to a profound reality, to a fundamental law of life that governs the functions of the human mind as well as the processes of nature. Our spiritual being, the Self, which is the essential and most real part of us, is concealed, confined and 'enveloped' first by the physical body with its sense impressions, then by the multiplicity of the emotions and the different drives (fears, desires, attractions and repulsions) and finally by the restless activity of the mind. The liberation of the consciousness from the entanglements is an indispensable prelude to the revelation of the spiritual Center. The agency for achieving it . . . is . . . both biological and psychological, that works with irresistible pressure *from within*.

Ideal scenes

Many self-therapy techniques, particularly Psychosynthesis, recommend a preliminary visualization exercise in which a psychic starting point, a base, is established. We are asked to visualize ourselves at rest in a favourite scene, real or imagined, in as much detail as possible. The sky will be blue, the breeze gentle, the flowers exuding their perfume, bees buzzing and so on. The scene should be a peaceful one, one in which we have been and are content and happy, at peace with ourselves and the world. This is a base that we should be able to recall at will, in which much may take place and from which much may flow. It could, for instance, be the base from which our walk up the mountain with a sub-personality may start.

Sub-personalities

A very helpful means of straightening oneself out is suggested by Roberto Assagioli in his concept of sub-personalities. Each of us, as you will recall I mentioned earlier, behaves in a different way according to the people we are with or the situation in which we find ourselves. It seems that we have a different personality or a different facet of our personality that we can produce in these different circumstances. Some are not pleasant.

Roberto Assagioli recommends that we 'meet' and 'befriend' these sub-personalities and Piero Ferrucci indicates ways in which we can do this. One is that we should concentrate upon one of our prominent traits or attitudes, allowing it to take physical shape in the mind. It may turn out to be a man or a woman or a beast, such as aggression appearing as a ravening lion or a bowler-hatted little weakling — anything at all. We are to get to know it, recognize the feeling that emanates from it, have a conversation with it. We should give it a name — the Complainer, the Bully or Macho Mac, for instance.

To transform the trait or attitude, Piero Ferrucci suggests that we visualize ourselves taking a path that leads through a valley and up a mountain (it is important that such visualized pathworkings take us to greater heights). We should visualize the surroundings — the grass and trees, imagine the chirping of birds, the sound of the wind. As we ascend, we should visualize the changes in the scenery — how the trees thin out, the air becomes purer, the sun brighter and warmer, for instance. Keeping in touch with our sub-personality, we can see, perhaps, subtle changes in it, perhaps even radical changes. We should stand in the bright sun at the top of the mountain and see if there are further transformations.

We shall meet this concept of visualized pathworkings in the Dreamworking section at the end of this chapter and again later in the book.

Best Therapist

Much of the therapy I have mentioned involves contact with that part of us that is called by various names — Higher Self, the Self, Super-consciousness, Cosmic Consciousness, for instance.

Abraham Maslow said about peak experiences that we have all felt at rare times that there is a feeling of being connected to our higher selves, feeling exceptionally high, clear, strong and so on. In *The Farther Reaches of Human Nature* he puts it like this:

> Talking of dimensions of psychological health, self transcendence, of mystical fusion . . . has had for me at least the one special advantage of directing my attention sharply to what I called at first 'the impulse voices', but which had better be called more generally something like the 'inner signals'.

It is possible, using visualization, to contact these inner signals. In our ideal scene, for instance, we can visualize meeting these inner signals in a personified form, which has been called by psychosynthesists 'the Best Therapist'. We can visualize him or her approaching the gate to our secret garden. We can go and greet this person, sit together and put questions to him or her, for this person is a means to tapping our own source of healing. This is a way in which we may, according to Roberto Assagioli, discover our own ability to improve our lives — but there are risks.

That such *inner* constructs may become *outer* is indicated in the works of Carlos Castaneda, the writings of Alexandra David-Neel and in the words of the prosaic Charles Lindbergh (*The Spirit of St Louis*, Murray, 1953) who felt himself to be like '. . . an awareness spreading through space, over the earth and into the heavens, unhampered by time or substance . . .' The fuselage behind him as he made his lonely way across the Atlantic Ocean in his plane 'The Spirit of St Louis' filled with ghostly presences, '. . . vaguely outlined forms, transparent, moving, riding weightless with me in the plane'. He 'saw' them behind him '. . . as though my skull was one great eye'. The ghostly presences conversed with him, advised him on problems in his navigation, '. . . giving me messages of importance unattainable in ordinary life'. For this reason Roberto Assagioli says in *The Act of Will*,

> On the other hand these 'inspirations' and inner urges are not to be accepted and followed without being subject to careful scrutiny . . . do these promptings to act *really* come from the exalted level of the superconscious? . . . We live immersed in a psychic ocean, enveloped in a psychic atmosphere: we are continually subject to influences of every kind and source. Therefore, a cautious attitude of continuous discrimination is necessary.

On the other hand, there is a real tendency to ignore the 'promptings of grace'. As Shakti Gawain and others have said, we have a fear of power and responsibility — and of enlightenment.

Dreamworking

Dolores Ashcroft-Nowicki tells in *Highways of the Mind* (Aquarian Press, 1987) of the Senoi Indians who live their whole lives by the power of their dreams. Each morning, every member of the family will tell the content of their dreams and these are then interpreted by the father or, if thought to be very significant, by an elder of the tribe.

Dreams are more important to our psychological health than is often realized and have long been a means of self-therapy. (Those who claim not to dream, or not to be able to recall their dreams, should try a simple visualization exercise in which they wake up and *do* remember!)

Those who, like Jung, the Gestalt psychologist Fritz Perls and many others, see dreams as messages from the interior and thus believe that dreams are meaningful and indications, sometimes, of deep-seated and unadmitted problems, can use a visualization technique to make their dreams work for them.

If, through Focusing or Psychosynthesizing or some other method, we become aware of a problem that needs attention, Dolores Ashcroft-Nowicki suggests a procedure for using dreams. This is to visualize the beginning of a story that involves the problem — perhaps a walk up the mountain with the sub-personality meeting a rock-fall or some other barrier. Visualize the climb to that point and leave it at that point of decision. Go over the story to that point again and again as you go to sleep. With practice, the story will be taken up in a dream and the problem explored or even solved.

Dreams *can* be controlled. Walt Anderson writes of Tibetan dream-therapy in *Open Secrets* (Penguin, 1980),

> The next step after you have learned to recognize dreams is to begin to direct them while dreaming. It is suggested that you can try transforming the objects in dreams into other objects, as sorcerers do in fairy-tales and also to transform yourself into an animal, another person, an inanimate object. You can also learn to 'rewrite' your dream scripts while they are unfolding and carry the events in your dream life towards more satisfactory conclusions. You can meditate while dreaming and you can also enter into altered states of consciousness.

One of the curses of our modern age is its speed, and our demand (which affects all but the most otherworldly of us) for instant remedies. There is no such thing as instant self-therapy, unless that is, we find ourselves surprised on a road to Damascus. We need, therefore, to persevere in whatever method we choose, to give it a fair trial. After all, people who go to guru or ashram therapy go for years, at vast expense. In doing so, they gain faith that it is working, adopt a basic belief in its efficacy and stay with it. Whatever method we choose, we should also stick with it for a reasonable time. Our neuroses are deep-seated and have survived by adopting strong defences, one of them being that familiar feeling of despair, of discouragement, that feeling that one is getting nowhere. Such feelings are often a sign that we are, in fact, getting somewhere and should encourage us to go on. Perhaps a spell recuperating in our secret garden is in order and a meeting with our Best Therapist there will alleviate the feelings of loneliness. Perhaps a spell of focusing will also help.

If we have made the decision to avoid outside help, that decision in itself is worth taking up a mountain to examine. Besides the dangers that exist, Joel Kovel also sounds a note of caution in his *A Complete Guide to Therapy*: 'To break through all this [the ills of the modern world] requires more than meditation, it demands a coherent system of belief, discipline to tame the unruly self and a social fabric to support the whole enterprise.' Necessary to that coherent system of belief is faith, in the last analysis, but today for most people that is to be found in the achievements of science (though even this is declining). Discipline to tame the unruly self is, in the early stages, like pulling yourself up by your own bootstraps and where is the support of family and friends these days for navel-gazing?

Perhaps it is the last of these factors that poses the greatest difficulty. Systems of belief of greater or less coherence exist and it is not impossible, once embarked on a path, to acquire habits of self-discipline, but isolation is often the lot of a seeker after his or her own truth and the right to love him- or herself. When all is said and done, though, fulfilment is an *individual* achievement, reached finally *without* a Master, who, at best, can only point the way.

9.
To Woo the Muse

Successful therapy frees creative forces that were before bogged down in neurosis. As Joel Kovel says in *A Complete Guide to Therapy*,

> Like neurosis, creativity is a highly idiosyncratic solution to life's paradoxes and while creativity is the antithesis of neurosis in that its laws are those of freedom rather than compulsivity, it is also a close relation, since the freedom or compulsivity in each case describes the disposition of unconscious forces that have broken loose from repression.

Indeed, one of the potential problems of professional therapy is that it is aimed at a return to normality — or perhaps we should say imposing a state *called* normal in our particular culture. If creativity is undervalued in a society and the society's methods of schooling reinforce this undervaluation, therapy, too, will be concerned to repress creative impulses.

Theft of innocence

All children are creative geniuses: they draw, sing, learn a language, make up stories, dance, invent imaginary friends and do any number of other very creative things most of the time. It is sad but true that most developed education systems concentrate on developing the rational powers of their minds at the expense of the intuitive and that almost the only educational establishment in which the flowering of creative genius in children is to be seen is a good nursery or kindergarten. Here, an experienced teacher provides a wealth of material (from sand to sugar, from paint to a peaceful corner to dream in) and allows the children to pursue their interests, interfering as little as possible, secure in the knowledge that the children know what they need — even if it is to raise hell for a while. What is important from our present point of view is to see what it is the children are really doing as they carry on in the ways they have been for a year or two before entry into nursery school and which is behind the practice of their creative genius.

Give a child a block of wood and, before very long, that block of wood will be a doll or a car or some food or a rocket ship . . . In other words, the block of wood becomes a symbol for something else. What we don't know is what the child is seeing as he or she handles the newly-invented doll, car or whatever. Ask them and they will say 'It's a rocket,' but what do they actually see, what are they visualizing?

We have, of course, no way of telling as their other skills are not up to telling us, as we can see from looking at their drawings, such as the one below. It is unlikely that mother or father actually looks like this to the child. What they are drawing is possibly an attempt to delineate the important features of their parent, but who can say for sure? If they see the block of wood as a symbol of mother, what are they seeing then? For seeing they must be and visualizing they are.

Child's drawing of parent

This point is explored further by Jonathan Miller and Slade Professor of Fine Art, Professor Gombrich, in Miller's book *States of Mind* (BBC Books, 1983):

> Miller   Yes, but the point is that one should never run away with the idea that because a child *represents* its world like this, the child is in fact *seeing* its world like this. If the mother were to walk in looking like the child's picture of its mother, the child would be frightened.
>
> Gombrich   It would be very frightened and rightly so. The main point here is . . . that we live in a three-dimensional world . . . The problems of transposing this on to a flat piece of paper or canvas is much more formidable . . . You simply can't represent the world as you see it . . . What you have to perform is a reduction of a very complex character.

Imaginary friends, too, are said to be a therapeutic feature of children's private lives and the power of visualization is tremendous in this case. Daydreaming, too, which we discussed at the beginning of the book, involves much visualizing and is often therapeutic as well as highly creative.

Children are great visualizers. It is their great strength, second only to their acquisition of language, to which it is related in its utilization of the symbolic function. They devote much more of their lives than we do to creative visualization, creating their world within the framework of the adult one and gradually drawing closer to it.

What happens when they climb the ladder of schooling is a shameful acceleration of this process of coming to terms with the 'real' world — whatever that is. They are inducted into a picture of the world that is selected for them by dominant adults. Their creative urge is channelled and blocked. Even in so-called 'creative writing', certain bounds are imposed. For example, it is all right to catch the robber, but not all right to be one. Soon the stories become stereotyped and left-hemisphered. Again, in a creative, free subject like art certain conventions are imposed with some subjects being acceptable, some not, to say nothing of techniques. Again, left-hemisphered stereo-typing is too often the result for a great many children.

Creative writing and art are, in any case, less important to the dominant culture than the acquisition of facts and processes. We see more computer terminals than easels in schools today and even where software is available to encourage artistic endeavour, it is likely to be lower down the scale of requisition priorities than those programmes that lead to measurable results. Schools knock the creative impulse out of their students, but they cannot take all the blame — the home will often do the same, the telly acting as a mental pap to go with the frozen pap they are given to eat.

It is the creative imagination, however, as much as the possession of language, that separates human beings from their companions lower down the phylogenetic scale. Indeed, it can be said that it is humanity's most distinctive trait, for it makes our creativity possible. We have been creative from the earliest times of which we have any trace, for early people used visualization a great deal in coming to terms with the world and in efforts to control it. The same may be seen to be true for primitive peoples in our own time — where they survive in the face of the greed of their more 'developed' neighbours. In their use of symbolism — and therefore of visualization — they were and are like the children of our own times.

It is interesting to note that the ability to produce representations is confined to the human race, for not even the higher primates have it. In children, Jean Piaget and others have shown that the skill is associated with that other great symbolic system, language — also confined to humans. In primitive peoples it is very possible that it was associated with the exercise of symbolic magic.

Like young children, our early ancestors were creative artists and just as young children use their powers of visualization in coming to terms with the surrounding adult world, so, too, did these primitive people to come to terms with their surrounding threatening world. Evidence of this and their great representational skill may be found in the cave paintings of southern France and northern Spain (see the example overleaf). Their drawings are superb representations of the animals they feared and hunted — accurate not only technically (although we can only guess at that), but in feeling and tone, the latter to an extent that immediately qualifies them to us moderns as works of art rather than technical or working drawings.

Painted as they were sometimes as much as a mile from the entrances of deep underground caves, it is clear that their creators were true artists, able to keep the animals in mind, to visualize them and then reproduce them. Perhaps they were also more than artists, for it is well recognized now that such paintings were almost certainly the means by which Cro-Magnon people sought magically to control the animals represented and to bring about good fortune in hunting them. It was a means by which the hunter could 'get inside' the animals, empathize with and understand them, the better to control them.

A feature of these drawings, the possible significance of which will be apparent from what follows, is that, according to Stan Gooch in

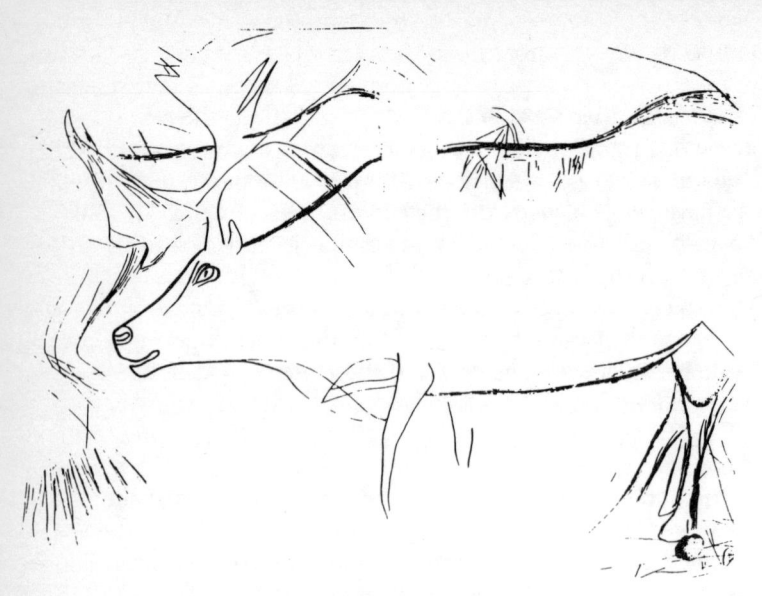

The outlines of a reindeer engraved on the cave wall at Sainte Eulal in the Lot valley, southwest France.

Total Man (Abacus, 1975), the majority of the paintings appear to have been executed by left-handed artists. 'There would seem to be grounds for believing it [left-handedness] to have predominated among cave-artists (cave-artist-priests, if such there were) and possibly among the makers of tools also.'

In primitives and in children, we can see how creativity is used as a means of mastering the environment. This is a human trait. Animals survive, while humans invent; animals react, while humans create.

Rainbow bridges

Creativity is defined as that state or quality of being creative, of having the ability to create. The ability to create means the ability to bring into being or form out of nothing, to bring into being by force of imagination. It is not the prerogative of the creative artist, but necessary for the full release of talent in any vocation, profession or trade. Without it we are but dull or competent technicians.

To bring out of nothing? This is poesy. To spring from the void, to harness creative cosmic energy may be what happens, but even bricks are not made without straw, there has to be a substrate of the material even in the most ethereal of creation. What is fundamental to creativity is for the two hemispheres of the brain to be worked in harness.

Viewed from above, the brain can be seen to consist of two halves. Through experimentation, it has been shown that (in right-handed people) the left hemisphere has to do with processing logical thought and language, while the right has to do with processing intuitive thought. This table shows some characteristics of the two hemispheres.

Left hemisphere	Right hemisphere
Control of speech, verbal functions	Spatial, musical
Logical, mathematical	Holistic
Linear, detailed	Artistic
Sequential	Simultaneous
Intellectual	Intuitive
Analytic	Synthetic

It appears from all this that intuitive and creative ability is a function of the right brain, but, of course, for creativity and intuition to emerge in any useful form, the left brain must also be involved. To be operating totally in the intuitive mode of thought would mean that one was unable to communicate the insights in any way logically or in a readily understandable, non-symbolic manner. Conversely, to be operating totally with the left brain would mean that intuitive insights would be denied expression.

Kurt Goldstein in Jonathan Miller's book *States of Mind* describes what happened when the union of the two hemispheres was destroyed in a woman hospitalized for bizarre behaviour:

> Her left hand would come up to her own throat and would start to choke her . . . she complained that her left hand was bad and beyond her control.

Professor Geschwind comments in the book as follows:

> If you think about it for a moment, however, you suddenly realize that it was not the whole woman who was talking. Since it was disconnected from the right side, the left side could not give a correct account of what the right was thinking or feeling . . . The right side of the brain almost certainly has a very rich mental life, but because it does not speak, one

is easily deluded into thinking that it is not active when in fact it is every bit as alert, attentive and active as the left side.

The two halves are equally involved in any act of creation and so there has to be a balance, a bridge between the two. This bridge exists in the *corpus callosum*, a thick bundle of nerve fibres that run between the two sides of the neo-cortex. (Interestingly, it is said to lie in the area known to mystics and meditators as the 'third eye'.) Again and again, though, the right hemisphere — the intuitive side — is ignored, too often regarded as the source of non-productive daydreaming. Intuitive insights only occur when the dominant (generally the left) hemisphere is quiescent in states such as occur in daydreams, dreams, meditation and hypnotic trance. Creative scientists recognize this to be true as much as do artists, yet both, in common with most other people, tend to regard intuitive insight as an unusual one-off occurrence. It may be, but it may also be true to say that such occurrences could be more commonly achieved than they are.

Creativity often needs a period of hard left-brain work, followed by a period of incubation in which the unconscious processes are allowed to get to work. The target has been fed into the cybernetic system and the system then needs a time to programme itself. While not forgetting that much creativity can, and must, take place at a conscious level, it is nevertheless true that paying too much attention either to the aim or to the process at this time disturbs the smooth flow of the process. One of Roberto Assagioli's laws outlined in *The Act of Will* states that all the various functions and their manifold combinations in complexes and sub-personalities adopt means of achieving their aims without our awareness and independently of, even against, our conscious will. A creative person can, however, connect with and consciously use the intuitive side of the brain and thus allow spontaneity free rein.

There are ways in which this ability may be fostered. Perhaps the best-known collection of methods is that introduced by Edward de Bono, under the general term 'lateral thinking', a term that he himself coined. Such exercises encourage the thinker to relax his or her everyday left-brain control of thinking and so accept weird, off-beat thoughts. This method is best exemplified in the well-known group exercise called brainstorming. A problem is set and the members of the group throw in ideas, fast, without any censorship of weird, outlandish or ridiculous notions. This allows ideas from the right side to get across the bridge, like a spy crossing a bridge in a crowd. Often such 'spies' bring valuable despatches from the foreign land.

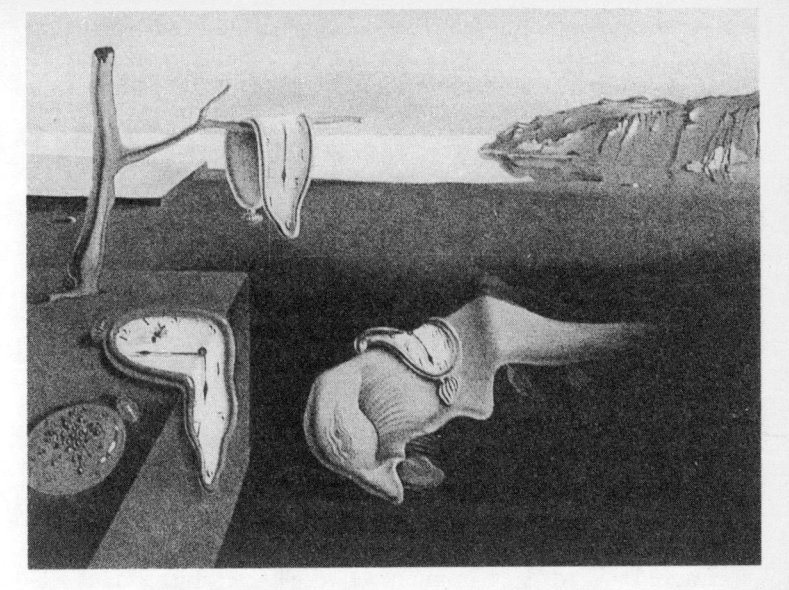

Salvador Dali's *The Persistence of Memory*, 1931

Exercises such as these encourage the freer use of the right brain. Such an achievement does not mean that we give up use of the rational, left hemisphere, even if it were possible. The aim of them is that where there is an imbalance between the hemispheres in favour of the left hemisphere, to create more of a balance between them.

In the painting above by Salvador Dali, that arch-surrealist, who depended more than most on the right brain, but who never neglected the left, this balance is apparent in the representation of the irrational and dream-like soft watch (from the right brain) by means of rational use of pigments, perspective and blue sky (from the left brain) to attempt to create conceptually common ground between artist and audience.

Perhaps Dali, with his extremely weird life-style, is a poor example to use because he may exemplify the common fear that many non-creative people have that a loss of control occurs. 'Here be monsters' is the feeling many have who become aware of, but do not venture far into, the *terra incognita* of the hidden powers of the unconscious, a feeling that Freud did much to foster. Yet practitioners of Taoist, Mahayana Buddhist, Jewish, Islamic and Christian mysticism can practise a living meditation in everything they do without any loss of everyday effectiveness — indeed, the opposite may be true. As Ben Willis writes in *The Tao of Art* (Century, 1987),

Since intelligence is not verbal, it is possible to live in a wholly spontaneous consciousness without any loss of mental acuity and [one] is, in fact, far more creative and natural.

Alternatively (in a manner reminiscent of recommendations of Eugene Gendlin), it might be as well to get right out of the way, to stand aside a while and, as RW Gerard in PE Vernon's *Creativity* (Penguin, 1970) says,

> By [such] various mechanisms, then, great masses of nerve cells — the brain as a great unity — act together; and not merely to do two or a million units sum their various contributions, but each is a part of a dynamic fluctuating activity pattern of the whole. This is the orchestra which plays thoughts of truth and beauty.

We underrate the innate powers of the brain, not least those of the right hemisphere and its fruit, intuitive awareness and it is in spontaneous thought and action that intuition becomes apparent.

Salvador Dali had a high opinion of himself as an artist and his self-concept, while strange, was nevertheless plainly displayed in his work and in his life-style. Paradoxically, his personality was well integrated. In his work and life he had access to the intuitive and resulting spontaneity.

Anyone who seeks to utilize their faculty of intuition and resultant spontaneity needs to learn to reduce conscious verbal thought to a minimum so that their creative intuition can awaken and become a real, significant and worthwhile part of their lives. It is necessary to allow a free flow between the hemispheres and it is the Chinese concept of *wu wei* (to be examined shortly) that may further open up our understanding of this necessary condition for creativeness.

In the remainder of this chapter I shall examine the nature of intuition, spontaneity and *wu wei* and the conditions that may best bring about the full use of our powers of creativeness, without which a person may be said to be living a less than fulfilled life.

Intuition

The dictionary defines intuition as '... the power of the mind by which it immediately perceives the truth of things without reasoning or analysis' or as '... a truth so perceived, immediate knowledge in contrast with mediate'. The branch of philosophy known as Intuitionalism goes so far as to state that the perception of truth is, in fact, only achieved by means of such immediate knowledge.

There is little doubt that many, if not all, of the fundamental discoveries that the human race has made have involved at least a degree of intuition at some stage or other. This is true, whether the discoverer is artist or scientist. Indeed, examples are most often cited in the field of science, if only because it is so often a surprise, being least expected in such a rigorous field.

The power of our minds and our need to trust to that power is nowhere brought out more clearly than in the well-known words of Henri Poincaré when he described a state of utter intellectual fatigue in which the left brain was so exhausted by its own exertions that it allowed the spies to gather at the end of the bridge (*The Foundations of Science*, Science Press, 1924):

> For 15 days I strove to prove that there could not be any functions like those I have since called Fuchsian functions. I was then very ignorant; every day I seated myself at my work table, stayed an hour or two, tried a great number of combinations and reached no results. One evening, contrary to my custom, I drank black coffee and could not sleep. Ideas rose in crowds; I felt them collide until pairs interlocked, so to speak, making stable combinations. By the next morning I had established the existence of a class of Fuchsian functions . . . I had only to write out the results.

I will not attempt to detail how the unconscious mind is said to perform its miracle of bridge-crossing, but will merely remark that Poincaré himself later speaks of the will not choosing ideas at random, but of pursuing '. . . a perfectly determined aim'. It is as though he was dimly aware of a cybernetic mechanism at work in his brain.

Characteristics of intuitive thought are many and include direct apprehension, insight, a feeling of rightness and conviction. It is often marked by an instantaneous 'eureka' feeling of happiness. There is, too, often a feeling of having been spoken too, a hint of the presence of the Best Therapist in the guise of expert.

That such intuitions, particularly those in which such a direct inner dialogue has taken place, have to be backed up by a lot of logical thinking in order to confirm them goes without saying. This is particularly true of those forms and fields of scientific knowledge that demand rigorous proof before acceptance. No doubt artists and writers, too, apply a deal of logical application of technique in order to transform their on-going apprehension of truth into a form that may be communicated. Indeed, much of the trouble with intuition is this difficulty of communicating insights. Artists, writers and other creative people may be content to allow their works to be the means, but scientists are obliged to justify by logic the truths of which they have become convinced through non-logical means.

Intuition springs from the non-logical side of the brain, but the dominant, verbal, analytic side, even though it may have no direct part to play in the breakthrough, is, none the less, important for two reasons. First, it is used to check any distractions (by the exercise of concentration and mindfulness) and, second, it keeps the questions that initiated the process alive in the mind.

Wu wei and the creative act

I turn now to the act of creation itself, concentrating for the moment on pictorial art and the artist. One such artist, Kwo Da-Wei wrote in *Chinese Brushwork* (Allanheld Osmun, 1980),

> When one starts to write or paint, one should keep going without any hesitation, for once the continuity is interrupted, the life force is broken.

This is true of all painting, but peculiarly so in the case of Chinese painting and its near relative, the art of calligraphy. The use of a brush on watery paper or silk demands an immediacy of action. As JC Cooper wrote in *Taoism* (Aquarian Press, 1972),

> Using a brush on silk, the strokes had to be quick, sure and unhesitating, there was no second chance, no possibility of erasing, modifying or painting over a mistake. Both were subject to the same immediacy as life itself; the movement, the choice, was irrevocable.

The artist has a vision — mental or actual — of the ideal whole. As Eugen Herrigel said in *Zen in the Art of Archery*, '. . . spend ten years observing bamboos, become a bamboo yourself, then forget everything and — paint.'

In addition, as I shall suggest more than once, the artist is monitoring progress with a series of mental models of the results of her brushstrokes, each one perhaps only a microsecond or so in advance of execution, but mental models nevertheless, to which she is persuading her eye and muscles to conform. In the same way, a perfect musical performance has this immediacy and this conformity to models. It has nothing to do with musical notation except at the novice stage. Instead, the performer forms a mental representation of the piece, explores that and experiments with it.

The Chinese have an expression — *wu wei*. It covers their centuries-old pursuit of creative living. The truly autonomous man, the Taoist Sage, the Confucian Superior Man, is one in whom the flow of circumstances is allowed to act out with interference, is one who has a heart like '... a placid lake unruffled by the wind of circumstance'. With such harmony a fully realized person is able to react directly and creatively in the most difficult of situations.

Characteristic of such a person is a sure appropriateness of response to all circumstances such that few people attain. It is marked by spontaneity and quietude and, as far as a Taoist is concerned, spontaneity is the principle of all ideal human activity and conduct, for all human activity and conduct is marked by moment-by-moment creativity. Such spontaneously appropriate behaviour is characteristic of *wu wei*, which may be roughly translated as 'letting go' or 'no action'.

As I've shown previously, the mind of the average man or woman is taken up by incessant, almost feverish, mental activity — a mishmash of hopes, fears, daydreams, feelings, emotions and half thought out plans. The result is a condition of unmindfulness.

Concentration on logical solutions can improve matters — it may, indeed, be a preliminary requisite as problem-solving strategies of a sort may be developed by the left, or dominant, hemisphere. As I have indicated elsewhere, however, really effective problem-solving involves visualization and the right hemisphere. In addition, really effective problem-solving (and control of the mind in general) needs an easing of tension (or surrender as in the case of Henri Poincaré) to increase receptivity to the intuitive spark.

It is this receptivity that *wu wei* brings about. Ben Willis realizes this in *The Tao of Art* when he says,

> *Wu wei* is the habit and discipline of stilling the mind so that intuition, the voice of spirit, will penetrate to our consciousness and supply a creative or spiritual solution to every problem of life. Such solutions can include a judicious doing nothing about the problem and it is often extraordinary how things have a way of righting themselves if left alone. It may be that creative intuition suggests some other course — if action becomes necessary, it is the *right action* in the *right* amount that characterizes proper *wu wei*.

As Alan Watts wrote in *The Way of Zen*, 'In judo, for example, one uses muscle — but only at the right moment, when the opponent is off balance or has overextended himself.'

What can we learn from the practice? The Taoist sage does not sit around doing nothing like a clod of clay. He can be lively when necessary — though never overstrained — and will act completely adequately according to the demands of the moment. What the sage is able to do when practising the gentle discipline of *wu wei* is to suspend the will, to reduce the interference of the rational process and thus release spontaneity.

Fostering intuition

Some people see themselves (and are therefore seen by others — a self-perpetuating cycle) as non-creative, as plodders without a spark of spontaneity or any flashes of intuitive wisdom. As I've shown, children possess and use both, before schooling too often represses them and so it is the lucky adult who rediscovers the spark.

People vary in their ability to utilize non-verbal thinking. There are variations between artists and between scientists. Whether this is due to innate differences or whether the differences are cultural is a moot point. Anne Roe, for instance, writing in a 1952 issue of *Scientific American*, described how she had found among 64 scientists that biologists and experimental physicists tended to depend more on visual imagery in their thinking than theoretical physicists. The latter tended to verbalize more — '. . . a kind of talking to themselves' and seemed obviously to be utilizing the left brain more than the former — and perhaps losing some magic in the process.

Poets, too, may be expected to verbalize a great deal, but it is noteworthy that Stephen Spender (as quoted by PE Vernon in *Creativity*) in describing the making of a poem says, 'At this stage, a poem is like a face which one seems to be able to visualize clearly in the eye of memory . . .' Such words will tend to be dismissed merely as the words of a poet and thus not worthy of attention in the 'real' world — again, we come across this cultural obstacle to recognizing the importance of intuition. Nor is its connection with other psychological processes recognized. Instead it is devalued and, indeed, actively rejected. This results in its repression, to the loss of both society at large and individuals within it, in spite of work done by people such as de Bono. It is certainly possible to learn techniques of non-verbal thinking and to reduce conscious verbal thought to a minimum so that our creative intuition can emerge and play a vital part in our lives and the lives of our fellows.

Throughout this book I have been at pains to foster the belief that we can reshape our lives by reshaping our personalities, our personalities being that aspect — or aspects — of ourselves that we choose, consciously or unconsciously, to present to the world. So it will be no surprise to you when I claim that it is by deliberately and consciously using the psycho-cybernetic system with which we all operate that this sorry state of affairs can be altered.

Striking the creative spark

Ritual

The rare people who have learned to rely on intuition often have rituals by which they hope to activate it. Stephen Spender (quoted by PE Vernon once more) wrote,

> Schiller liked to have the smell of rotten apples, concealed beneath the lid of his desk, under his nose when he was composing poetry. Walter de la Mare has told me that he must smoke when writing. Auden drinks endless cups of tea. Coffee is my own addiction, besides smoking a great deal, which I hardly ever do except when I am writing.

Such rituals may range from lighting a stick of incense, to clearing the desk, to strolling in the park, to rewriting the last page of writing. All such practices are means of stilling the monkey mind and of focusing the attention. Many people tend to play music as they work and this, again, is a means of stilling the mind. Perhaps behind this ritual lies the conscious or unconscious thought that such a linking with the fruits of another's creativity may be of advantage and may permeate the person's mind by some process akin to osmosis. Such encouragements, whatever they may be, imply a need to discover and respect our own idiosyncrasies, flows and rhythms.

We all have our temporal rhythms and a respect for these individual personal characteristics are a necessary adjunct to fostering intuitive creativity. Such a respect gives a new slant on the use of time, allowing for periods of gestation. Trust in these rhythms allows unhurriedness to emerge without the guilt that may afflict you in these days of concentration on, and near-worship of, productivity. As Ben Willis says in *The Tao of Art*, 'The birthing of a work of art or the birthing of a soul is just that — birthing. It has all the time of eternity and will not be rushed or produced in a clumsy panic.'

Meditation, rituals, respect for rhythms, all lead to an upsurge and the emergence of spontaneity — but the possibility must first be a part of your self-picture.

Meditation

The idea of yourself as a person able to create includes, first, being in a state of tranquil emptiness, of a natural and unstressed frame of mind — though Henri Poincaré at first glance hardly seemed to fit this criterion, second, being receptive and, third, admitting the appearance in the mind of ideas from 'elsewhere'.

Serenity, tranquility, receptivity — these are words I have frequently used before and they are words that describe the characteristics of a meditative mode of being and of *wu wei*. It is in the cultivation of these qualities that there lies not only the secret of creativeness, but the mastery of material life. Such a way of alert receptivity implies a trust in inner resources and a consequent readiness to suspend (but not abandon) logic.

The practice of meditation is indeed a high road — many would say the only road — to the growth and development of the intuition. Intuitive insights only occur when the left or dominant hemisphere is quiescent in states such as daydreams, dreams — or meditation. Creative scientists sometimes recognize this to be true as much as some artists do, yet both — in common with most other people — tend to regard intuitive insights as unusual, one-off occurrences. It is an uncommon artist — and perhaps an even more uncommon scientist — that regularly practises meditation as a means of tapping intuition. This may be because, as I've remarked before, there is that unknown territory marked 'Loss of Control', yet, once foot is set down on that unknown shore, the picture changes, and the sun shines upon a gold-mine of creativity.

Visualization

Roberto Assagioli writes in *Psychosynthesis*, 'By means of meditation we can modify, transform and regenerate our personality.' To do this he recommends the use of what he calls the 'ideal model' exercise. He continues, 'Now you see that in imagination you can perform the role, be the model, quite easily . . . Now go ahead, live and relive it in imagination and then seek to play it in reality; you can go ahead with a good prospect of success.' In this exercise there are five basic steps for effective and deliberate visualization aiming at the release of the creative spark, the utilization of the intuitive side of the brain and they are as follows:

- relax into a state of tranquility — perhaps into your ideal scene
- set your goal — in this case the release in yourself of intuition
- create a clear idea or picture of yourself as creative, thinking of that state as happening *now*, create a vivid picture of the successful

outcome as already achieved, see yourself exercising your new-found abilities, feel yourself feeling triumphant in discovery
- focus on it often until it becomes an integrated part of your life, and
- give it positive energy and affirmations.

As usual, merge the desired self-concept with the unconscious, for it is in the unconscious that the psycho-cybernetic system works.

It may be that Roberto Assagioli's procedures for dis-identification might be useful here also. It is the other side of the coin as we need to divest ourselves of our old, less useful non-creative personality before replacing it with the new.

In these dis-identification exercises, he recommends these affirmations and visualizations:

- 'I have a body, but I am not my body'
- 'I have an emotional life, but I am not my emotions'
- 'I have an intellect, but I am not that intellect'.

These he recommends, should be followed by a process of identification:

- 'I recognize and affirm that I am a centre of pure self consciousness, a centre of will, capable of will, capable of using all my psychological processes and my physical body'.

Visualization in the creative act

I have so far looked at methods for reshaping your picture of yourself as creative, but can the same sort of technique be equally effective in the actual process of creation, invention and discovery?

At the risk of repetition, almost everything we do, we first visualize. Our intention to act is first rehearsed in imagination. The intention and the act are so often so close that any gap is not apparent, yet the gap *is* there. It follows that such a gap must be present in the spontaneous act of creation. For example, the artist when painting or sculpting has a vision or a series of visions, each one apparently only a second or two in advance of successive executive acts, but there is nevertheless an evolving series of mental models to which eye and muscles conform. In the same way, a perfect musical performance by a virtuoso has an apparent immediacy that is nevertheless conforming to a model, which, except at the novice or early rehearsal stage, has little to do with the musical notation. Instead, it is as though the performer forms a mental representation of the piece and explores, experiments and flows with that model, directly and creatively. So, too, with composing music — there is a model towards which the artist strives. For example, Tchaikovsky, as PE Vernon reports in *Creativity*, wrote, 'I never compose in the *abstract*; that is to say, the musical thought never appears otherwise than in a suitable external form.' The striving, however, is there and he continues, 'Therefore I expressed myself badly when I told you yesterday that I transcribed my works direct from the first sketches. The process is something more than copying; it is actually a critical examination, leading to correction, occasional additions and frequent curtailments.'

This may be getting some way away from visualization — defined as the evocation of visual mental images — but the principle is the same. A problem exists and the mind is aimed at, is programmed towards, its solution. The material is to hand, but needs to be put together in a novel way. This may seem, too, a far cry from that explosive 'Eureka' of insight, yet, even in that, a psycho-cybernetic model is explicative. Reducing the rational process allows the psycho-cybernetic system freedom to find its target.

Anyone planning to increase their creative powers through visualization will, then, be best advised to trust thereafter to *wu wei* and allow circumstances to flow with confidence that the target will be achieved.

10.

Towards Wider Horizons

In previous chapters, we saw examples that could well be included in this chapter, which is about the paranormal. To take just one instance, I noted that some healers 'tuned into' their patients in order to 'see' what was the matter with them by some form of remote visualization. Such a phenomenon is surely in the province of the paranormal.

Most of us have had some kind of experience of the paranormal. We may have experienced telepathy, for instance, when we have 'known' what someone close to us has been thinking. Many of us have had experience of clairvoyance, dowsing or some other psychic phenomenon.

Scientific examination of the paranormal has been going on for about a century for there has always been a strong interest in the subject. Like orthodox science itself, it is seen, along with sociology, psychology and other 'ologies', as yet another means of control that relatively few humans have employed in order to impose order on a chaotic world. Many cases of fraud have been exposed, but there is, nevertheless, a large body of evidence that is not fraud and cannot be explained by any of our usual frames of reference.

The paranormal is defined as 'Abnormal, especially psychological' and refers to those apparently inexplicable phenomena such as telepathy, clairvoyance, precognition, memories of past lives, hauntings, poltergeists, psychokinesis and so on. In general, it is not to do with the occult (hidden, secret, esoteric, magical, supernatural), though some overlap does occur. Nor are paranormal events unearthly or 'supernatural', they are merely phenomena that lie beyond present understanding. The paranormal is, therefore, a shifting concept. As JB Rhine, the great scientific pioneer into such topics, observed about parapsychology, the 'para' gets dropped as oddities are explained. I hope in this chapter to show that those limits are on the move outwards and that visualization can perhaps help to explain — and can certainly expand our ability to tap — such phenomena. The subject covers a wide field and consists of five major categories. First, there is telepathy — the direct interchange of information between minds — second, there is clairvoyance — the acquisition of information by a mind from an inanimate object — thirdly, there is precognition — the acquisition of information about a future event — fourth, there is psychokinesis — setting objects in motion by mental power — and last, there is psychic healing, which we have already discussed.

The theme of this chapter, which has already featured elsewhere, is that matter and energy are not fundamentally distinguishable and that the energy of thought can affect matter. Much of the chapter is devoted to the examination of recent scientific thinking that has a bearing on this belief. Danah Zohar joins a growing band when she writes in *Through the Time Barrier* (Heinemann, 1982),

> The Principle of Complementarity established that matter and energy are two sides of the same coin and if, as seems likely, consciousness itself is some sort of mental energy, then it no longer seems so far-fetched to consider that the mind might be able to exert some influence on matter.

I shall return to Danah Zohar in a moment in order to discuss her thoughts on the subject of precognition.

It has often been noted that precognition is a faculty shared with us by animals but most humans are much less sensitive to such hints than animals. Here and there, though, there are individuals who seem to have a paranormal sense and who develop an inexplicable knowledge of things to come in the same way that animals sense the coming of an earthquake, springing from an obscure perception of something going on in the present that may burst out with overwhelming force in the future.

In spite of such claims, and others to the opposite effect that right-brained human intention and visualization can affect the material world (for example, the disposition of particles in a cloud chamber, the growth of crystals, the rate of radioactive decay and the rate of growth of bacteria), such thinking is not yet mainstream. The paranormal has always been explained away. Aspects of it have been seen, for example, as being the result of subliminal cues, vibrations, dim awarenesses of the earth's magnetic field, of dim racial memories and the like. However, at the end of his 50-year career devoted to proving the principle that matter was prior to mind, that mind was completely dependent on the brain, Wilder Penfield wrote that all his experiments 'proved exactly the opposite'. The realization of the extent to which the brain and the body in general is dependent upon the mind and the way in which mind appears to be able measurably to affect matter, has resulted in many scientists and laymen believing that they are witnessing a turn of the tide towards an acceptance of the validity of the paranormal. This tide is turning ever so gently but perceptibly towards other less hard-nosed alternatives than the conventional wisdom of scientists. Indeed, in Russia, the paranormal has been taken up by science as a respectable and perfectly valid study in its own right.

In Brian Inglis' book *The Hidden Power* (Jonathan Cape, 1986) is the story of an experiment. On October 10 1984, the *San Francisco Examiner* reported that a Soviet scientist, the healer Djuna Davitashvili, who had never left his country, would '. . . close his eyes today, clear his mind and attempt to use his psychic power to "see" — from 10,000 miles away — an undisclosed site in San Francisco where an American researcher stands'. The experiment in remote visualizing succeeded to the satisfaction of the researcher — though 'satisfaction' is perhaps the wrong word in relation to the possibility of remote espionage of this kind.

Some uses of paranormal faculties

It is possible that, if they could be developed further and produced to order, telepathy and the following faculties would be of immense value to society:

- second sight — in the detection of criminals (already being tried as was seen in the notorious case of the Yorkshire Ripper) and the early warning of disasters (very frequent phenomena in everyday life)
- psychokinesis — to provide light and heat without tapping other sources
- remote viewing — possible uses could be, for instance, to intuit dangerous mechanical faults in your car; being in the right place at the right time for worthwhile opportunities
- healing — physical and emotional
- green fingers
- dreamwork — understanding the hidden content of dreams, at present filtered out by 'the censor'. There is some evidence that supports the hypothesis that reception to the paranormal is

heightened during sleep and I have shown how it is possible to use dreams for the solution of scientific problems, in the field of creativity and in psychotherapy. An extension of this would be becoming aware, while awake, of the messages constantly being pushed through from the intuitive and mostly ignored.

Scientific hints

I turn now to look at insights from some of the fringes and leading edges of scientific thought for, at any rate, the beginnings of explanations of paranormal phenomena, wherever possible from the viewpoint of the workings of visualization. I offer them as little more than hints.

Left and right brain

We saw in the last chapter that the source of intuition and creativity is in the right hemisphere of the brain. There is little doubt that we moderns have handicapped ourselves by ignoring the benefits of access to this hemisphere. The mystical, intuitive side cannot be ignored and, indeed, modern physics increasingly finds itself crossing the bridge between the two hemispheres.

As I have shown previously, there are many ways of summarizing the position and perhaps one of the most succinct is the Taoist belief that this left/right balance (this equilibrium of the *yin* and *yang*) harmonizes the flow of what they call the *ch'i*, which is their name for the creative energy that pervades the universe.

By listening to, and rationally acting upon, the promptings of the right-brain intuition, we have seen how men and women can not only release spontaneity, but open themselves to the promptings of the collective unconscious and its archetypes. The door to the paranormal also opens and we shall see in the next chapter that mystic intuition and magic are fruits of the use of the neglected hemisphere.

Parapsychologists acknowledge that their observations lead them to acknowledge the importance of the Rainbow Bridge. As Renée Haynes wrote in *The Seeing Eye, the Seeing I* (Hutchinson, 1976), 'It seems overwhelmingly likely that extra-sensory perception, which emerges into consciousness in the same way as creative impulses and "inspirations" do, is mediated by the right-hand side of the brain . . .', bringing balance to the resolution of the chaos that otherwise appears to underlie the world of sensation.

Mental filters

Of course, it is not the world that is chaotic, it is our inadequate apparatus for receiving and interpreting the mass of stimuli that bombards us. We are limited to five senses, each of which operates over a limited range. In hearing, for instance, birds and animals are able to hear high-pitched sounds that are inaudible to humans. In sight, out of 50 octaves of electromagnetic radiations, our eyes pick up but one.

The human brain acts as a filter and, for most of us, this is fortunate. We are, all the time, waking and sleeping, subject to a bombardment of stimuli and we have to filter out those stimuli that are not immediately relevant. We look for order and what is not orderly will tend to be rejected, so that any stimuli that does not accord with everyday experience will be filtered out.

Sometimes, however, this is to our loss, for the forces that are responsible for paranormal phenomena may act as regularly as any of those more commonly accepted, obeying regular laws. It was William James who wrote, in 1902,

> Our normal waking consciousness . . . is but one type of consciousness, while all about it, parted from it by the flimsiest of screens, there lie potential forms of consciousness entirely different. We may go through life without suspecting their existence; but apply the requisite stimulus and, at a touch, they are here in all their completeness.

Lyall Watson in his book *Lifetide* (Sceptre, 1987) goes so far as to suggest that psychic phenomena are all the result of flaws in the normal filter system.

Most of us have brains that act as small-mesh filters that bar entry to many stimuli, regarding them as being irrelevant to our survival or other, shorter-term needs. Some of us have slightly different filters and are more sensitive than others to the paranormal. Such people can see, for instance, auras around living things, commonly experience telepathy, can 'feel' colours, are natural healers, and so on. They are more open to what the rest of us call the supernatural. Sometimes normal filters break down and hints of a wider world obtrude onto our unwilling consciousness. Not uncommonly such breakthroughs *have* been shown to have had a survival value. Very often, they are not noticed, being put down to hunches or inexplicable last-minute changes of plan. How different, though, our perception of the world would be if even *one* of our senses was to have its range extended. At the end of this chapter, I shall give an example of claims that this has been done and that visualization plays its part.

Carl Jung

Carl Jung, as we have seen, provides a number of points of contact between Eastern mysticism and twentieth-century science, so I see him as providing a suitable general explanation of many paranormal phenomena. Much of what he said many years ago is being validated to varying degrees by later insights, as I shall hope to show.

The basic notion running through all of Carl Jung's work is that human beings share common memories and experiences that exist as archetypes, or, formal patterns of psychic energy. Carl Jung argues that all of our unconscious life (dreams, impulses, mythologies and artistic creativity) mirror the world of pure archetypes, drawing psychic energy from them and diffusing their patterns throughout our personalities and behaviour. As Danah Zohar puts it in *Through the Time Barrier*,

> The psychic energy patterns focused in the archetypes lie at the root of Jung's attempt to explain the dynamics of telepathy and precognition. At those moments when we are using, or when we find ourselves using, these faculties, we are experiencing, he says, not the perception of events in the outer world of objects arrayed in the fiction of space and time; rather we are in touch with something deep inside ourselves. The precognitive psyche is relating to its own extended self by way of the spaceless, timeless, collective unconscious. There, being attracted to some archetypal pattern . . . the psyche gathers in some of the meanings (images, thoughts, scenarios of events) relevant to the emotion which first put it in touch with that particular archetype. These meanings may have come from far afield, from other centuries or other continents, but the psyche finds them bound together in the archetypal vortex and 'in time' communicates them to its own conscious self as events 'in the future'.

All possibilities are thus present in the here and now.

One means of tapping into the 'precognitive psyche' that attracted Carl Jung is the ancient Chinese oracle, the book known as the *I Ching*. By means of tossing coins, the enquirer is directed to the text about one of the 64 hexagrams. Somehow, the hexagram invariably speaks to his condition, that is, the meaning in a seeker's question seems irresistibly to be drawn to the meaning lying at the heart of the most relevant of the 64 hexagrams of the *I Ching*.

Quantum physics

Quantum physics promises much, yet the breakout from its mathematics and preoccupation with the discovery of yet more particles seems a long time a-coming out of its closet, whose door was set ajar by writers such as Fritjof Capra in *The Tao of Physics* (Fontana, 1976) and David Bohm who has explored ideas that are to do with bringing the mental and the material together as two sides of one overall process. Such writers join with Jung in bringing the East closer to the West.

A lesser-known writer whom I have already mentioned who has tried to marry the insights of quantum physics with the paranormal is Danah Zohar. She takes precognition as the central theme of her book *Through the Time Barrier*. In it, she takes quantum theory as her jumping off point, drawing parallels between the mechanics of quantum theory and the mechanics of precognition in particular. As she says, '. . . we now know that it is at least *theoretically* possible to look towards relevant quantum phenomena when attempting to explain any proven psychic phenomena which researchers might produce.'

She takes as read that matter and energy are not fundamentally distinguishable, that both are subject to the 'uncertainty principle' — more closely and obviously, she believes, than might be suspected. The central tenet of the uncertainty principle is that it is impossible ever to pin down a quantum event with precision. We are reminded of chaos theory when we observe how the effect of the light, for instance, in an observing instrument immediately and inevitably alters the very thing being observed. Similarly, each element of a process of thought partakes of the same uncertainty.

The brain, being a part of the universe, is sensitive to quanta jumps by the electrons of the atoms of which it is composed. This has been shown experimentally. As Danah Zohar says in *Through the Time Barrier*, '. . . it has been known for decades that the visual cortex of the human brain is sensitive enough to register a single photon of light . . . a single quantum process . . .' Experiments in the first half of the twentieth century showed that single neurones in the brain were subject to an uncertainty principle so quantum uncertainty was, unsurprisingly, built into the workings of the brain itself.

The observations of quantum physicists, then, are not confined to the esoterica of physics, but are also true of the brain and so of the weft and warp of our everyday thinking, resting as they do upon a substrate of particles and waves. Most of the time, though, such tiny phenomena are masked by the massive injections of stimuli from the ordinary business of living. The brain's neurones have a low sensitivity threshold. Danah Zohar once more has some interesting facts about this in her book.

> In the ordinary course of perception, neurones are being excited at or beyond their stimulation thresholds all the time by the very strong electrical impulses generated by the surrounding environment . . . Only those which are stimulated at or near their stimulation thresholds will be sensitive to the quantum level excitation of the surrounding fluids. If the stimulation comes at a higher level, as it does in normal perception, then it will drown out the more delicate, quantum level stimuli.

If, as I shall show, such tiny excitations are relevant to explaining paranormal phenomena, then the need for relaxation, peace and quiet in exercising them is very necessary.

There is not a predetermined outcome of a disturbance, for such precognitive phenomena occurring at the threshold are random. As Danah Zohar says,

> If an atomic system is disturbed (either internally or externally), the resulting electron transitions occur in a completely random way . . . It would be accurate to say that one event was *related* to another, but quite wrong to describe one as a cause and the other as an effect.

There is not a predetermined outcome of a disturbance. What does appear to happen is what could be called a series of mini-experiments that endeavour to cope with the unpredictability. Danah Zohar again:

> Marshall's Theory recalls that a sub-atomic system is always at any given time, a mixture of possibility and actuality . . . An elementary particle within the system, such as an electron, tends when disturbed to throw out 'feelers' towards its own future state when faced with the problem of adjusting to some new energy level . . . [and will] simultaneously cover all the possible energy states the particle might actually choose to occupy — i.e., they simultaneously act out all of the particle's possible futures.

Precognition could be explained if there was a way that the brain could 'tune into' these virtual (and mind-boggling) dips into the future. Each electron transition is, as it were, an experiment to find the best outcome. To rely on Danah Zohar once more,

> Thus, if there is any similarity between pattern formations in the brain and patterns building up in the virtual transitions of quantum phenom-

ena, the increasing tendency towards a pattern amongst the virtual transitions (the theory holds) is going to create an increasing similarity in the patterns building up in the brain's reverberating circuits. This concept of resonance is similar in many ways to Jung's synchronistic notion that 'like attracts like' . . . thus creating a precognitive image which mirrors the increasing probability of some quantum event pattern.

It is also similar, as we shall see below, to Sheldrake's concept of 'morphic resonance'.

In a faint echo of what Roberto Assagioli and others have said, Danah Zohar later suggests that it is possible, also, that the act of visualization *increases* resonance between thought and the physical world. She says, in respect of this, that fantasy seems almost to be designed for us to throw out feelers into the future and this enables us to live out in our minds possible future situations. All possibilities are present here and now.

If there is anything to all this, then it would seem to be apparent that precognition is not so much a matter of coming events casting their shadows before them, but of short-term memories of the multiplicity of possibilities arising as a result of the particle transitions. Danah Zohar puts it like this,

> . . . if quantum mechanical approaches to the subject are correct, precognition (our memory of the future) would necessarily contain an uncertain mixture of 'memories' of actual events and 'memories' of lost possibilities.

The holographic paradigm

Holograms 'work' by using a laser beam to reconstitute the interference patterns formed by other laser beams reflected off objects. They have the property of being able to be split asunder and for the fragments to contain all the information of the original and this provides a model of how the brain delocalizes memory. Gone are any traces of the old picture of memory as a gigantic filing system, instead the concept is taken out of the field of space and time — from the material world, indeed — and transmuted fairly and squarely into mathematical calculations performed on the frequencies of energy that the brain receives via perception and disturbed particles.

This makes it more possible to see the paranormal as normal, of the transcendent as part of nature. Perhaps, Karl Pribram is reported as saying by Marilyn Ferguson in *The Aquarian Conspiracy* (Tarcher, 1980), the material world is a collection of representations of frequencies. Arthur Eddington it was who said in *The Expanding Universe* (University of Michigan Press, 1958), 'The stuff of the universe is mind-stuff.' The universe is immaterial, but orderly.

Buddhists and others have long said that a material object is merely a 'standing wave', a flux in the stream of energy. Today's physicists say matter has only a *tendency* to exist and can easily be redistributed as purer energy. Paul Dirac summarizes the enigma when he writes, 'All matter is created out of some imperceptible substratum ... nothingness, unimaginable and undetectable. But it is a peculiar form of nothingness out of which all matter is created' (quoted by Marilyn Ferguson in *The Aquarian Conspiracy*). This nothingness is none other than concepts met with in such as the Buddhist 'Void' and the Tao. In the Void, form is emptiness and emptiness is form. The Tao expresses itself in the world by means of *ch'i*, energy, constantly streaming and returning.

When energy is seen as 'constantly streaming', it is no longer separated from matter. The fundamental building blocks of the cosmos are those slippery wave-particles: mathematical symbols, concepts in a Tibetan Lama's mind. Constantly returning, space and time are seen in theory as curved and returning in upon themselves. Past and future disappear. David Bohm indicates that what we normally see is the explicate order of things. Under this order there is an implicit, enfolded order, much as the DNA in the cell directs the nature of unfolding life as it becomes explicit, much as morphic resonance does and much as a hologram enfolds its image until it is made explicit by the use of a laser light. As the physicist Karl Pribram once said, surprising himself a little at the time, 'Maybe the *world* is a hologram.'

If the universe *is* holographic, then it follows that the universe is contained in every part of itself. In such a scheme of things, psychic phenomena can easily be seen as a by-product of universal simultaneity and Carl Jung once more makes sense. All possibilities are present here and now and under certain conditions, individuals may obtain access not only to some, but to all of the information in the system — the Oceanic Experience.

Rupert Sheldrake's morphogenetic field theory
Rupert Sheldrake introduces readers to his ideas by telling us about a very difficult laboratory procedure whereby new crystals are created or discovered. Such a procedure may take much time. However, and this is the nub of his theory, once a procedure has been successful and a new crystal has emerged for the first time, he remarks that

similar crystals start popping up very easily in many other previously unsuccessful laboratories. He notes that this phenomenon of action at a distance is sometimes explained by puzzled scientists as the effect of dust particles floating on the breeze. He rejects this and puts forward his theory of 'morphic resonance', analagous to the sympathetic vibrations of stretched strings to sound waves.

Whatever explanation is chosen, we are apparently dealing here, in this sympathetic resonance between laboratories, with a paranormal phenomenon, that is, with action at a distance without the transmission of energy.

Normal growth, according to Rupert Sheldrake, is not so much a matter of following a genetic blueprint, but more of being shaped by morphogenetic fields connecting across space and time so that embryos develop by 'tuning in' to the forms of past members of the species. It is this sort of field that makes a rabbit grow up to be a rabbit and not a man or one salt crystal to look like another — it is another kind of blueprint.

The same is true of behaviour. Once a new behaviour has been learned by any member of a species, that behaviour becomes more likely in all others. Again, Carl Jung makes more sense.

Rupert Sheldrake himself cautiously says in *A New Science of Life* (Paladin, 1987) that,

> It is not inconceivable that some of the alleged [paranormal] phenomena might turn out to be compatible with the hypothesis . . . in particular, it might be possible to formulate an explanation of telepathy in terms of morphic resonance and of psychokinesis in terms of the modification of probabalistic events within objects under the influence of motor fields.

Direct knowing

Jean Piaget, a Swiss psychologist, made his name in his experimental and theoretical work to do with the development of logical thinking in children and adolescents. He traced the development from what he called the Sensori-motor stage of the young baby, through a Pre-Operational (pre-logical) stage in the infant, through the Concrete Operational stage of the child, to the Formal Operational stage of some adolescents and adults.

His work has been developed by others, such as Jerome Bruner and Herbert Koplowitz. The latter claims that there are two stages beyond that of Formal Operational Thought. The highest stage, 'Unitary Operational Thinking', is a stage in which the thinker understands that the way in which he has been conditioned to see the external world is only one of many possible constructs. As Marilyn Ferguson explains in *The Aquarian Conspiracy*,

> Opposites, which had been thought of as separate and distinct, are seen as interdependent. Causality, which had been thought of as linear, is now seen as pervading the universe, connecting all events with each other.

These, however, are observations, not explanations, yet Marilyn Ferguson quotes Koplowitz as saying,

> Just as mysticism is not a rejection of science but a transcendence of it, science is not a rejection of mysticism but a precursor of it . . . Mystic traditions such as Taoism may offer the most thoroughly developed bodies of Unitary Operational Thinking.

Bypassing our normal, constricting perceptual mode in mystical states, such Unitary Operational thinkers may be attuned to other perceptions or indeed to the source of reality.

So, from this brief survey of hints, it appears that science may be able to provide some explanations of paranormal phenomena. We are at the edge of knowledge. As for visualization's place in all this, we have to content ourselves with Danah Zohar's opinion that it may be used to '. . . increase resonance between thought and the physical world' and the general mystico-religious thought that brings past, present and future together into the here and now.

Learning to be psychic

Is it possible to learn how to increase psychic powers? Perhaps there has to be a certain predisposition. The shaman, the clever man, the witch, the medium — most are singled out as being possessed of powers. Some develop the powers by trial and error, some are trained and all cultivate continuous attention to their own inner sensations.

It is not certain where such powers come from, whether they are primitive throwbacks, a natural but neglected part of our normal psychic make-up or whether they represent an emerging faculty that marks the next stage in the evolution of our species. Perhaps it does not really matter. What is more important is that such powers should be developed, either for purely pragmatic reasons, such as for use in crime detection, or for reasons to do with the full development of the human race.

From an examination of the somewhat sparse literature, a small scrap of advice emerges as to how this may be done. It not unexpectedly includes the need for preliminaries such as relaxation and the need to develop vivid visual imagery, powers of concentration and the ability to provide feedback on mental states.

Such introspection always lends itself to scorn and attack by sceptics and nowhere more so than in this search for wider horizons. Bob Couttie, to take a typical example, says in *Forbidden Knowledge* (Lutterworth Press, 1988) that the greater the concentration on internal processes, '... the more meaningful they tend to become and the more one notices correlations with what is going on in the outside world, thus reinforcing a spurious link between the two'. This assumes that the link is spurious in the first place and not an example of Herbert Koplowitz's Unitary Operational Thinking. Nevertheless, gifted psychics such as Matthew Manning have helped ordinary people to develop their paranormal faculties in as short a time as two days. As Andrew Stanway reports in *Alternative Medicine*,

> It was simply because they [then] knew *how* to do it, in what order to do things, how to visualize images. The only people it doesn't work for are those who have a conscious block.

José Silva in his chapter 'How to Practice ESP' in *The Silva Mind Control Method*, describes how ESP can be used in healing by means of visualization exercises. The trainees first visualize the physical properties of their own homes and then move on to visualizing themselves entering the wall of their home and testing its internal properties. During the training course they devise 'psychic instruments', as we saw earlier, such as sieves for filtering blood, delicate brushes for sweeping away the white powder (calcium) '... that can be seen psychically in arthritis', baths for washing away guilt and so forth. They finish the training course by being able to visualize the imaginary ailments of an imaginary patient from the bare details supplied by a partner.

If sceptics would enjoy mauling *that* example, they would have a field-day with the next example, yet none of them have, as far as I know, attempted to explain it away.

In this chapter we have been looking at the shadowy world of the paranormal and it may be that now we step into the secret world of the occult — the boundaries are often obscure. Either way, we are dealing with phenomena that lie outside the boundaries of the normal. Sometimes those boundaries are set by science, sometimes they are set by religion. Meditators, for example, are constantly being warned against the heady seductions exercised by the *siddhis*, those powers and other psychic phenomena they often meet with. Perhaps this is an example. It is to do with the creation of a spirit-body by Alexandra David-Neel, who spent 14 years in Tibet and who wrote of her experiences there in *Magic and Mystery in Tibet* (Souvenir, 1967). First comes the visualization:

> I chose for my experiment a most insignificant character: a monk, short and fat, of an innocent and jolly type. I shut myself in *tsams* and proceeded to perform the prescribed concentration of thought and other rites. After a few months the phantom monk was formed. His form grew gradually fixed and life-like looking. He became a kind of guest, living in my apartment.

The rites she mentions will be looked at further in Chapter 12. In the meantime, the story takes us to the limits of the paranormal and perhaps beyond. At any rate, I shall leave to a later chapter the further and somewhat unpleasant development of this story and content myself here with remarking that if such a phenomenon can be achieved by visualization and taking thought, the achievement of other paranormal skills is certainly possible.

11.
Wider Horizons

The previous chapter would have been much easier to write if we had been able to move easily into and out of a fantastic world of our own creation — for that is what occultists do. The line between paranormal phenomena and occult phenomena is a thin one, but it does exist.

Paranormal phenomena get a good press because people are interested: tales of the unexpected abound and science is beginning to provide explanations. The occult gets a mixed press as tales of the unknown abound, but explanations are less clear and less forthcoming. By definition, the occult is hidden, secret, esoteric, unknown, and, therefore, often feared. It is also very dependent on strong powers of visualization, as I shall show in this chapter.

Science and the occult

Most men and women are trapped in the 'triviality of everydayness' as Martin Heidegger the German philosopher has it. It may be that we urgently need to develop our knowledge and awareness of those unseen forces that open wider 'the vistas of meaning that surround us'. Such powers as divination, bilocation, telepathy, precognition, psychokinesis and the like are but Western names for Eastern *siddhis* — those gifts that are attained through deep meditation or the disciplined suffering of the shaman. Even though these powers are often discounted as being of no real importance by their Eastern possessors, we in the West do have some catching up to do.

Quantum physics and Jung with his concepts of the collective unconscious and synchronicity may have some bearing on our scientific understanding of the *siddhis*, but the mysteries of quantum physics are only just beginning to percolate into the consciousness of the West and certainly have not percolated to the extent necessary to recall to modern sophisticates the sense of the numinous, of magic and of the consciousness of unseen powers that can be tapped. The same may be said of Jung's ideas, though they are now becoming more respectable.

The occult shares with the paranormal a widening of consciousness. Where the student of the paranormal is more often an observer caught unawares, however, occultists are those that set out deliberately to extend still further that widening.

The occult is generally regarded as opposed to science. Up until very recently, anything that could not be explained by science was automatically marginalized by being put into the category of the super (beyond) natural, was therefore completely discounted and often regarded as the province of women, the dark underground of the left hand and the right (intuitive) brain. It is thus likely still to be discounted by men-centric sciences. Now, though, there may be the dawning of a change of emphasis, brought about by some of the scientific gropings in the field of the paranormal described in the previous chapter. Interest in the occult may now indicate a desire to find a *scientific* explanation of things regarded heretofore as supernatural.

The Chambers Twentieth-Century Dictionary's definition of 'occult', besides the conventional '. . . hidden; secret, esoteric; unknown . . .' is '. . . *not discovered without test or experiment*' as an obsolete meaning, thus half-heartedly pulling it into the range of science, before going on: '. . . beyond the range of sense; transcending the bounds of natural knowledge; mysterious, magical, supernatural . . .'. As I have said, once upon a time, magic was all we had with which to try to explain and control natural forces. As Aleister Crowley once wrote, '. . . magick has always been the mother of science'.

It is as though there has been a conspiracy by a gang of two — traditional religion and modern science — each, for its own reasons, desirous of abolishing the occult sciences.

As history has progressed, at any rate in the West, myth, magic and mystery have been transformed — myth into history, magic into science and reason and mystery into technology and domination of the natural world. Historian Theodore Roszak succinctly describes this process as one that turns its back on the visionary sources of our culture. Science has narrowed our perceptions by becoming the dominant frame of reference, but, it is not the only, nor necessarily the most important of such frames.

An effort to drag magic, supernormal powers and the like back into scientific respectability is sometimes made. Charles Tart, for instance, recognizes that science is normally conducted within the conceptual boundaries of the reality that we all accept as necessary for normal communication and daily activities (I have asked before what it is that we mean by 'reality'). Charles Tart is a clinical analyst and so continues to accept and urge the need for rigorous scientific investigation. However, he also recognizes the existence of altered states of consciousness in which several of the consensual rules of normal perception and causality do not seem to hold good or appear to apply. As a result, he introduces the notion of 'state-specific sciences' in the hope that the purview of science will be widened.

Science is the belief system that is at present the dominant one so this means that the analysis of reality that is made by scientists is likely to be heavily contaminated by the rules of this belief system. However, there is a deeply felt and growing need for alternative, equally acceptable, equally valid, belief systems that allow for a sense of identification with the earth, the environment and the forces of nature, seen and unseen. Colin Wilson has this to say in *The Occult* (Hodder & Stoughton, 1971)

> So-called magic powers are a part of this underground world: powers of second sight, prevision, telepathy, divination . . . He [man] must somehow return to the recognition that he is potentially a 'mage' . . . the message of the symphonies of Beethoven could be summarized: 'Man is not small; he's just bloody lazy.'

This is a difficult chapter to write, as I have little knowledge of magic and, indeed, find myself reluctant to embark on it even to the extent of seeking help by using the Tarot and so forth. In this I am an average member of my race and class in this period of history. We are, if we dabble at all, happier with the *I Ching* and it may be that this is because this 'Book of Changes' is less symbolic and more down to earth. It is also, of course, a divinatory technology, as opposed to a transformative one. One of our difficulties in the West is that we are looking (if we look at all) for a *safe* religion, for a belief system that will tell us how we ought to behave, rather than a transformative belief system, that is, one that will transform our way of seeing the world and that will therefore transform our very selves. Nevertheless, I would be less than honest if I did not share with the reader the little magic I believe I have been able to perform. I write with trepidation of my first experience of controlled visualization.

I first became aware of the possibility of magic in myself some years ago in Dorset. I was on a week's holiday and the weather was only so-so. As the clouds gathered *again* on the third day of the week and threatened to spoil the whole holiday, I found myself visualizing those clouds. I was relaxed, my eyes were closed and I was somewhat emotionally roused. I visualized the clouds as moving, melting, the blue sky behind them appearing and the sun breaking through. I opened my eyes and there they were, those clouds, moving, melting, breaking up, and the sun was shining more and more. We laughed, my companion and I, and enjoyed the splendid day that followed.

Since then, believe it or not, I have repeated the experiment and, more often than not, have succeeded (to my own satisfaction at any rate) in controlling the weather.

I rest my case, except to say that the experience encouraged me to try my hand at self-healing and healing others, both with moderate success (how do you distinguish natural from psychic healing?) and finally to write this book.

It is little wonder that we in the West opt for divination, for we are frightened of what we may find in the transformative aspects of the occult. Pink Floyd put it so well in their song,

> And if the dam breaks open many years too soon,
> And if there is no room upon the hill,
> And if your hand explores with dark forebodings too,
> I'll see you on the dark side of the moon.

Self-transformation

It will be becoming apparent that we have been dealing with the occult quite often in this book, whose theme is the transformations we can make in ourselves and in our circumstances through visualization. Such changes as have resulted have, in the main, been explicable in terms of rational discourse. With the occult, and in the remainder of the book, I deal with the same subject, but explanations are harder to come by. Nevertheless, we cling to an article of faith, which is that the universe, in its subtle as much as in its gross aspects, is a field of constantly changing energy and that it is possible by a variety of means to control these changes. Magical operative models of the universe, the subject of this chapter, are only other methodologies concerned with the transmutation of that energy.

One of the main reasons for the study of magic is the hope that it will enable the achievement of self-fulfilment. Self-fulfilment is implicitly about the exercise of greater power over your destiny. The self, which here means the self-concept, and the skills possessed by the self have both to be transformed.

There are many non-scientific belief models extant. Consequently, there are differences between peoples in the operative belief models of the universe that they embrace. There are differences for example, between the Buddhist and the cabalistic inner worlds that provide the psychic power of their respective models. We are able to a limited extent 'to try models on for size' as it were to see which may be compatible with us, but it is important to give time to the experiment. We need to remember that our reality is a world that demands instant gratification, instant success and this cannot happen with self-transformation. In addition, a certain suspension of everyday belief is needed.

To opt for an occult model is to embark on a path that not only has psychic dangers as well as rewards, but physical ones as well.

The occult path

Dion Fortune has written in *Sane Occultism and Practical Occultism in Everyday Life* (Aquarian Press, 1987), 'Occult science is really a branch of knowledge that is hidden from the many and reserved for the few.' It is said by these few to be a philosophy of science and life. Like classical music, it is reserved for those few whose training and natural gifts enable them to appreciate it. *Why*, though, are magic procedures kept secret, reserved for the few? It is, after all, open to anyone at all to try for him or herself the delights of classical music and to turn away freely. It is not up to some secret brotherhood of classical musicologists to admit the individual or not. In this there is a marked difference from entry to the occult. Has someone, or some group decided to limit membership, perhaps because they think that such powers can be misused? Or is it merely thoughtless elitist priestcraft? Or is it for purposes of group protection and the need to guard against *agents provocateurs* (occult groups are often threatened not only by dark interior forces, but by the forces of what Alan Watts once mockingly called 'lawn order' in its straight tidiness or by the rise of newer, more powerful or more socially acceptable religious groups)?

What is quite certain is that occult powers are not easily developed and need much concentration and practice — in itself, one would have thought, a factor likely to limit membership. That having been said, it is true to say that in the latter half of the twentieth century there has been an opening up in the West of esoteric knowledge. Some knowledge, as always, has been misused — one has only to think of the Mansons for instance — but nevertheless the interest continues to increase, as a browse in a bookshop will testify. Why is this?

Perhaps it is the death of religion, which has left a gap that is only partially filled by new gurus of all kinds. Perhaps it is an instinctive, atavistic return to older beliefs. Whatever the reason, it appears that it is not the time for group conversions, but more a time for individual development. As Colin Wilson says in *The Occult*,

> Civilization cannot evolve further until 'the occult' is taken for granted on the same level as atomic energy . . . we have to learn to expand inward until we have somehow re-established the sense of *huaca*, until we have re-created the feeling of 'unseen forces' that was common to primitive man.

Even if ordinary people are not able to partake of occult powers, the fact that such powers are more popularly recognized is a valuable inward step for modern humankind to have made.

Witches and shamans

Such people are ones who, by one means or another, have become adepts. Shamans suffer long torments of physical and mental suffering in order to attain such powers; witches very often have, or have had to, endure long torments of isolation.

The word 'witch' comes from the Old English word *wiccian* that means to practise sorcery. Witchcraft itself is a legacy from pagan times, being a nature-based religion. It appears to have been carried on mainly by highly regarded wise women or witches. Paracelsus is said to have burned his textbooks of drugs in 1527 declaring that he had learned from the sorceresses all that he knew. It is, therefore, little wonder that a male-dominated society has tended always to issue stern warnings against the practice of magic, particularly when in the hands of women, even though the purposes of the craft, whose watchword was 'do as you will and harm no one', was to use the psychic power mainly for healing, black witches being regarded as a sick fringe.

Like witches, shamans (most, though not all, however, being male) were, before the coming of civilization, able to exercise paranormal powers, such as telepathy, clairvoyance, clairaudience, telekinesis and psychic healing. That being so, it is not difficult to believe that shamans were able to employ psychic force against enemies and appeared to be able to use visualization when necessary.

A consideration of visualization as employed in the visions of the North American Indian shamans takes us forward to the subject of the next chapter. Suffice to remark here that shamans, particularly in the suffering endured in their initiations, may well have suffered from hallucinations — it would have been strange if they had not. Such visions would be remembered in all their stark detail, would have been a well-defined mental image, particularly by one who had not the modern advantage of demarcation lines between the 'real' and the 'unreal'. They became a tool for future magic and would have needed to have been recreated by means of visualizations. Thus, I venture to suggest that very often when 'visions' are mentioned in the literature of occultism, self-created visualizations are meant.

So, in the West, the magician, as Neville Drury has it in *Inner Visions* (Routledge & Kegan Paul, 1979),

> ... knows the scope of his hierarchy of gods and goddesses, his spirit allies and archangels [and can invoke them by the power of his imagination] ... He imposes upon the vast range of visual and auditory possibilities ... a particular set of images [which may often be those of the Tarot] ... 'Formed pyramid over me. Went through it ... and saw Ahepi in the centre of the brilliance, and himself light and white ... I said I wanted to interview the Sphinx of the pyramid ... I saw him easily and at once but his colours were not brilliant.'

The Tarot cards are used quite specifically in Western magic as a basis for such visualization, which, according to Neville Drury, may be effective enough when taken as objects of meditation, but are much more effective when undertaken as part of an out-of-the-body experience, such as was experienced by Oliver Fox, described later in this chapter.

An additional source of inspiration for adepts is the theological, metaphysical and magical cabbala. This and the Tarot are commonly worked in tandem. The cabbala was developed by Jewish rabbis in the eleventh and twelfth centuries who read secret symbolical meanings into the bible with the use of numerology. Its aim is to relate the finite and the infinite (as in some pathworkings), and this, cabbalists say, is brought about by emanations from the Absolute Being (Jahweh, the *Tao, prana*, the Life Force). From the later Middle Ages, cabbalists were chiefly occupied in concocting and deciphering charms, mystical anagrams and so forth and, most importantly, in searching for the Philosopher's Stone. They make much use of the mandala, The Tree of Life. Within cabbalist teachings are found rituals, magical invocations, pathworkings and so on. In the latter great significance is placed on Hebrew letters as psychic way-marks.

Working magic

What is needed to work magic? First, there must be confidence, born of faith and experience.

Second, there must be a firm grasp of reality. When a person has completed a pathworking, for instance, certain procedures are recommended so that everyday reality is firmly recalled.

Third, intense powers of concentration are needed. As Da Liu says in his discussion of Taoist magic in *The Tao and Chinese Culture* (Routledge & Kegan Paul, 1981), '... to be able to control the powers of magic, it is necessary to develop a very intense level of mental concentration for which rigorous discipline and unceasing practice are essential'.

Finally, and most importantly, a strong and precise imagination is needed. Imagination is the key to all magic because it is able to stir mental energy and to use pre-existing mental models. We are reminded of the words of Roberto Assagioli in *Psychosynthesis* that 'Images and mental pictures tend to produce the physical conditions and the external acts corresponding to them.' Assagioli is here very near to the twin concepts of the *Tao* and the plenum field of quantum physicists, both of which indicate that we live in a field of energy that can take subtle or gross form, but which is identical in both forms. Pictures created in the imagination invariably affect the physical, the latter being another form of the same energy.

Mention of the Tarot reminds us of the powers of divination and clairvoyance that may accompany the acquisition of occult powers. This art of ascertaining future events through tapping into the flow of universal energy can be brought about either by subjective means through dreams, trance, automatic writing and so on or by objective means, such as casting lots, consulting texts, such as the *I Ching*, omens, entrails and so forth.

Carl Jung looked into the mysterious way in which the *I Ching* was able accurately to predict change in the context of the total situation pertaining at the time in *Synchronicity* (RKP, 1972). In his researches, he detected what he called an '... acausal connecting principle, in which events and feelings were often clearly connected even in the absence of any direct cause-and-effect'. He called this principle 'synchronicity', which was that often a dream or vision (later verified) coincided with a distant event. Certainly he found the *I Ching* to be full of such inexplicable connections.

The *I Ching*, however, is an oracle and as such is not to be asked direct questions. At best it will give relatively direct clues, but normally its answers have to be worked on by the enquirer.

Healing

We have discussed the topic of healing at some length elsewhere and it is only mentioned here to remind us that healing is at the centre of very much magic work — healing of oneself or of others. Rebecca Clark gives some good advice in *Macro-Mind Power* that will encourage the use of a little magic. It is to avoid giving a sick person advice on what they should or should not be doing to make themselves well again. Better by far, she says, to '. . . use the scientific, psychological and cosmic way of picturing the person whole in mind, body and affairs . . . Picture a thing and bring it through, rather than trying to force it through.' Tribesmen, after all, did not believe that they were sticking a sword into the side of an enemy when they pricked models with a pin, but instead believed that they were invoking a psychic force that would kill him. What interests me, however, is the question as to when it was discovered that a doll was not needed, but that a visualized picture of the enemy was sufficient.

Benjamin Walker writes in *Tantrism* (Aquarian Press, 1972), 'The [first] object need not actually be touched, but in that case, the touching must be powerfully visualized.' He gives an example of the way in which energy is drawn down in tantric ceremonies by the placing of the worshipper's fingers, for instance, on the stone phallus before touching his own phallus.

Magicians have long known that the imagination is powerful in that it first directs the consciousness and then directs the material world. It is, they believe, a powerful means and as Neville Drury says in *Inner Visions*, 'Shamans in the West have long known that the imagination is itself a form of direction — it can lead one into wonderful and awesome spaces that are both illuminating and terrifying.'

There are two related ways of employing the imagination to transform ourselves and our world and they are sufficiently distinct to warrant separate treatment here. One is by means of visualization and affirmations, the other is by means of pathworkings.

Visualizing

In general terms, Da Liu crystallizes popular thought on this when he says in *The Tao and Chinese Culture*, 'The success of those who have practiced such magical arts traditionally has depended on their ability to divert and manipulate the imagination of the observer'. In fact, of course, the boot is often on the other foot, that is, it is the magician's imagination that is manipulated.

Dion Fortune echoes much of what Maxwell Maltz, Shakti Gawain, Roberto Assagioli and a host of others have said when she writes in *Sane Occultism and Practical Occultism in Daily Life*:

> We must rise above fear and nervousness by learning to control our imagination, for fear is entirely the product of the imagination . . . We should therefore train the imagination not to dwell upon the things we fear, but rather to picture a happy issue out of all our afflictions and ourselves as sailing triumphantly into the port of our desires. This happy daydreaming plays a far more important part in the lives of successful men and women than is generally realized . . . The person who habitually indulges in happy daydreams develops a peculiar mental atmosphere which is best described by the word glamorous.

Similarly Dolores Ashcroft-Nowicki has this to say in *Highways of the Mind*,

> . . . the language of unconscious gesture is an extraordinarily eloquent thing . . . when our subconscious gestures announce that we expect a welcome, that we expect unquestioning acquiescence, nine people out of ten will respond . . . if . . . our habitual daydreams have been concerned with our triumphant success, we hang out unconscious banners of triumph, and nine out of ten persons will line up and march behind them.

Again she says,

> We can create a finished image inside our heads, change it if we are not satisfied and then manifest it on the physical level in metal, wood, stone, gold, silver, cotton and even flesh . . . thought is creative and fantasies are thoughts that need only a strong emotional push for them to become as real as the hand that carves or shapes the dream into reality.

Every moment of our lives we live in a field of energy, energy that may manifest itself as thought or substance. It is all one. Everything any man or woman ever made or did, however trite or terrible, was first conceived of in thought.

Colin Wilson in *The Occult* describes how a certain Oliver Fox experienced in a dream the ability to leave his body and how he determined to achieve the same while in a waking state. He put himself into a trance, would feel his body becoming numb and the room assuming a golden hue. 'He had then to *use his imagination*, and picture himself hurtling towards the "pineal doorway" . . .' the site of the third eye, the *corpus callosum*.

Tibetan lamas have a view of the mind as lying on a continuum of energy that embraces all physical manifestations. WY Evans-Wentz suggested that in their view matter was a development of thought, was in fact 'crystallized mental energy' — another extraordinary link between ancient Eastern and modern Western thought.

Such crystallized energy, thought-forms, they called *tulpas*. Alexandra David-Neel describes in *Magic and Mystery in Tibet* how she, on a public occasion, and therefore with many witnesses, saw a lama step out of a sedan chair in which he was riding, walk up to a statue and fade into it. The sedan chair was empty and the lama had, in fact, been a thought-form, never actually there at all. Her own experiments in this field have already been mentioned.

Such a *tulpa*, that is, a visualization that had taken on a human form, might have been what they call a *tulku*. This is a 'phantom body', born in the usual way, but conceived by a focusing of thought and will by a superior being or by several people co-operating. A *tulku* would live a normal life of birth, maturation and death, be in no way distinguishable from ordinary people, but be instead an embodiment of a god or an ideal. This is how the Tibetans would explain the passing on from body to body of the incarnate Dalai Lama and we shall see in Chapter 11 how this belief is utilized in the religious practices of Tibetan Buddhism.

Such mental projections or personifications may not be confined to the roof of the world: photographic evidence of fairies literally thought up by two little girls in Yorkshire caused a sensation when brought forward by Conan Doyle in 1920. Mika Waltari, a Finnish novelist of this century, was apparently persecuted by one of his own female characters who got completely out of hand.

Geoffrey Ashe in *Miracles* (Routledge & Kegan Paul, 1978) suggests that it is possible that the risen Christ's body was such a *tulku*, incarnate mind-substance, substantial enough for doubting Thomas to feel His wounds. Medieval Cathars, believing as they did that matter was evil, could not understand how goodness could be embodied in matter and thus believed that Jesus had not been crucified and that his earthly form was a phantom. His miracles could equally well be classified in Tibetan terms as *tulpas*, transformations of energy by taking thought.

We shall see in the next chapter how meditation on a mandala can convert it into a powerful focus of psychic energy that may then be used as a healing picture.

Affirming

There is a universal belief in the power of sound in words. Many a spell has been cast to the accompaniment of occult chants and mantras. In Hinduism, the sacred syllable Om is said to keep the universe in being and in Egyptian death ceremonies the exact pronunciation of magical formulae is of the utmost importance.

The use of mantras is spreading again in the West. A growing number of people in both East and West believe, for instance, that they find a source of power and realization in chanting the mystic formula *nam-myoho-renge-kyo*.

We do not have to go far these days to see magic in use. An American spiritual counsellor, Rebecca Clark, for instance, in her book *Macro-Mind Power* claims to harness '. . . the miraculous cosmic force of the ancients . . .' and in it she relies heavily upon the twin arts of visualization and, especially, affirmation.

The publisher's blurb for what is a breathlessly exciting book asks the reader to 'Harness the *Limitless Power* that can bring you abundant wealth, radiant health, love, happiness — and everything else your heart desires! Learn the five easy steps for developing *Macro-Mind Magnetism*; discover your body's twelve *Healing Centres* . . .' and so on. The book is very moral, even religious, but makes use of magical techniques to a very great extent, largely through the use of the twin techniques just mentioned and, as such is a useful primer for beginning magicians. For instance, her section 'How to Implement a Seven-Day Macro-Mind program for Exerting Greater Influence over Others' begins 'As you are getting dressed each morning, *look into your mirror and give yourself a great big SMILE*! Then say to yourself, "I look wonderful. I feel wonderful, for this is a glorious day! For the precious time allotted me this day, I am going to act in a courteous, charming and magnetic manner."'

Pathworkings

We met these before in Chapter 8 and they have been defined as imaginative journeys between this side of the mental worlds and the other side. They may be based on mythology, such as mentally visiting the abode of the gods, or be constructed by the individual, as in visiting an idealized, peaceful place for purposes of contact with your own higher self: '. . . pathworking is a term used to describe the trained use of the imagination and such journeys within the mind can inform, calm, heal, relax.'

One such pathway described by Dolores Ashcroft-Nowicki is a visualized journey in which you are taken by that messenger of the gods, Mercury, to visit those gods, cold and silent on an abandoned Olympus. You are enabled to wake each god and to talk with him or her about what they represent on Earth (and in the psyche). The journey ends with a promise by you to try to bring back to suffering Earth some of the values the gods represent. She goes on to say,

> We know also that [a pathworking] can cause events to happen in accordance with the will . . . One of the most important occult truths is this: all things stem from the inner places. If you want to change yourself, start by changing the inner you through the medium of pathworking, then, slowly, the change will seep through into the everyday world . . . It has been said that it takes about 21 days for the beginnings of change to be seen on the physical level . . . provided it is built correctly and worked with emotional force behind it, the inner self will see and accept the image you have given it . . . We are what we imagine ourselves to be.

The shaman is initiated into his art by means of pathworkings. He or she follows an initiatory path, and such a path can be viewed either as a literal description or as a journey of the imagination (and who, in such a culture and in such agony of mind and body could distinguish between the two?) Pathworkings then continued to be a part of his work. In officiating at a death for instance, Mircea Eliade writes in *From Primitives to Zen* (Collins, 1979), 'Equally stirring is the voyage of the shaman to the other world to escort the soul of the deceased to its new abode; the shaman narrates to those present all the vicissitudes of the voyage as it takes place.'

Odds and ends

Auras
One of the advantages of clairvoyance to an adept of the occult is the ability it grants to detect the aura that is said to surround all beings. The aura's purpose is to protect you from harm — physical as well as psychic. Some are stronger than others and Rebecca Clark has a visualization designed to increase its protective power. In *Macro-Mind Power* she describes the procedure as follows: 'Draw a mental picture of yourself encased in a radiant energy balloon — enclosed within a circle of intense white light.'

Alchemy

Alchemical practices are, of course, very much the province of the magician. It is a practice apparently very much concerned with the material world and its transformation. That being the case, there might not appear to be very much in it to do with our present concerns. However, Carl Jung found that very many of the dream symbols and visions that he encountered rising up uncontrollably in his mind during the middle years of his life did have numerous parallels in the alchemical literature that he studied extensively. One of the criticisms that is made of Carl Jung in these matters is that he dismissed the work of alchemists by accusing them of projecting their fantasies into matter. I've remarked before that Carl Jung might here have missed an area of investigation that he may well have found fruitful.

Dreamwork

People have always regarded dreams as being significant and have thought of them as messages from the gods or the unconscious. Wherever they come from, we have seen that dreamwork can be a means of psychological self-therapy and an entry into the realms of the paranormal, for dreams can also be used magically as a means to self-transformation. Dreams can even be commanded to order. By creating in your 'quiet place' a 'Dream-Sender' as Janette Rainwater calls him or her in *You're in Charge*, it is possible to ask for a dream that will answer a specific question or show the way to a desired end. The fact that so many dreams are ambiguous and apparently misleading can also be corrected by asking the Dream-Sender to explain them, perhaps by means of a dream the following night.

Astral travel

Then there is the phenomenon known as astral travel in which the body appears to take charge, as it were, and acts without conscious thought. Joe Cooper writing in *The Guardian* on 27 April 1988 gives an example, the gist of which follows:

> It is a wet, dark Bradford evening. C is frustrated at not being able to get through the traffic to the bus stop at the other side of the road. Suddenly she is there. 'I seemed to be walking over and through the car radiators, but nobody appeared to be taking any notice.'
>
> A is walking in India on a path beside a muddy rutted field. She wears a dress and bright white court shoes. She looks across the field and sees a man beating a donkey with an iron bar. Passion rises within her and next second she is beside him, wrestling the bar from his grasp.

Her shoes are still white and unmarked. It takes her five minutes to stumble back through thick mud. She is up to her ankles in it when she gets back to her astonished friends.

Joe Cooper goes on to offer explanations based on the theory that thoughts and emotions combine to dematerialize and materialize the body in response to external stimuli. He suggests that an extension of the theory could be applied to cases of bilocation.

An alternative explanation is that strong emotion is a necessary component in successful visualization. Perhaps A, for instance, seeing the plight of the donkey, visualized herself wresting the iron bar from the man with emotions so strong that, in a way similar to the creation of a *tulpa*, she caused her body to jump the gap between wish and reality.

Warning notes

Clearly there are dangers lurking in the practice of magic. Not everyone who partakes fulfils the second of the criteria for success mentioned above in having a firm grasp of reality. There is very real danger for the unwary individual who is prepared to dabble, unguided, in the occult.

Dreams, for instance, may put the sleeper into direct contact with what Carl Jung calls the 'Shadow' and with other aspects of the personality that are suppressed in a waking state. It is here that the experienced adept knows what he or she is meeting — may indeed, have summoned it — and can certainly exercise control in such a way as to protect the psyche from the bad effects of such a dream.

Colin Wilson in *The Occult* defines magic as a spontaneous manifestation of the forces of the unconscious. Much magic may be, given enough emotion as a motive force, and much may happen — witness the astral travel mentioned above. He gives an example of a Japanese man who, to embarrass local monks, said that on a certain day, a dragon would appear from a pond. The day came and no dragon appeared. The local people grew angry, the monks grew worried and the man himself became affected by the tense expectancy around. He stared eagerly at the surface of the pond, which, suddenly, boiled and frothed and a dragon appeared, shooting off into the sky.

Many witches doubtless did surprise themselves by performing magic. Colin Wilson explains this as the results of sexual frustration or loneliness and, certainly, if you set up circumstances that arouse strong pent-up emotion, then magic may well result, but much magic is, in fact, a controlled manifestation of the unconscious, achieved through conscious effort.

I asked earlier, when I spoke of healing, whether such a power for good could also be used for evil. There are enough stories of witches and the like to persuade us, if we needed it, that certain people *do* have the ability to *harm* others by means of magic. Common sense would indicate that there is always an opposite side to every coin. If you can visualize a person bathed in light, it is no more difficult to see them bathed in darkness or blood or whatever. Indeed, such is the power of the emotion of intense hate, it would seem to be reasonably simple, given confidence in the basic method. Witches and witch-doctors have killed.

It seems that visualization, then, is a two-edged weapon and this is a fact that is not often recognized by present-day exponents of success-programming that use the technique. Shakti Gawain and Marcus Allen insist that visualization can work *only* for good and base that belief on the law of karma, which states, according to Marcus Allen in *Tantra for the West*, that

> . . . the Universe is set up so that whatever you do comes back to you. Think loving thoughts and you live in a loving world. Think hateful thoughts and you live in a hate-filled world. Try to injure someone else and you will be injured.

This is all fine and good, but does not actually prevent evil being done. Equally, it ignores the fact that the concept of karma is linked with the belief in reincarnation, so that causes set up in this life do not automatically result in their karmic effects manifesting in this life — its effects may lie many lives away.

If they do not have complete faith in what can only be described as a dangerously optimistic view of karma, Marcus Allen does at least suggest that at the finish of every visualization session, the following sort of phrase is said: 'This, or something better, now manifests itself for me in totally satisfying and harmonious ways for the highest good of all concerned.'

Conclusion

If it has done nothing else, this chapter has emphasized the necessity of enlisting strong emotion if visualization is to lead to change. Magic, black or white, depends on it. It has also, I hope, indicated the need for thoughtful preparation and, just as a spiritual aspirant often needs a guru, so an aspirant for occult powers needs an instructor, a well-chosen guide.

In the next chapter, we move further into the field of the use of visualization in matters of the spirit. Much magic may appear to border on the miraculous, yet the fact is that miracles are not generally regarded as magical. Nevertheless, they do partake of the same nature in that they involve mind over matter, in other words, the transmutation of thought energy into material energy.

12.

Eastern Horizons

This chapter is about ways in which visualization is used to expand spiritual consciousness. It is therefore about prayer as prayer involves visualization. In intercessionary prayers, visualization of the nature of a desired change is present and in worship, visualization of the adored is also basic.

In the West, visualization is less deliberately used than in the East. In the East, there is no difficulty in believing that thoughts can become externalized objective facts and, conversely, that there is little difficulty in internalizing objects, such as images of deities.

I shall therefore consider in this chapter only those Far Eastern religions that set out to foster the use of visualization, that is, Hinduism and Buddhism in particular and, to a lesser extent, Taoism.

In Hinduism, for instance, people's imaginations create or find a huge pantheon of gods and goddesses whose incarnations and deeds are collected in epics of vast dimensions.

The Hindu knows that all of these gods are creations of the mind and yet, at the same time, entirely real so that the basis of Hinduism is the knowledge that the multitude of everyday things and events and gods around him are only varied manifestations of the same ultimate reality — Brahma, the Ground of all Being. Not to know this is to be in the realm of *maya*, in the grip of illusion.

The underlying fact of which Hinduism reminds us is that the cosmos is all of a piece, organic, growing, fluid and ever-changing. Good goes hand in hand with evil and the destructive aspect of human nature may emerge, for instance, as the Goddess Kali, in which visualized form it may be worshipped and which in being given this form may sanction the externalization of evil in such practices as Thugee. While we in the West may deplore such extremes (while we continue to kill and maim on our roads in the name of individual freedom), the Hindu knows that it is all *maya*, that what happens to individuals is their *karma*.

The central channel

We saw in Chapter 3 how the physical organs of the body may be affected for good (or ill) by means of visualization. Eastern traditions in general have it, as I have shown, that there are psychic organs and channels in the human body that are equally subject to manipulation by means of imaginative thought.

As a preliminary, and to heighten the differences I have suggested, it is important to know that much Eastern practice centres on energy and its transformation through the visualization and activation of channels and of energy centres known as the *chakras*.

A *chakra* is said to be a centre of energy in the subtle body at a point of contact with the physical body. There are a number of them and each is a centre of energy distribution. Much as our own tradition tends to centre certain emotions in the heart or in 'gut' feelings, so the East sees parts of the body as similar centres of emotions.

Belief in them has a long and wide history, from ancient Egypt and the Middle East, India, China, fourteenth-century Christian Hesychast monks, and even among the Mayas of Central America.

The *chakras* are said to be centred in the body along a central channel that runs from the coccyx to the crown of the skull. They are often visualized as lotus flowers — always a potent symbol in the East of ethereal enlightenment arising from the damp mud of the material earth.

In the average person, these *chakras* and the central channel or channels are blocked, so that psychic energy cannot pass freely. For a person to become enlightened it is said that they must be activated and the central channel that connects them must be cleared. Each of the religions I am looking at has its own method for doing this, each involving concentrated visualizations.

Once the central channel is cleared, the transformation of the meditator into a deity is enabled. It goes without saying that such a concept is anathema in the West. As I shall show, differences in terminology do not hide marked similarities between my three chosen traditions in their practice and achievement. In all traditions, for example, the visualization of fire and heat is to be noted.

Hinduism

Hindus count 88,000 *chakras*, but of these only seven are considered to be of supreme importance. Peculiar to Hinduism is the belief that the lowest of them, said to be found between the anus and the genitals, is the seat of a mysterious spiral of fire-energy called *kundalini*. Elaborate yogic techniques arouse this fire-energy and it ascends by burning through the other *chakras*, causing their petals to open, until it reaches the crown of the head. Physical sensations that are said to accompany this ascent include roaring, thundering, tinkling and humming. Visual phenomena include dots of light, flames, colours and geometrical shapes. Experts warn of dangers associated with this practice of arousing *kundalini* energy and say that it should only be done under the guidance of a Master.

Upon the fire-energy reaching the crown comes the Great Awakening, The Immortal Draught, Supreme Bliss, unity with a godhead.

Buddhism

Buddhists in general, more than the practitioners of any other religion, have spent much time in a study of the mind and its workings and have realized that the mind can be tamed, its stormy surface stilled, its calm depths plumbed. Those of the Mahayana (Great Vehicle) and Vajrayana (Diamond Vehicle) have realized the spiritual value of its natural propensity for visualizing as a way to stillness and Supreme Bliss. They, too, use visualization in the clearing of the *chakras*. (In addition, we shall see that they use it in the worship of deities, and in the effort to identify with such deities.)

Buddhists experience blockages in the *chakra* system at the base of the spine, navel, heart, throat and crown of the head. The method of clearing them I choose to describe is that used by Tibetan Buddhists of the Vajrayana tradition.

The procedure can merely be outlined here and these few words hardly do justice to the scope of the full method. You may like to refer to Geshe Kelsang Gyatso's *Clear Light of Bliss* (Wisdom Publications, 1982), which gives a fuller picture than I can here.

The channels (there are three) should be visualized and the visualization held and stabilized for as long as possible. To quote Geshe Kelsang Gyatso from his aforementioned book,

> Imagine that you are actually inside the indestructible drop. Think that if you were to turn on a light it would shine down the corridors of the eight spokes of the heart channel-wheel. Look down these spokes carefully, inspecting each one closely until you can conclude, 'Now I have seen the eight petals of the heart channel-wheel clearly.'

Next, the imagination is directed to pluck a tiny red-hot glowing ember of coal from a fire and place it in the central channel at the level of the navel. Its intense heat should be imagined. By means of contraction of muscles and directed breathing, the temperature of the ember is increased in such a way that it explodes into flames and burns away the blockages so that the silvery blissful energy at the crown *chakra* may be free to flow and fill the body.

Taoism

Again, there are three channels: the central channel, the *Tu Mai*, corresponding to the spinal cord, and the *Jen Mai*, corresponding to the central nervous system.

Much of Taoist sexual alchemy, one of the two methods by which Taoists hope to attain immortality and to join the gods, involves perfectly clear impressions of force flowing within the body through these subtle channels. Of the two, the more important appears to be the *Jen Mai*. This channel is prepared, in Taoism, by regulation of the mind and sexual activity.

As regards the mind, the alchemist is advised to calm it by careful regulation of his or her breathing, diet and emotions. The Emperor Hwang Ti was advised, 'Do not overwork your body, do not allow your vitality to become agitated. Then you will live long.' Chapter 16 of the *Tao Te Ching*, similarly, says 'Attain to the goal of absolute vacuity; keep to the state of perfect peace.'

As regards sexual activity, the sexual fluids of both sexes, called *ching*, have to be conserved. In men, this requires careful control of ejaculation and much advice is available to them that will achieve this. The stored *ching* is drawn up into the *tan tien* (just below the navel) where it is transmuted into *ch'i*. From this, what is described as a golden pill is formed and drawn up the *Jen Mai* into a cavity close to the top of the skull. Then, as Wen Kuan Chu in *Tao and Longevity* (Samuel Weiser, 1984) relates, '. . . he or she will feel as if there is a line of force that moves through the inside of the pubis, rushing up the lower *tan tien* . . . The abdomen becomes as hot as fire, the *ch'i* rushes to the spine like steam.'

Once the *Jen Mai* has been cleared, it is possible for immortality to be achieved. No special practice is needed as the mind is then ready to dissolve into the pure spirit of the 'Void'. You have then acquired a body beyond a body and so you are then able to leave this body at will and 'soar among the stars'.

A diversion into fairyland

Taoism is a gentle philosophy, more worldly and less intellectual than either Buddhism or Hinduism and is ready to use visualization in a more overtly magical way than them, as can be gathered from this quotation from John Blofeld's book, *Taoism: the Quest for Immortality* (Unwin, 1979):

> To obtain charms, provided you have won to the way, rise at dawn, burn incense in your courtyard, offer prayers and rites, then visualize a lovely youthful lady immortal, richly dressed and girdled with a belt of jade. In her hand she grasps the 'Genuine Jade-Clarity Purple Cloud Charm of the Sun Emperor'. Beholding it, your mind will become one-pointed, free from idle thoughts. Then will the truly efficacious charm you seek appear in your mind.

Elsewhere John Blofeld tells how one Chou Shao-hsien, an ancient, describes these charms as being visible in the mind as written on red and coral clouds. They are so vivid that the adept beholding them feels that they must be visible to all, in other words, they seem to exist objectively. John Blofeld is another who remarks that it is a pity that these descriptions were never commented on by Carl Jung.

How different, though, and refreshing was this gentle tale, so typical of the traditional view of the Chinese Taoist living remote in a mountain hermitage, and how far from Tianenmen Square.

Though classical Taoism had as its core the emptying of the mind, some later schools of the period when Taoism had become the state religion had detailed descriptions of gods and goddesses, their clothes and the colours of their clothes and these descriptions were used, according to Da Liu, to induce the deities to dwell in the mind.

Taoism is about the Way and the Way is found through quietude. That being so, it is not surprising to find this description of a pathworking, taken from Alan Watts' *In My Own Way* (Random House, 1972):

> Out behind the temple another staircase goes higher into the forest, suggesting that one has not yet come to the end of the mystery. Climbing, one reaches not a Chinese gate, but a *torii*, a Shinto arch that originally served as a perch for sacred birds, and this gives access to a plain wooden shrine with a thatched roof. Looking inside, one is faced — and given pause — by nothing more than a mirror, a disk of polished bronze on a lacquered stand. Yet it is not quite that, for behind this the stairway goes on, narrower and less imposing, winding up through the trees to come out into a level clearing planted with rows of stone and wooden posts inscribed with Chinese characters. The obvious message seems to be that it all comes to this — the cemetery. But as you are about to conclude that the tedious and depressing moral of this ascent is that 'the paths of glory lead but to the grave', it appears that there is still another stepway, rough and little used, going yet higher. You climb on. The path

levels out a little and then vanishes. Put into *haiku* —

> This is all there is;
> the path comes to an end
> among the parsley.

Aids to meditation

The gentleness observed in Taoism serves to remind us that spiritual development may be attained by other means than *chakra-yoga* and this section is to do with material aids to meditative visualization.

In them, although the aids start out as gross objects, they are used as means to increasingly subtle contemplation and end by being themselves completely internalized.

Kasinas

A *kasina* is an object — it might be a fruit, a candle, a bowl of water — upon which a meditator concentrates his gaze, from time to time closing the eyes and visualizing the chosen object, repeating the process until it is possible to visualize the object perfectly. As practice proceeds, the visualized object becomes spiritualized — idealized — so that any imperfections of the original are done away with and a perfectly conceptualized object remains, to be recalled at will.

Kasinas are thus emblematic of the quality embodied by the object, which may be symbolic of earth, water, fire, air and so on. They may be of various colours, each of which may set up vibrations influencing consciousness. If the object is light or space, they will expand consciousness.

Pictures

Pictures such as the top one overleaf to be used as aids to meditation may be artistically impressive, but they were intended for use, not admiration, being made expressly to stimulate psychic energy. At first they are used as they are; later, after many years of visualization and assimilation, they will be internalized.

In picture below there may be seen the Tibetan letter *ah*, signifying *sunyata*, or emptiness, that has to be concentrated on for several periods each day, its outline being firmly impressed on the mind's eye. After about six months, a perfect representation is obtainable and the image may be used in self-healing of parts of the body by visualizing it placed upon the appropriate part of the body.

The Tibetan letter *ah*, a symbol of sunyata

Mandalas and yantras

These are diagrams, generally circular, that are sacred and powerful centres for psychic operations. Certainly they appeal to deeper layers of the psyche than pictures. This is because, according to Carl Jung, they relate directly to archetypes and it is worth reminding readers that much of Jung's therapeutic work resulted in the spontaneous production of mandalas by his patients. Probably the most famous mandala is the Tibetan Wheel of Life (opposite), which combines the force of a picture with the far greater energy of a mandala.

Mandalas and yantras have been referred to as maps of the cosmos (cosmograms) or as maps of the secret pathways into the human mind (psychograms) and it is this interpretation that is much favoured by Jungian analysts. Tantric yogins refer to them as 'seeds', for, when planted in the mind, through visualization they will grow and flower.

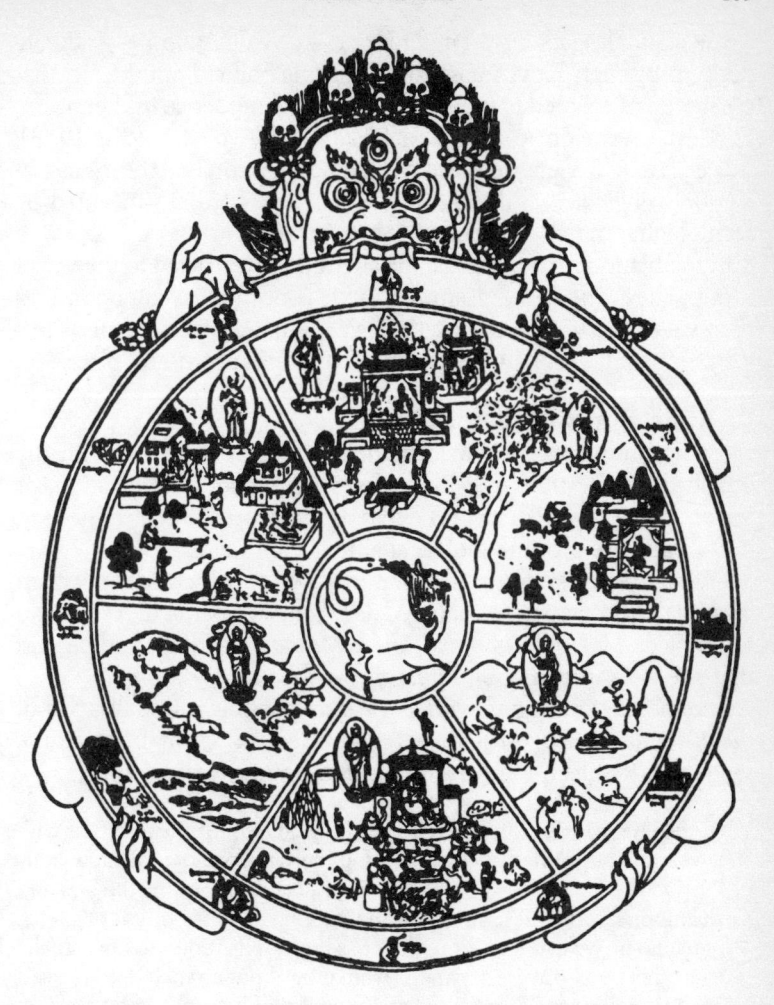

The Tibetan Wheel of Life

They may be drawn on paper, animal skins or sand; engraved on bone, wood or metal or become the ground plan for religious buildings. They may also be visualized — constructed in the mind's eye, often in a form that is unique to the individual meditator. This ability to construct an interior mandala, as indeed, the creation of any meditational object, has obvious advantages. There is no need to be in any special place to meditate for one. Many forms of meditation, therefore, can be done independent of time and place. Indeed, Carl Jung was told by Lingdam Gomchen, a *rinpoche* he met in India, that a true mandala is *always* an inner image — a visualization — gradually built up through active imagination. Having pointed out the fact that all mandalas seemed to be subject to cultural influence in their form, Carl Jung went on to say in *Collected Works, Vol XII* (RKP, 1968), however, that 'It seems to me to be beyond question that these Eastern symbols *originated in dreams and visions* and were not invented by some Mahayana church father.'

In meditation on a mandala, the attention is restricted to the visual input. They should be examined with concentrated attention and then visualized with eyes closed. The copy-image will become as real as the original and may be produced at any time, in any place.

Identification with deities

Most religions have as part of their ideals, that of union with the godhead. In the three religions I have examined, identification, or literal union, with deities is what is practised. Needless to say, visualization is a prime tool in attaining such heights.

The following example is of the method by which identification with the Buddha may be managed. (For a fuller treatment, I refer you to Kathleen McDonald's book *How to Meditate* and it should be said that she is a practising Buddhist of the Tibetan tradition.)

The meditation begins with as clear as possible a visualization of the Buddha seated on a throne seven feet or so in front of the meditator. Kathleen McDonald describes the next stages thus:

> At the level of your forehead . . . is a large golden throne adorned with jewels and supported at each of its four corners by a pair of snow lions . . . On the flat surface of the throne is a seat representing the sun and the moon . . . Seated upon this is the Buddha . . . His body is of golden light and he wears the saffron robes of a monk. His robes do not actually touch his body but are separated from it by about an inch. He is seated in the vajra, or full lotus, posture. The palm of his right hand rests on his right knee, the fingers touching the moon cushion.

Once this visualization has been stabilized, a request is made to the Buddha for his blessings to free the meditator of negativities and then a stream of purifying white light is visualized as flowing from the heart of the Buddha to the crown of the head of the meditator.

While reciting the deity's mantra — *tayata om muni muni maha munaye soha* — the throne is visualized as dissolving into the Buddha, who now comes to the space above the meditator's head, melts into light and dissolves into the meditator's body, so that he or she becomes one with the Buddha. Such methods attain their full heights in Vajrayana. I rely on Kathleen McDonald again:

> At your heart are a lotus and a moon. Standing upright around the circumference of the moon, reading clockwise, are the syllables of the mantra, *tayata om muni muni maha munaye soha*. The seed-syllable *mum* stands at the moon's centre.
>
> Visualize that rays of light — actually your wisdom and compassion — emanate from each letter and spread in all directions. They reach the countless sentient beings surrounding you and completely purify them of their obscurations and delusions and fill them with inspiration and strength.

Similarly, there are visualizations leading to worship of other deities, for instance, the worship of the powerful Buddhist deity, the Lady Tara. One of her many aspects is as Goddess of the Underworld, in which she rules the demons of the hells. In modern parlance, she may be said to rule those demons of the psyche such as greed and avarice. Yet another of her aspects is as the Goddess of the Earth, ruling all plants, animals and human beings. Her domination of wild animals again symbolizes the possibility of her restraining the instinctual drives of the human psyche and of her worship giving the devotee some possibility of first meeting the devils in the unconscious depths and then of restraining, repressing or sublimating them. She should be visualized and evoked by means of her mantra, which is *om tare tuttare ture soha*.

Mind substance

As we saw in Chapter 11 on the occult, the Tibetan Buddhists in particular believe that the mind's power of imagination is part of a continuum of energy — thought being a less dense and concentrated form of energy that can just as easily manifest itself in material form. They believe that thought can be so concentrated as to emerge in material form, as we saw, as *tulkus*. I told how Alexandra David-Neel herself created such a *tulku* in the form of a monk, who/which materialized in her room. Unfortunately, the being got out of her control, as she says in *Magic and Mystery in Tibet*: 'Sometimes I felt as if a robe was lightly rubbing against me and once a hand seemed to touch my shoulder . . . The fat, chubby-cheeked fellow grew leaner, his face assumed a vaguely mocking, sly look.' He/it had got out of its creator's control and had to be dematerialized — a process that took six months of hard struggle.

Geoffrey Ashe comments on *tulkus* in *Miracles* (Routledge & Kegan Paul, 1978), which, he says, by giving

> ... a special focusing of thought and will — by a superior being, or by several people together — a human *tulpa* can result which is an actual person, able to live a complete life from conception to death. Such a person is born in the usual way and is called a *tulku* or 'phantom body'. A *tulku* child need not be visibly different from other children, but embodies a god or a demon or someone who has never lived before or perhaps simply a hope or an ideal — whatever it was that the creator or creators may have been thinking about. This is the clue to such puzzling notions as the mystic succession of Dalai Lamas.

Such succession is not confined to the Dalai Lama. There are living now several reincarnated lamas and a full account may be found in Vickie McKenzie's book *Reincarnation — the Boy Lama* (Wisdom Publications, 1989).

Geoffrey Ashe goes on to say that the resurrected Christ's body also behaves like a *tulpa*. 'It could be composed of what [a lama] called the radiant form of matter, mind-substance.'

Implications for the West

The creation of mental pictures in minds untrained in their use is most often involuntary, such pictures rising like flotsam in the sea to the surface of the mind and then sinking, sometimes without trace, never to be seen again.

Whatever their immediate cause, many of these wandering mental pictures rise from the deepest depths of the collective unconscious. They may thus be those mental creations that Carl Jung recognized as archetypes such as are most often acknowledged in analytical therapy and present more nakedly in our memories of dreams. Most often they lie unacknowledged and unrecognized behind everyday waking thoughts and actions — dim, shadowy and potent. In contrast to the East, such potency is less immediately interpreted as the presence of gods who can be praised and appeased. Instead it may feed into our everyday unease, our 'existential angst', for the archetypes are culturally loaded. Carl Jung wrote in *Collected Works, Vol XIV*, for instance, of the 'redeemer-figure' universally present in human psyches, 'Whether the redeemer-figure be a fish, a hare, a lamb, a snake or a human being; it is the same redeemer-figure in a variety of disguises.' So, where we moderns now have lurking in the depths of our psyches the threat of nuclear or ecological destruction, the Greeks had Nemesis to punish their hubris, the Hindu has Shiva and the Tibetan Buddhist has an aspect of Tara.

It is in the East that the archetypes surface more readily. Where we *repress* our angst, the followers of Eastern religions *acknowledge* theirs and acknowledge and sublimate their fears. From this point of view, so called 'reality' is merely the result of our need to measure and categorize those things that our limited powers of perception and cultures persuade us are there, often having been passed through the filter of the collective unconscious.

There appear to be two layers of unconscious. There is a layer — in Carl Jung's terminology, the collective unconscious — in which are found the mythic archetypes and there is another layer — Sigmund Freud's 'id' — in which our animal history lives on. Among other characteristics, an aspect of human beings is that we are highly developed animals and our animality, our brutishness, is driven underground.

Both layers are found within our minds, affecting our daily conscious lives. Too many people 'live lives of quiet desperation', at the mercy of the id and the collective unconscious. Psychotherapists and mystics aim, each in their own way, to control them and to grow towards fulfilment or enlightenment. It is a path that, if undertaken without a guide and/or deep understanding, may be fraught with danger.

All appearances are *maya*, illusory concepts, and it is in Hinduism, of all the Eastern religions, that we find ourselves in territory that is the most far removed from the Western Judaeo/Christian/Islamic tradition.

The 'dark night of the soul', or even Bunyan's 'Slough of Despond', which figures so prominently in the biographies of Christian saints, may be brought on by the mystic's near approach to the devils that lie within and a consequent repression of their appearance, for there is little, it seems, in the Christian and Islamic traditions that leads an individual to being able to face, acknowledge and control these demons. Acceptance of the devils within is as much a part of Eastern religion as it is a part of Western psychotherapy.

It is Carl Jung who points up the distinction most aptly. He draws our attention to the fact that in the Western, theocentric religions, we exalt God and worship Him on high, whereas in Hinduism and, to a lesser extent, in all Far Eastern religions, we withdraw inwards. Westerners exteriorize while Easterners interiorize. Where the West has the High Altar and steeples and pinnacles reaching to heaven, all typifying the 'way of ascent', the East (in Hinduism, as an example) has the *lingam*, the phallus, placed in a pit, under ground level, all typifying the 'way of descent'. Where we hear 'thou shalt not', in the East we are more likely to hear 'it would be better if . . .'

Carl Jung claims that these differences reflect another fact of our cultures. He says in *Psychology and the East* that the West's working principle is that '. . . nothing is in the mind that was not previously in the senses'. (In passing, I draw your attention to the fact that in Chapter 3 we saw that the mind may reconstruct its mental models, so that, in fact, what is in the mind is often many steps removed from the original sensory perceptions.) Jung goes on to develop his principle with the statement that, 'Indian thought and Indian art merely *appear* in the sense world, but do not derive from it.' (What a world of sensual spectacle, though, what an abundantly writhing mythology is revealed in Hindu temple carvings.)

The implication of this is that any visualization done by a Hindu swims up, as it were, from the depths of his or her psyche, whereas a Westerner's visualization, where it is used, is designed to swim down to those depths. The former emerges as a statement about the existing inner being of the devotee, while the latter is designed to modify the inner being.

A study of Indian (that is Hindu and certain Buddhist) practices leads me to the conclusion that for them reality is not based primarily on sense perception, but on a sinking, a withdrawal into that ground we share, the ground of the collective unconscious and ancient mythic symbols. From these arise visions that are consciously adopted and invoked by means of *mudras* (gestures), mantras and the like, as we have seen.

The images that spring to mind in the imagination during, for instance, a meditation on a mandala may be either beneficent or terrifying and are the products both of our interior consciousness and of our need to bring order to our experience.

The underlying fact Eastern religions seek to persuade us the truth of is that the cosmos is organic, growing, fluid and ever-changing. Fulfilment, then, or enlightenment, may be achieved by deliberately colluding in the creation of another aspect of *maya* than the everyday, thereby discovering more of its nature. As Thubten Pende says in *The Mandala* (spring 1989),

> Likewise, nothing exists as it appears to my senses and, instead of sheepishly following the illusory display of ignorance — something I have yet to profit by — I let it go and create instead a theater of wisdom

and compassion: still illusory, but having a much better effect on myself and others.

On the other hand, the everyday may be taken to extremes and transformed, as in Tantra, some schools of which encourage excesses in mundane appetites of all kinds as a path to the light.

The foregoing is not to say that there are deep-seated psycho-biological differences between East and West. Some have suggested that such differences as are found are due as much to climatic differences as anything else — the Northern European being a fighter of the elements, going out to conquer them, the Southern Asian submitting to them, for example. That said, we have already noted that Western magicians are as likely to invoke gods and goddesses discovered in the depths of the psyches as any Indian swami.

Preliminary practices

For anyone wishing to experience such visualization techniques and their meditations as I have described in this chapter, general advice would be to find a guide, someone who has travelled the path and who has experience of advanced meditation. How this can be done is not always easy — it is not like reaching for the Yellow Pages and picking out a furniture shop or a dentist. What generally happens, strange though it may seem, is that a guru emerges when the time is ripe.

What follows are some of the simpler meditations you can do that may serve to accelerate that ripening. Kathleen McDonald's book *How to Meditate*, referred to from time to time throughout this book, is an excellent introduction to Tibetan Mahayana and Vajrayana practices. A more general introduction may be found in Lawrence LeShan's book bearing the same title.

Beginners are often discouraged, when reading of the elaborate visualizations that advanced meditators can evoke, by being unable to visualize clearly. Even though they know that this is only to be expected, they have the natural human wish to be able to run before they can walk. They should stick at it. However fuzzy and ephemeral their first efforts may be, things *will* improve, as I hope you will have understood from Chapter 6.

As I constantly reiterate, the most important thing to remember is perseverance. Having chosen a meditation it is important that the meditator sticks to that meditation for, at the very least, a fortnight, practising at a regular time, for a regular time and in a regular place, remembering all that has been said earlier about the tricks that the monkey mind will get up to. To help you, here is an introductory programme that will last about a couple of months.

In all meditation, remember that it is advisable to sit with your spine straight, body relaxed and mind alert. Your breathing should be natural.

The programme begins with what some have called the simplest of all visualization meditations for a naïve Westerner to try and, though simple, it is said to be conducive to great inner tranquility.

The cloak of light

Sit with your eyes closed, simply visualizing a bright, pure white light covering your entire body and wrapping around your head. Sit like this for 20 minutes. This sounds easy, but your monkey mind will have a lovely time. Stick at it, though, for the fortnight.

Crystalline water

This meditation is one described by James Hewitt in *Meditation* (Hodder & Stoughton, 1978). The aim is to dissolve the ego and reveal the self.

> You sit motionless with the eyes closed and then picture every part of your body being filled slowly with water of crystalline clarity, commencing with the head. Next the water slowly fills the space between the throat and the stomach. Then the arms and legs are filled from shoulders to fingertips and from pelvis to toes respectively. The cool, pure water also slowly fills the room in which you sit from floor to ceiling.
>
> The second stage of the meditation is to reverse the process witnessed by the inner eye. The water drains slowly from the room, from ceiling to floor. Then the water slowly leaves the legs, the arms, the trunk and the head. Last of all it disappears from within the skull. At this point it may be that the false ego slips away also and pure existence remains.

Body of light

The idea is to imagine a sphere of light in front of, and slightly above, you. It will be slightly smaller than your head. The sphere is representative of mental, physical, spiritual and emotional qualities that you most wish to embody at this moment in time. Visualize the sphere as decreasing in size until it is about 1 inch across. Then it will descend in the imagination into the top of your head, when it will begin to expand again until it fills your whole body. All solid parts of your body dissolve into it and themselves become pure light.

Concentrate on the body of light just created for as long as possible so that negativities fade away and any distractions that float into the mind are themselves transformed and dissolved into the light. You will clearly see similarities to the identification with the Buddha exercise.

Purification meditation

You should start by being comfortable and relaxed and aware of all parts of your body settling. Breathe normally, watching the exhalations and inhalations. When exhaling, try to imagine all negativities in your life, present and past, leaving your body with your breath. Visualize the negativities as black smoke coming from every part, every cell, every atom and disappearing into space, dissolving there.

Upon inhaling, imagine all positive energy from the universe as a whole entering and filling your body with pure white light, flowing to every part, every cell, every atom, until you experience a feeling of lightness and contentment, even joy. The exhalation of black smoke and the inhalation of white light should be concentrated on for as long as possible. Distracting thoughts should be seen, transformed into the black smoke and dispersed along with the rest.

Conclusion

It is not necessary these days to wander the Himalayas in search of a guru or monastery. The East is now firmly a part of the West and it is not difficult to find some group who will welcome a seeker. It is easier in the large towns, of course, but small groups and isolated individuals are around and will not reject approaches.

You will find a list of contacts in the Appendix on page 201.

13.
Beyond the Horizon

Death is my Beloved,
I look for her at each new turn in the road of life.
Her arms are gentle and her lips warm.

Anonymous ancient Egyptian poet

Western ways of death

Nowadays terminally ill patients are all too often drugged right up to the point of death and death-bed scenes are now a thing of the past — it is all sterilized. We miss the poignancy of being able to say such things as, 'When my grandfather died, he spoke of the most beautiful music.'

Death today is seen more and more as an obscenity, a defect, a failure of scientific materialism and there is today a virtual denial of the absolute fact of death. As a result, people are forcibly kept alive in intensive care units when all reasonable hope has gone, kept from dying by frightening machinery and tubing. Relatives, other visitors, and fellow-patients are too often unable to act authentically in the face of the fact of the coming death of their loved one. Indeed, they often do not know if the illness is terminal, but, if they do know, they often do not know if the patient knows. Alternatively, the patient may know, but is unable to talk of it in case the relatives do not know. This is cruel madness.

Ironically, we are very familiar with death — we see it daily on our television screens. Such pictures, though, are second-hand, safely sanitized behind a glass screen, capable of being recorded and even shown again. Editors decide what our image of death is to be, giving us pictures of hungry children and despairing mothers, floods and famine in faraway places, slow starvation before our very eyes — but these pictures are, somehow, not real.

We are very seldom given images of the usual natural dying process. Seldom do we see pictures of dead bodies at peace. Seldom do we see dead bodies being shown respect and regard. Most often we see violent death, torture, atrocity, moments of extreme agony. No previous culture has even been subjected to such terrifying spectacles, so productive of dismay and fear.

Death is not always violent, yet because we are all of us witnesses to so much horror that we cannot fully comprehend, we find ourselves unable to give meaning to the death and dying of fellow human beings. What is all this doing to our imaginations? When we picture death it becomes ever more likely that we see it in terms of blood and horror, distant, not quite real. *Actual* death, though, death next door, everyday death, ordinary death, this is hidden from us as though obscene. What a strange reversal of values this is, that the ordinary deaths of ordinary human beings in ordinary circumstances are kept from us.

Thanks to the effects of TV and tabloids we all of us have an immense repertoire of images of violent and unnatural death upon which to draw as our own death draws near. Yet, of the innate character and individual intimacy of everyday dying we certainly understand far less than members of primitive cultures and our own ancestors.

Not only the medical profession, but the church has failed in this, too. Once clerics were the professionals who prepared people for death and held their hands as they passed on. There is a tendency now for theologians to discourage dwelling on life after death in case it detracts from the business of trying to improve the lot of people on Earth now, yet religions are founded upon the fact of death. Where religion *does* take death seriously, this emotionally sensitive subject is treated to theological restructuring and so becomes surrounded by a penumbra of fear of judgement. It is no longer a simple matter of returning to the womb of the Earth, but is instead a journey to a judgement hall. Pluto, for instance, once the god of riches and abundance, is now the guardian of hell and so religion is here distorting primary myths. The ancient gods who represent the archetypes and who could once have helped stand cold on Olympus.

If death is not, in fact, the end, but only a stage in existence, such a denial is unnecessary. Doctors and clergy could, instead, prepare people for their deaths and people could be given time to prepare for their death (as well as tidying up their present lives). Families, too, could be given time to prepare and tidy loose ends. Instead, to a doctor, a dying patient is regarded as a medical failure, a fact to be glossed over, shrugged off for as long as possible, and the remaining life prolonged at the terrible cost of quality and respect. However, a belief in life after death clears the decks, sharpens up and makes our lives more rounded. It enables us to make more informed choices to do one thing rather than another. It also, very importantly, means that we are able to die more healthily, more humanly.

If we had the experience of good deaths that people find in such places as hospices, we'd all be healthier. Where doctors insist nowadays that life is only evidenced by brain activity, if they are surgeons, or by heart failure, if they are neurosurgeons, those that work to *comfort* the dying, those that *accept* death, believe that such materialism and professional demarcation makes a mockery of all that humans can be and are and that there are realistic alternatives.

In this final chapter I shall hope to show how, even at the point of death, visualization can help and comfort. A deal of ground has to be gone over, however, before I can do that, particularly in trying to answer the age-old question of whether there is, in fact, life after death.

Near-death experiences

Evidence of a sort that life may continue after death is found for many in what are called 'near-death experiences', which are those experiences that many, but not all, people have had when apparently close to death. Enough of these have been reported for some generalizations as to their nature to be ventured.

All who claim to have been through a near-death experience say that everything at first becomes dark, that it is like going down a long tunnel, that they experience a bright non-blinding light and often meet a person in white, perhaps a dead relative, smiling and happy as they were in life. Some people report getting a sort of flash-back, a sort of cinefilm of their life. The dead relative often says something very matter-of-fact like 'Well, that's that'. There is no comment, no judgement. Then there is the return, often to feelings of intense sadness, as the person is told that he or she has to go back.

Sometimes these people are in their bodies, sometimes they are floating as if on the ceiling watching their body before returning to it.

The matter is summed up and perhaps confirmed by such works as George Gallup's *Adventures in Immortality* (Souvenir Press, 1982) in which the characteristic features of out-of-body sensations that occurred during a verge-of-death incident were that people were:

- likely to hear noises during the early stage of the experience

- inclined to feel that they were going through a tunnel
- inclined to see their physical body from a distance
- apt to sense that there were other beings in non-physical form with them (especially loved ones who had died)
- likely to encounter a communicative being described as a brilliant light
- likely to feel after the experience that there was a purpose associated with it, that it was an experience of lasting benefit, that it was a spiritual or religious experience and that their life had been changed by the experience.

Sometimes there are negative experiences, such as:

- featureless, sometimes forbidding faces
- beings who are merely present, but who aren't at all comforting
- a sense of discomfort — especially mental or emotional unrest
- feelings of confusion about the experience
- a sense of being tricked or duped into ultimate destruction
- fear about what the finality of death may involve.

Explanations of near-death experiences are many. They are largely rationalizations, illustrating the need to make sense of an experience and so a bright light, for instance, will be interpreted in a manner most likely to be least frightening.

Explanations include:

- the results of prior religious conditioning — Christians don't see the Buddha, for instance — however, people who have had this experience are not all particularly religious or devout
- side-effects of medication, but many have not been under medication — such as accident victims — and drugs give rise to many varieties of experience, whereas near-death experiences have many points in common
- hypoxia (lack of oxygen), but some near-death experiences occur in hyperventilating conditions
- Freudian wish fulfilment and other explanations along these lines
- prior preparation such as will be illustrated below.

Sceptics are thus saying, in effect, that all instances of subjective experiencing are fantasy, which are, by definition, accidental, coincidental and trivial. Those who are less sure, however, such as many quantum physicists, who understand that the real world is only one version of reality, agree with mystics and most members of Eastern religions, who say we live in a 'veil of *maya*', illusion.

As Rupert Sheldrake wrote in *The Guardian* on 4 April, 1989,

The materialist orthodoxy of biology, established in the late nineteenth century, was shaped by notions of matter which have long since been abandoned by physicists. In modern physics, matter is no longer fundamental, but rather consists of energy bound within fields. The fields of relativity and quantum theory have properties undreamt of by nineteenth-century physicists. And perhaps there are fields at work within living organisms with properties as yet unrecognized by contemporary physics.

To my mind, this certainly does not exclude the possibility of life persisting beyond brain- or heart-death. Certain primitive tribes treat killed animals with respect, postponing skinning and dismembering, in the belief that the animal survives in some way for several hours.

One possible extension typical of the kind of thinking expressed here by Rupert Sheldrake is that emotion is one such field, helping to provide the motive power of the physical universe, generating waves of energy that operate on subatomic particles. Emotion would thus pull together particles that then form electrons, atoms, molecules and so on and so the world of physical reality would be built up from emotional energy. Who is to say when feeling is dead in the body?

Life after death

Heber D Curtis, writing in the *Los Angeles Times* on 31 December, 1926, asks,

> I personally find it impossible to regard Handel's 'Largo', Keats' 'Ode to a Grecian Urn' and the higher ethics as mere by-products of the chemical interaction of a collection of hydrocarbon molecules. With energy, matter, space and time continuous, with nothing lost or wasted, are we ourselves the only manifestation that comes to an end, ceases, is annihilated at three score years and ten?

This is a common *cri de coeur*, but some who take a rational/materialistic view of death would say 'yes, it is annihilated'. They argue that we know of no life form that does not have some material basis, that is, a body, and that since mind and body are inseparable, so, upon the dissolution of the body, the mind and thus the personality, dissolves too. As Rupert Sheldrake wrote in the article just cited,

> ... for materialists, there is no such thing as the soul. Therefore, memories cannot be aspects of an immaterial psyche, but must be stored as material things in the brain, the memory traces. And if memories are

stored in brains, they must of course be lost as the brain decays. On death, the individual, personal consciousness is obliterated forever as the brain breaks down and all conscious and unconscious memories vanish.

It would be a dogmatic person, indeed, however, who would argue that the self, the personality, is entirely dependent upon the body, entirely at the mercy of microscopic changes that take place in its physical tool.

Until recently, science had indeed seen matter and energy as separate — neither one invading the other's territory. Nowadays, however, it is increasingly recognized that matter and mind are one, that matter is a denser form of energy, mind a less tangible form of it. No atom of matter/unit of energy is ever lost, so the constant transmutation of energy into matter and vice versa constitutes some support for the idea that life in some form *can* continue after physical death.

We see energy at the centre of stars and trace its descent into atoms and complex molecules, into dense matter and into living creatures. This dissolves and the whole returns to the source. So, in a living organism, there is birth, youth, maturity, old age, death — and birth once more — in some form or other.

Such beliefs may go back to the beginnings of agriculture some 10,000 years ago, though cave paintings predate that by some 20,000 years. We saw in Chapter 9 how these paintings can be taken to be the earliest evidence of human efforts to control our environment by means of visualization and magic — or was it religion? (The first real archaeological evidence for what we understand by religious belief is to do with burial customs. Often a foetal position was forced on the corpse, as though for rebirth.)

Neanderthal man was certain that death was a phase in the lifecycle and that some element of the dead person would survive. So sure was he that he made quite certain that the dead body was made safe from danger, such as marauding wild animals and the weather, and took the trouble to equip the dead person with all that he or she might need on the way to the next event in the cycle and yet, so many centuries later, death — and its effect on the personality in particular — remains one of the barriers that man has yet to explore in any scientific manner. The point is crucial.

With the possible exception of reincarnated lamas, no individual of a later generation has been proved to continue the conscious personality of any individual of a previous generation in the same way as the later days of an individual continue his childhood ones. So, in the absence of any evidence to the contrary, the process of individuation that produces this ongoing incarnation now called Michael Page may, after my death, produce in the course of time a new personality called, say, Jim Smith. This is not a reincarnation of Michael Page.

Humans share many characteristics, such as bodily form, organs, hopes and fears. Though variations between individuals are certainly found, for each of us, unless we are a twin, is unique in this respect, our chief claim to individuality is found in our personality, in which even a twin may find uniqueness. If personality does not survive, can we speak of rebirth at all?

Rebirth

In both East and West there has been a continuing belief that something of each of us must go on after death. Is it only a by-product of our level of consciousness that makes us say that it is unlikely that we are the only manifestation that comes to an end, *finis*, is annihilated after such a short span? Is it only an effect of our feeling of having achieved so little in this life that makes us pine for another chance?

Whatever the answers to such questions, it is probable that a belief in rebirth has been held by more people than by those who reject it. In the *Bhagavadgita* it is written:

> As leaving aside worn out garments
> A man takes other, new one,
> So leaving aside worn out bodies
> To other, new ones goes the embodied.

Carl Jung suggested that there were five main types of rebirth in *Collected Works, Vol IX Pt I* (RKP, 1968).

- metempsychosis (the passing of the soul after death into some other body): Pythagoras believed that this was what happened and Herodotus, too, believed that people are reborn successively over 3,000 years through all forms of animal life before becoming human again, in which belief he seems to have been echoed by Empedocles: 'For already have I once been a boy and a girl, a fish and a bird and a dumb sea fish'
- resurrection (to rise from the dead complete in original body and mind)

- rebirth within one life (a belief that many Buddhists embrace, seeing as they do that existence can be construed as a series of 'now-points' of which death is but another in the series)
- transformation (the birth of the hidden immortal within the mortal man) as exemplified in Taoist alchemical transmutation of bodily fluids to spiritual golden pills.

We have seen that Taoist sages aim at transformation, at a continuation of this very life with increased powers that verge on the supernatural. There is little doubt that the Chinese have tried very hard to find a means to immortality. This fits with their hard-headed pragmatism — better the life you know than the rebirth you don't. There is little doubt, either, that many Chinese sages have attained to very great ages. A well-attested example of this is of Li Ch'ing Yuen, whose obituary appeared in *The New York Times* in 1933, observing that he had been born in 1678, had been married 14 times and appeared at the Imperial Court on the occasion of his 150th and 200th birthdays. It is strange to realize that he could, if he had wished, have observed the whole of the history of the United States

- reincarnation (to be born again, personality preserved, in another body or form).

Reincarnation

The nature of reincarnation covers a wide spectrum of opinion, including the beliefs that each person has three incarnations — woman, man and finally as the sex in which the spirit fared best — that there are an indefinite number of reincarnations, that reincarnation involves instantaneous rebirth or periods of, for example, purgatory or limbo, that reincarnation is always as the same species, that it can be as a member of any species.

In the West, historically, the Druids had reincarnation as a basic tenet of belief, as did Gnostic sects including Manichees and Cathars. Early Christianity also accepted reincarnation until the Second General Council of the Church at Constantinople in 553 AD declared that 'If anyone shall assert the fabulous pre-existence of souls and shall submit to the monstrous doctrine that follows from it, let him be anathema', and hoped thereby to have killed the idea stone dead.

The actual mechanics of reincarnation have naturally always been vague. For instance, there is the theory that everything ever experienced is stored in the subconscious mind and transmitted to the child of the next incarnation (including, of course, all transmitted memories from ancestors). Then there is the mystic 'Akashic Record', which is said to be a subtle substance totally enveloping the Earth and acting as a recording medium for every thought, feeling and act that ever occurs, which can be tapped by psychics.

We are returned to the question posed above: is it possible for this Michael Page to be reincarnated with a personality that is still recognizably Michael Page? Mentors of reincarnated lamas say that even young children do exhibit personality traits that were possessed by the lama they are claimed to have been in a previous life, but the Jesuits have an answer to that one: 'Give me a child before he is five . . . and I will shape his personality in such a way as to prove anything.'

For rebirth to be reincarnation it is necessary that the personality survives, that memory survives the physical dissolution of the body. Rupert Sheldrake sidesteps this materialistic argument when he suggests in his *Guardian* article of 4 May 1988 that memory might '. . . turn out to depend on morphic resonance rather than on memory traces', so this is at least a lead in to the subject, a non-materialistic theoretical possibility emerging from twentieth-century scientific thinking.

Karma

Plato wrote: 'They say that the soul of man is immortal. At one time it comes to an end — that which is called death — and at another it is born again, but is never finally exterminated. On these grounds a man must live all his days as righteously as possible . . . Thus the soul, since it is immortal and has been born many times and has seen all things both here and in the other world, has learned everything that is.'

Such thinking may lead, depending on the person and his acculturation, to a number of consequences. In a Christian culture, it may lead to thoughts to do with retribution from on high, while in an Eastern context, the question of *karma* will be uppermost.

Any nursery teacher knows that individual differences between the children in her care are often seemingly inexplicable. Very often children from the same parents and home are as distinct as chalk is from cheese. As Paracelsus said, 'Some children are born from heaven and others are born from hell, because each human being has his inherent tendencies and these belong to his spirit and indicate the state in which he existed before he was born . . .' Children, then, trail more than clouds of glory — they bring with them traces from their actions in previous lives, to be worked out, perhaps, in this one.

Even in this life, from moment to moment we face the consequences of our previous actions, but not all are worked out before death supervenes. Thus *karma*, for it to make sense and achieve a balance in the actions of any one individual, must be continuous past death. Only some belief in reincarnation makes sense of the concept of *karma* and thus of this life itself and only these twin beliefs make sense of the enigma of evil and the need for it to be balanced by good. Only this makes sense of our need for personal responsibility if we are to progress either individually or, consequently, as a species.

Ongoing personal responsibility implies an ongoing personality, for there can be no escape either from fellow creatures we have harmed or from ourselves who did the harming. This is not a system of rewards and punishments, but the working out of consequences. Nor is it that somehow, somewhere, a total of evils is balanced by a total of impersonal goods. Personal responsibility must surely persist on both sides of the grave. Thus the concept of reincarnation was born and with it two consequent implications. One is that personality persists from life to life. The other is that there is always a physical existence of a vehicle for the soul.

Death paths

All religions and most cultures (that is, with the exception of our own largely secular one) have some form of initiation of the individual into the fact of lonely death. Need it be lonely, though?

Just as our worldly friends are often largely figments of our own emotional needs as we walk the way of our lives, so it may be that companions on the final way may be created. Often there seems to be an expectation that beings will be met with, as in the kindly welcomers to the path observed in near-death experiences. Mercia Eliade's *From Primitives to Zen* (Collins, 1979) states:

> So Ishtar passes through seven gates of the nether world, at which the gatekeeper removes crown, ear pendants, chains around her neck, breast ornaments, girdle of birthstones at her hips, clasps round hands and feet and the breechcloth of her body.

There is a well-known story of the traveller on a mountain who is chased by a tiger to the edge of a cliff. He goes over the edge, clinging to a thick vine. Below him, he can see another tiger waiting for him. Then he sees two mice nibbling away at the roots of the vine. What does he do? He sees a wild strawberry growing beside him. He takes the fruit and pops it in his mouth.

One of the points of the story is the importance of living the moment of death in full consciousness — an extension of the true art of living, which is to be alert and aware of what is happening in the present moment.

Death is the great unknown and some idea of the process, of the pathway, is helpful. Such a pathway is described in a number of traditions, the best-known being those of the Tibetan Buddhist, described in the *Tibetan Book of the Dead*, the *Bardo Thödel*. This describes a series of three stages, *bardos*, the challenges of which have to be surmounted by the soul. Buddhists become familiar with the death path and may visualize its stages in advance.

The work is meant to be a guide for the dead person during the period of his *bardo* existence, symbolically described as an intermediate state of 49 days' duration between death and rebirth. The text falls into three parts, firstly the *Chikhai Bardo*, which describes the psychic happenings at the moment of death, the second part, the *Chönyid Bardo*, which deals with the states that supervene immediately after death, and the third part, *Sidpa Bardo*, which concerns the onset of the birth-instinct and of prenatal events prior to reincarnation. Each one descends from the height of joyful enlightenment in the *Chikhai Bardo* to the last and lowest region. This region is where the dead person, unable to profit by the teachings of the *Chikhai* and *Chönyid Bardo*, begins to fall prey to sexual fantasies and is attracted by the vision of mating couples and thus to reincarnation.

A Buddhist sutra, crossing the divide between the *Bardo* and Freud, quoted in Mercia Eliade's *From Primitives to Zen* (Collins, 1979), says,

> He sees his [future] father and mother making love and, seeing them, a thought crosses his mind, a perversity arises in him. If he is going to be reborn as a man he sees himself making love to his mother and being hindered by his father; or if he is going to be reborn as a woman, he sees himself making love with his father and being hindered by his mother.

The *Egyptian Book of the Dead* describes the path in 'The Book of Coming Forth by Day', a guide-book for the deceased through Amenti (Hades) to the Kingdom of Osiris.

Dolores Ashcroft-Nowicki in commenting on the Egyptian rites in *Highways of the Mind*, tells us that in the actual burial chamber would be portrayed the death, burial and judgement of the dead person. All the required passwords, actions and responses would be painted on the walls for the soul to read. Crossing the bridge between life and death, a priest or priestess would lie down beside the dying person and take their hand. Another priest would then begin to describe the journey the dying one would soon be taking. Rebirth was not automatic, however, for in the presence of Osiris, the judge of gods and men, the heart of the deceased was to be balanced by the jackal-headed Anubis in judgement scales against the weight of an ostrich feather. If it was a heart made light by goodness, and so did not weigh down the scale, then the soul was allowed to pass on into the blessed fields of Osiris. If the scales showed the heart to be heavy with evil, then the soul was destroyed.

For us in the West, however much we might wish to, it is unlikely that our cultural conditioning will allow many of us to adopt these particular paths to the next stage of our existence, yet some form of guided visualization could be helpful.

The urge is there, as Roberto Assagioli says in *The Act of Will*:

> The process of death and rebirth was symbolically enacted in various mystery rites and has been lived and described in religious terms by many mystics. At present it is being rediscovered . . . this process often occurs without a clear understanding . . . But a conscious, purposeful, willing co-operation can greatly facilitate, foster and hasten it.

Perhaps it might be a helpful thing, as old age approaches, to write your autobiography. It need not be a long story, for what is searched for is some meaning to your life and what is found is some unfinished business. This discovery could help us as our passage through death is negotiated, for we have seen that for many there is an assumption that people after death do in fact steer their own way back to a suitable rebirth. An atom liberated from its molecular bonds is described as manifesting an unwonted activity, technically known as a nascent state, but still it does not recombine indifferently with the first free atom that it encounters, only with one for which it has an apparent affinity. It does not seem all that strange a notion that each person enters into a body that it is most fitted to be connected with, for a free spirit can be expected to have rather more *nous* than a liberated atom.

The same effect as writing a biography can be brought about by meditating on one's future death, as in this example from Ean Begg's television series *Is There Something After Death?* (1988):

1 Close your eyes.
2 Breathe slowly and repeat the word, 'relax'.

3 Imagine you are told by the doctor that you have contracted the most acute form of adult leukaemia. You are unlikely to have more than a year left to live. You go home, your mind racing.
4 What thoughts and feelings arise? What bodily sensations?
5 Visualize the response of family and friends. Pick one person in particular and imagine their reaction to the news of your imminent death.
6 Now try to decide who you want (alive or dead) to help and support you in your last days.
7 Finally, imagine you're lying awake at night, unable to sleep. Facing this ultimate aloneness, what do you think the purpose of your life to have been?

What follows now is part of a meditation devised by Stephen Levine in *Healing into Life and Death* (Anchor Press, 1987) to be read later, at the point of death, by someone close to the dying person:

Find a comfortable position and allow the attention to come to the breath.
Let the mind and body begin to still.
Let the body soften. Let the breath come all by itself.
If the in-breath is longer than the out-breath, let it be so.
If the out-breath exceeds the in-breath, so be it.
Nothing to change, nowhere to go, just this much.
Moment to moment softening the body, opening around the sense of the solid.
Feeling the pull of gravity on this earthen body. Feel its denseness, its solidity beginning to soften and melt at the edges.
Let your arms and legs lie loose by your sides. You have relied on these hands, these arms, your whole life to pull the world closer or to push it away. Now let go of the strength in your arms and allow it to converge in your heart. Let the tension in the hands and arms melt into the spaciousness in which each sensation floats.
Sensations from the legs, from the torso, from the shoulders, from the head received in soft belly, in spacious heart.
Like an ice-cube melting, let this body soften from its hard solidity into the soft, open flowing of its essential fluidity. The body no longer frozen in form, but melting into the sweet waters of a sense of greater spaciousness and fluidity.
Pain disappears, the body of awareness, the light body within, beginning to float free of its dense earthen vessel.
As the sense of solid body dissolves into the quality of liquidity, the senses turn within.
Receiving life moment to moment as it gradually leaves the body behind, floating free.

The edges melting, the solidity softening like a crystalline ball of ice melting away, evaporating into air, distributed equally throughout the spaciousness.

Letting the heart melt each holding as it arises — letting go of name, letting go of reputation, letting go of family, letting go of form — mercy pervading each moment of existence.

Do-it-yourself death path

Dolores Ashcroft-Nowicki in her book *Highways of the Mind*, remarks that in these days of sudden death in unexpected circumstances, some people may find it advantageous to prepare for their entry into the next stage by a simple pathworking.

As regards your own preparation for death, a pathworking may be constructed in the same way as for another person or it may be entirely imaginative, an amalgam of all your dreams. It will consist of a visualization of a location that is 'heavenly' for you, with people of your choosing to welcome you. This is where you will spend your time immediately after your passing, where you will sleep a lot and relax and prepare for the next step, a halfway house where you will go over the life you have just left. It will have a distinctive pathway to it and beyond it, and this is important, a gate to the next stage.

When the visualized scenario is perfected, go over it again and again, then lock the gate and put the key where you can see it clearly. Dolores Ashcroft-Nowicki says in her book,

> If by chance the change comes suddenly, the pathworking will snap into action at once without you doing anything . . . Follow the familiar path, you know where the key is and you are bound to find someone there already, waiting for you. Place yourself in their hands and rest.

The road to the tennis club

In the case of preparing another for that step, she recommends encouraging the other to reminisce about their past lives until a particularly happy episode occurs on a number of occasions. She suggests that we should get them to repeat that and to fill out the details, what they were wearing, who else was there, the weather, the time of the year. Perhaps it would be, as it was for one old lady of my acquaintance, the memories of playing tennis as a girl for her school with her dear and life-long friend. It was easy to build in the road to the tennis court, the court itself and to imagine a gate on the far side of the court leading to the club pavilion where all her friends were waiting for her. When the time came close for her to go, she was led to the court and left there by the gate to the club, with reassurance that she would not be alone there. On the last occasion, she would be urged to go on, with the reassurance that her guide would be following her before too long. It was important that there were people in the working that she knew and Dolores Ashcroft-Nowicki says it is not important whether they are either alive or dead.

There is clearly a cultural convergence between this sort of thinking (that has existed down the ages and is just now surfacing to a wider public than the esoteric groups to which it was previously confined) and that of the Ancient Egyptians, Buddhist and Taoist sages, Gnostics, Greeks and Celts.

Choosing future life

If it is possible, though scientifically unproven, that you can build a pathway into death, is it not equally possible (and even more lacking in scientific proof) to build a pathworking out of it on the other side — in other words, to choose your future life, at least in general terms?

Tibetans would say that, in fact, there is empirical proof and it is mistaken to speak merely of a possibility. They would say that a proof that this can occur is to be found at the very least in the successive reincarnations of the Dalai Lama. In this case presumably the dying one in the series directs his 'soul' to choose a suitable time, place and parentage for the next incarnation.

If all thoughts and manifest objects are indeed aspects of the underlying cosmic energy field it does not seem out of the realms of possibility that certain highly evolved personalities may have such power to control their own karma and that of others.

It seems, given the initial premise, to be the logical last step for us all.

A Final Vision

A book is a path of exploration. This particular path, the one I share with you, started, as I said in Chapter 10, on holiday in Dorset some 10 years ago.

Where has my path led me so far? To this book. Outwardly it is just some pieces of paper, cardboard and glue, but it is also very much more — it is a map. It is, I hope, a map that people can scan, is a map pointing people in an interesting and, I believe, a worthwhile direction towards a goal that is fundamental to their happiness.

What sort of map do Western navigators want? What sort do we need? What Eldorado do we persuade ourselves is the final goal?

I have already suggested that many moderns are interested in neither the metaphorical nor the actual end of life (which latter, in spite of, or because of, the death of God seems so final), but in getting what they can out of it here and now. 'How to Influence People', prosperity visualization, programming for health — all these are indicative of the way in which Western people use the ancient art. Very well, so that is the starting point, the entry to a path, the first tentative steps along that path.

Throughout history the story has been much the same. Even in Lao Tsu's day, 3,000 years ago, it is clear that most people were off track, interested in consuming, in war, concerned about death and how to avoid it (an explanation no doubt for the Taoist interest in immortality). They, like us, were concerned to hold on to life and those of its passing pleasures in which they found their identity. In all of this they were not so different from today and ourselves. Perhaps we have less of a grip on the numinous, have greater distractions; perhaps we are further from farm and field and are now all members of leisured classes — certainly so in comparison with those ancient Chinese — but perhaps our wealth of distractions will lead us in themselves back to seeking a path. There is a form of Tantrism that recommends overindulgence as a means of finding the way — indeed, Jean Jacques Rousseau advocated much the same in the natural nurture of children.

The taboo on gentle death in our (ageing) population seems to me to be the great Rocky Mountain range between us and our Pacific. It is the great range of mountains that we fear to begin to tackle, yet we have seen that some people claim to have been taken up and over them and through and back again and still we do not believe their calm-eyed stories of the immense peaceful sea beyond.

I have tried to make this a good map — clear, not too complicated and indicating practical steps, landmarks, obstacles and difficulties and the way around these. It indicates the nature of the final goal and it has to make the way beyond the Rockies and down to the Ocean beyond an attractive and feasible possibility.

The trouble is that this map-maker has not been very far along the path himself. My own map is constructed in part of my own explorations, but very much more of traveller's tales. I have only glimpsed with timorous eye the shining sea beyond. My hope and belief was that those other travellers would take me by the hand and direct me enough to be able to make a practical guide for others. So it has been my personal path, not in any exclusive sense, but my own in the way that all people have to find their own way up those mountain passes, may share those experiences, but finally have each to find their own way.

So this map has emerged of those distant vistas, and also of the nearby terrain, smooth paths and rough ones — all in the mind. The comparison and contrasting of success and failure in the completely worldly sense is crucial for readers, for pilgrims, who need to be convinced that it is in their own minds, within their own capacity, to succeed. Similarly they need to be convinced that their failures stem from their own inner being. Who could have been more likely failures than the paralyzed winner of a literary prize or the winners in a Paraplegic Olympic Games?

The mind, the imagination, the self-image, self-concept — these are what form, make, each and every one of us. It is of this that the book has tried to persuade its reader-pilgrims. It is about the power of the imagination to change the self-concept and the environment itself, that the book speaks.

The route I have traced is clear. It leads from the nursery slopes of everyday material success on to the whole area of health and healing, physical and mental. This latter is central to the book, leading as it does from better health for oneself and for loved ones and then, perhaps, to a realization that it is within your grasp to affect for good the lives of all people.

How is it that a mental act of imagination becomes concrete? How does it actually act upon the material world? The truth is, of course, we don't know. Explanations, if such they can be called, we have seen range from the poetic and the mystical through pure statements of faith to hints emerging from the leading edge of science.

Marcus Allen, for instance, writes in *Tantra for the West*:

> All things are contained within the 'Tree of Life'. The creation of the Tree of Life reflects the mysteries of all creation . . . The Tree of Life begins within emptiness, within the vast, shining void of space. Then it begins as a very subtle 'spiritual impulse' — the impulse to create. Then this very subtle spiritual impulse becomes something more tangible: a *thought*, a clearer, more definite impulse to create something. Once the impulse has become a thought, it gains momentum and becomes a *feeling*, an emotional impulse. This feeling supported by sustained thought, *soon becomes manifest in physical form*, as an object we can experience with our senses.

But how?

Then there's Rebecca Clark, who asks in *Macro-Mind Power*,

> Is there one fantastic Primal Power in the universe whose force can be harnessed and utilized to guide you to ultimate freedom and all the joys of triumphant living? . . . : [The answer] is an unqualified *Yes!* . . . there is the creative power of man's mind, which is a part of the Universal Creative Power, and this mind power can affect the elements of the Universe.

Again, we have to ask the question, how?

Poetry is all very well and this is indeed very poetic and for many people that is enough, the actual psycho-biological basis of it all for some people being interesting but secondary. However, most people of our scientific/technological age would appreciate some more rational basis on which to pin their faith. We turn, therefore, to the writings of a physician whom I have quoted already in this book — Maxwell Maltz. He says, for instance, in *Psycho-cybernetics* that, 'Thoughts bring organic as well as functional changes. We do know this much: mental attitudes *can* influence the body's healing mechanisms.' For an explanation of this, however, we saw that he, too, had finally to fall back on notions of cosmic consciousness and this does not appear to bring us forward. Indeed, none of this splattering of hyperbole appears to bring us very far forward.

Such an idea, that cosmic consciousness is everywhere present is found again in EH Shattock's writings. In *A Manual of Self-Healing* he wrote that,

> The whole body is alive and is a totality of consciousness. This is made up of the individual consciousness of the atoms, cells, organs, etc . . . The vestigial mind of the cell is not a separate piece of mind, it is simply mind as seen through the limits of the cell body.

We appear to be getting a little more into the twentieth-century idiom now and will even more with Roberto Assagioli, who writes, for instance, in *Psychosynthesis*,

> Every image has in itself a motor drive. Images and mental pictures tend to produce the physical conditions and the external acts corresponding to them.

We are forced to ask again, however, how?

Of course, it's easy to see the way in which, for instance, prosperity programming can appear to transform thought into money. The mere act of visualizing and affirming can cause a change in the mental set and attitude, so that the individual alters his or her way of acting in the world in order to bring change about. This may, at a pinch, explain healing and therapy, but beyond that such explanations begin to wear thin. Perhaps we really do then begin to think as I have hinted repeatedly, as lamas say and as Shakti Gawain writes in *Creative Visualization*,

> *The physical universe is energy.* The scientific world is beginning to discover what metaphysical and spiritual teachers have known for centuries. Our physical universe is not really composed of 'matter' at all; its basic component is a kind of force or essence which we can call *energy.*

This is better still, for it does begin to talk the same kind of language as that spoken by Fritjof Capra, David Bohm, RL Gregory and Rupert Sheldrake.

A summary of the thoughts of many quantum physicists and field theorists points to a realization that matter is not fundamentally distinguishable from energy. David Bohm, we have noted, has indicated that whatever meanings we have in our minds are inseparable from the totality of our bodies.

This, then, links with the sorts of thought I had in relation to some words of RL Gregory, in which he referred to the way in which self-observation — self-visualization — creates a cybernetic mental model that feeds back into the body-mind totality.

Then there is Rupert Sheldrake, with his notions of morphic resonance, in which states and changes of state are replicated non-physically, but in terms of meanings. I suggest that meanings are the province of mind — and where is that Master-mind? Are we back with cosmic consciousness already?

For a final example, I will quote Nirad Chadhauri, writing in the *Independent on Sunday*, 28 January 1990. In this, he says:

> What the physicists have finally established is that what we regard as the material universe is only a subjective illusion of man . . . the material universe is only the image which man's sense organs create out of an immaterial energy which is organised in patterns of motion . . . If this view of the nature of the universe is correct, there can be no room for materialism, for then we have to regard it as a process, as a flow of energy . . .

The boundary between the material and the mental becomes very faint, and the possibility of visualization affecting the physical increasingly believable.

The route leads, then, from a realization of the power of the mind to create success, to a realization that healing for yourself is possible, to the realization that healing is possible for others and from that to a realization that the problem of death itself is capable of solution.

The power of the imagination must stand or fall on the way it manages the final full stop, or what is imagined to be the final full stop. The pattern of the map has thus emerged: . . . worldly success, bodily health, mental happiness, happy relationships, death — and life. What is in those dots above? Did we have to get into the occult, the Spiritual Master, the collective unconscious, mandalas, mantras and yantras? What do these have to say to the lonely traveller? Well, at the least, they can provide a kind of companionship for that lonely soul, a comfort in the forest and the night. Must there be a forest? Is not this also existing only in the imagination?

All life is a pathway leading, in the end, to death. All life is a preparation for death, for the final path to — where? The next life in a series? Or to heaven or hell? One of the sub-themes of the book has been that there is a sort of shorthand code for a fundamental difference between East and West. The latter believes that there is but one life and its path is a straight and narrow one with Hell awaiting false steps, the former that this life is one of a series, with fulfilment awaiting the traveller at some time, in some place.

We moderns are all more or less lost. Some of us have more certainty, born of faith or experience, but most of our Western fellow beings have 'no interest' because the fact of being lost is a very frightening one — which of us has not felt, or been, lost or abandoned by our carer at some early stage of our life? It was then that we realized our essential aloneness and our essential ignorance about where to go, how to get there and whom to trust. Rather than risk abandonment, many of us prefer to blank the possibility from our minds, to avoid such troughs and sloughs of despond. Thereby much adventurous living is abandoned. Those who are prepared to take the risk are those who experience the heights of human achievement, the peaks of which Abraham Maslow wrote. Asked one day why such experiences were not more common, he answered that he thought we are just not strong enough to endure more. 'Our organisms are just too weak for any large doses of greatness,' he said in *The Farther Reaches of Human Nature*, and went on to say that we often avoid growth because of a built-in fear of being torn apart, of losing control, even of being killed by the experience.

We need therefore maps and we need an ability to read those maps, in other words to relate the map to the actual ground about us. John Bunyan's *Pilgrim's Progress* was just such a map — a medieval one whose dangers yet bore a relation to reality, the monsters in its contemporaneous world maps being denizens of *terra incognita*. While making no claims to comparison with Bunyan, I hope that this book relates a way of self-realization to the terrain met with in *today's* world.

Yes, there is a forest, a dark place full of traps and snares. Misuse of the power of the imagination, the power to grab success can, in the world as it is, lead to the Jonestown Cult, the Mansons, to people who prey in the night.

In the world of the spirit, the way to hell lies close — the misuse of *siddhis* being one. The misguided practice of tantric rites can lead not merely to moral degradation, but to disease, madness and premature death.

The subject of this book is not new. It is met with in Insight, est, Encounter Groups, Psychosynthesis, spiritual masters, meditation, ashrams, monasteries, and so forth. We are all on our personal path, and have been all our life or lives.

The reading of books is a solitary pursuit and I pray that the reading of this one leads not to solitary dreams turning to solitary achievement or solitary madness, but to a search for a better guide to take the traveller on to the next stage of his or her journey.

One thing is sure, whether alone or in company, the path, once commenced upon, will change the traveller irrevocably — it is a path on which there is no turning back. Its techniques demand effort and are, especially in the West, very much to do with achievement on a worldly level as much as on any mystical, heavenly level. They may, therefore, tend to be seen as a misuse of spirituality and even as demonic by the Western traditions — as, indeed, we have seen they sometimes actually are. Nevertheless, there are arguments here to do with the relationship between the individual on the one hand, and monotheistic religions and state authoritarianism on the other that result in public schizophrenia in the giving or the withholding of power — or in its taking.

Do we control our visions? If not, who does?

Appendix

Addresses of Eastern religious organizations

The Buddhist Society, 58 Eccleston Square, London SW1
Publish a useful yearbook.

Friends of the Western Buddhist Order, 7 Colville Houses, Talbot Road, London W11
Many branches.

Hindu Centre, 39 Grafton Terrace, London NW5

International Society for Krishna Consciousness, 10 Soho Street, London W1

International Taoist Society, 426 Charter Avenue, Canley, Coventry

Manjushri London Centre, 10 Finsbury Park Road, London N4
Affiliated to an international Buddhist organization.

Nichiren Shoshu Buddhism, NSUK, Taplow Court, Taplow, Berkshire
Claim to have 20,000 members in the UK.

Addresses of consciousness raising groups, non-religious

est Training, 10-14 Macklin Street, London WC2

Insight Seminars, 9 Spring Street, London W2

Local libraries and newspaper small advertisements are good sources of initial contacts.

Bibliography

Allegro, John, *Lost Gods* (Michael Joseph, 1970)
Allen, Marcus, *Tantra for the West* (Whatever Publishing, 1981)
Anderson, Walt, *Open Secrets* (Penguin, 1980)
Ashcroft-Nowicki, Dolores, *Highways of the Mind* (Aquarian Press, 1987)
Ashe, Geoffrey, *Miracles* (Routledge & Kegan Paul, 1978)
Assagioli, Roberto, *The Act of Will* (Turnstone Press, 1974; Crucible, 1990)
  Psychosynthesis (Turnstone Press, 1965; Crucible, 1990)

Benson, Herbert, *Your Maximum Mind* (Aquarian Press, 1988)
Berne, Eric, *What Do You Say After You Say Hello?* (Corgi, 1975)
Blofeld, John, *I Ching* (Unwin, 1976)
  Taoism: The Quest for Immortality (Unwin, 1979)
Bohm, David, *Unfolding Meaning* (ARK Paperbacks, 1987)
Bolen, Jean, *The Tao of Psychology* (Wildwood House, 1980)
Brohn, Penny, *The Bristol Programme* (Century, 1987)
Budge, Wallace, *The Egyptian Book of the Dead* (Dover, 1978)

Capra, Fritjof, *The Tao of Physics* (Fontana, 1976)
Carnegie, Dale, *How to Stop Worrying and Start Living* (Cedar Books, 1962)
Chang, Jolan, *The Tao of Love and Sex* (Panther, 1979)
Clark, Rebecca, *Macro-Mind Power* (A Thomas, 1980)
Cooper, JC, *Taoism* (Aquarian Press, 1972; Crucible, 1990)
Couttie, Bob, *Forbidden Knowledge* (Lutterworth Press, 1988)
Cox, Harvey, *The Church in the Secular City* (Penguin, 1962)

Da Liu, *The Tao and Chinese Culture* (Routledge & Kegan Paul, 1981)
David-Neel, Alexandra, *Magic and Mystery in Tibet* (Souvenir, 1967)
de Bono, Edward, *de Bono's Thinking Course* (BBC Books, 1982)
Drury, Neville, *Inner Visions* (Routledge & Kegan Paul, 1979)

Eliade, Mercea, *From Primitives to Zen* (Collins, 1979)

Ferguson, Marilyn, *The Aquarian Conspiracy* (Tarcher, 1980)
Ferrucci, Piero, *What We May Be* (Turnstone Press, 1982; Crucible, 1989)
Foot, David, *The Healing Word* (WH Walter, 1979)
Fortune, Dion, *Sane Occultism and Practical Occultism in Daily Life* (Aquarian Press, 1987)

Gallup, George, *Adventures in Immortality* (Souvenir Press, 1982)
Gawain, Shakti, *Creative Visualisation* (Whatever Publishing, 1978)
Gendlin, Eugene, *Focusing* (Bantam, 1981)
Geshe Kelsang Gyatso, *Clear Light of Bliss* (Wisdom Publications [361 Newbury St, Boston, USA], 1982)
Giles, Herbert A, *Chuang Tzu* (Unwin, 1980)
Gooch, Stan, *Total Man* (Abacus, 1975)
Gregory, RL, *Concepts and Mechanisms of Perception* (Duckworth, 1974)

Haynes, Renée, *The Seeing Eye, The Seeing I* (Hutchinson, 1976)
Herrigel, Eugen, *Zen in the Art of Archery* (Routledge & Kegan Paul, 1953)
Hewitt, James, *Meditation* (Hodder & Stoughton, 1978)
Hofstadter, Douglas and Dennett, Daniel, *The Mind's Eye* (Harvester Press, 1981)

Inglis, Brian, *The Hidden Power* (Jonathan Cape, 1986)

Jung, Carl, *Collected Works* (Routledge & Kegan Paul, various dates according to volume)
Psychology and the East (ARK Paperbacks, 1986)
Synchronicity (Routledge & Kegan Paul, 1972)

Kovel, Joel, *A Complete Guide to Therapy* (Pelican, 1978)
Kronenberger, Louis, *Company Manners* (Bobs Merrill, 1962)
Kwo Da-Wei, *Chinese Brushwork* (Allanheld Osmun, 1980)

Legge, James, *The Texts of Taoism* (Dover, 1962)
LeShan, Lawrence, *How to Meditate* (Turnstone Press, 1983; Crucible, 1989)
Levey, Joel, *The Fine Arts of Relaxation, Concentration and Meditation* (Wisdom Publications [361 Newbury St, Boston, USA], 1987)
Levi, Primo, *If This is a Man and the Truce* (Sphere, 1987) [quoted by permission of Bodley Head and the estate of Primo Levi]
Levine, Stephen, *Healing into Life and Death* (Anchor Press, 1987)

McDonald, Kathleen, *How to Meditate* (Wisdom Publications [361 Newbury St, Boston, USA], 1974)
McKenzie, Vickie, *Reincarnation — the Boy Lama* (Wisdom Publications [361 Newbury St, Boston, USA], 1989)
Maltz, Maxwell, *Psycho-cybernetics* (Prentice Hall, 1960)
Maslow, Abraham H, *The Farther Reachers of Human Nature* (Penguin, 1976)
  Towards a Psychology of Being (Viking Press, 1971)
Miller, Jonathan, *States of Mind* (BBC Books, 1983)

Needham, Joseph, *Science and Civilization in China* (Cambridge University Press, 1954)

Phillips, Deborah and Judd, Robert, *How to Fall Out of Love* (Futura, 1981)
Piaget, Jean, *The Origins of Intelligence in the Child* (Penguin, 1977)

Rainwater, Janette, *You're in Charge* (Turnstone Press, 1979). Republished as *Self-Therapy* (Crucible, 1989)
Reps, Paul, *Zen Flesh, Zen Bones* (Pelican, 1971)
Rogers, Carl, *On Becoming a Person* (Constable, 1974)

Sage, JAS, *Live to be 100* (WH Allen, 1975)
Samarpan, *The Feeling Good Book* (Turnstone Press, 1983)
Schneider, Meir, *Self Healing* (Routledge, 1987)
Shattock, EH, *A Manual of Self-Healing* (Turnstone Press, 1982)
  An Experiment in Mindfulness (Rider, 1958)
Sheldrake, Rupert, *A New Science of Life* (Paladin, 1987)
Silva, José, *The Silva Mind Control Method* (Souvenir Press, 1978)
Stanway, Andrew, *Alternative Medicine* (Pelican, 1979)

Thic Nhat Hahn, *The Miracle of Mindfulness* (Beacon Press, 1975)

Vernon, PE, *Creativity* (Penguin, 1970)

Walker, Benjamin, *Tantrism* (Aquarian Press, 1982)
Watson, Lyall, *Lifetide* (Sceptre, 1987)
Watts, Alan, *In My Own Way* (Random House, 1972)
  Tao: The Watercourse Way (Pelican, 1979)
  The Way of Zen (Pelican, 1970)
Wen Kuan Chu, *Tao and Longevity* (Samuel Weiser, 1984)
Willis, Ben, *The Tao of Art* (Century, 1987)
Wilson, Colin, *The Occult* (Hodder & Stoughton, 1971)
Wilson, Donald L, *Total Mind Power* (Camaro Publishing, 1976)

Zohar, Danah, *Through the Time Barrier* (Heinemann, 1982)

Index

Abundance programming, 10f
Act of Will, The, 45, 75, 109, 111, 120, 189
Acupuncture, 36
Adventures in Immortality, 180
Affirming, 25f, 100, 156
AIDS, 38, 41
Alchemy, 158
Allen, Marcus, 62, 65, 160, 195
Archetypes, 63, 98f, 136, 173
Ashcroft-Nowicki, Dolores, 43f, 112, 154, 157, 188
Assagioli, Roberto, 16, 21f, 45, 48, 66, 67, 69, 75, 91, 100, 109ff, 120, 128, 152, 189, 196
Astral travel, 158
Audio tapes, 87f, 106
Auras, 157f
Autogenic Training, 40
Autosuggestion, 26

Battered women, 68 *et seq*
Benson, Herbert, 21, 84
Best Therapist, 70, 110f, 123
Biofeedback, 105f
Bohm, David, 29, 140, 196
Brain, hemispheres, 52, 100, 107f, 119 *et seq*, 134
Breathing, 79ff
Bristol Programme, The, 28, 30, 36
Brohn, Penny, 28, 29, 30, 36
Buddhism, 21, 42, 43, 71, 83, 139f, 164f, 170ff, 188

Cabbala, 151

Capra, Fritjof, 137
Cave paintings, 117
Chadhauri, Nirad, 197
Chakras, 163ff
Ch'i, 36, 80, 98, 99
Child abuse, 65, 71f
Children and creativity, 114ff
Chuang Tzu, 22
Clark, Rebecca, 25, 153, 156, 157, 195
Clear Light of Bliss, 164
Collective unconscious, 98, 99, 145, 173
Complete Guide to Therapy, A, 93f, 95, 102, 104, 113, 114
Coué, Emile, 25f, 39
Creative Visualization, 32, 57, 196
Creativity, 114–30

Dali, Salvador, 121f
Da Liu, 152, 153
David-Neel, Alexandra, 144, 155
Death, 178–92
Death paths, 187 *et seq*
de Bono, Edward, 120
Dirac, Paul, 140
Direct knowing, 141f
Dreams, 112, 158, 159
Drury, Neville, 151, 153

Egyptian Book of the Dead, 188f
Eliade, Mircea, 157, 187
Emergencies, 23
Emotional scarring, 64, 96
Emotions, 25, 33, 38, 49, 86, 107ff, 129, 159f, 182

Experiment in Mindfulness, An, 40, 83

Farther Reaches of Human Nature, 111, 198
Feeling Good Book, The, 34
Ferrucci, Piero, 19, 67, 70, 71, 100, 109f
Filters, mental, 135
Fine Arts of Relaxation, Concentration and Meditation, The, 31, 35, 81, 82, 89, 90
Focusing, 88, 106ff
Foot, David, 53
Forgiveness, 65, 74f
Fortune, Dion, 149, 154
Freud, Sigmund, 32, 93, 95ff, 173
From Primitives to Zen, 157, 187

Gallup, George, 180
Gawain, Shakti, 32, 57, 58, 160, 196
Gendlin, Eugene, 88, 106ff
Gooch, Stan, 117f
Good fortune script, 23
Gregory, RL, 46, 197

Healing:
  AIDS, 38, 41
  Arthritis, 37
  Blindness, 36
  Blood pressure, 36
  Cancer, 37f
  Disease: reported cures, 29f
  Distant healing, 56f
  Group healing, 57f
  Pain, 34f
  Premature ejaculation, 73
  Slimming, 19f, 57
  Smoking, 40
Healing into Life and Death, 190
Healing Word, The, 53
Health check, visualized, 31f, 43f
Herrigel, Eugen, 22, 48f, 124
Hidden Power, The, 133
Highways of the Mind, 43f, 112, 154, 188
Hinduism, 162f
Holograms, 139f
How to Fall Out of Love, 66f
How to Meditate, 70, 79, 81, 85, 90, 170

Hypnotism, 39f, 52f, 94

I Ching, 136, 147, 152
Ideal Model, 100, 128
Ideal scenes, 103, 109
If This is a Man and The Truce, 7, 13
Inner Visions, 151, 153
Inutition, 122ff

Jealousy, 68f
Jung, Carl, 63, 93, 98f, 136, 152, 169f, 172, 173f, 184f

Karma, 63, 71, 160, 162, 186f
Koplowitz, Herbert, 141f
Kovel, Joel, 93f, 95, 102, 104, 113, 114
Kundalini, 163f

Laing, RD, 93f
Levey, Joel, 31, 35, 81, 82, 89, 90
Levi, Primo, 7, 13
Levine, Stephen, 190
Life after death, 182 *et seq*
Life-scripts, 17, 94f
Live to be 100, 30, 39

Macro-Mind Power, 25, 153, 156, 157, 195
Magic and Mystery in Tibet, 144, 155
Maltz, Maxwell, 11, 15, 38, 39, 47, 65, 195
Mandalas, 168f
Mantras, 84, 170ff
Manual of Self Healing, A, 30, 42f, 55, 56, 196
Maslow, Abraham, 98, 111, 198
McDonald, Kathleen, 70f, 79, 81, 85, 170ff
Meditation, 89f, 128, 175ff, 190ff
  aids to, 167ff
Mindfulness, 38f, 77–91
  techniques, 82ff
Mind's Eye, The, 46
Mind substance, 171f
Miracle of Mindfulness, The, 83
Morphogenetic Field Theory, 140f

Near-death experiences, 180ff

Occult, 145–61

INDEX

Occult, The, 147, 150, 154, 159
On Becoming a Person, 102

Pain, 34f
Paranormal, 131–44
Pathworkings, 156f
Perls, Fritz, 97
Piaget, Jean, 141
Poincaré, Henri, 123
Problem-solving, 45f
Psychic healers, 53f
Psychic healing, 55f
Psycho-cybernetics, 11, 21, 38, 39, 47, 65, 195
Psychosynthesis, 16, 45, 99f, 108f, 128f, 196
Psychotherapy, 90, 92–113
  Analytical Psychology, 98f
  Behaviour therapy, 94
  Directive therapy, 94
  Encounter groups, 102
  Existential therapy, 93
  Family therapy, 102
  Focusing, 88, 106ff
  Gestalt therapy, 97
  Group therapy, 103f
  Primal therapy, 96
  Psychoanalysis, 95ff
  Psychosynthesis, 99f, 108ff
  Reality therapy, 95
  Reichian therapy, 99
  Sex therapy, 101f
  Transactional Analysis, 94f

Quantum Physics, 137ff, 145

Rainwater, Janette, 17f, 72, 81, 90, 158
Rebirth, 184f
Reincarnation, 63, 160, 185ff
Relationships, 62–76
Relaxation techniques, 84ff
Ritual, 127

Sage, KAS, 30, 39
Sages, Taoist, 125f
Samarpan, 34
Sane Occultism and Practical Occultism in Daily Life, 149, 154
Schneider, Meir, 28, 30, 36
Self-concept, the, 15f, 59f, 92

Self Healing, 28, 30
Sexual relationships, 71ff
Shamans, 150f
Shattock, EH, 30, 42f, 55, 56, 83, 196
Sheldrake, Rupert, 140f, 181ff, 186, 197
Silva, José, 20, 36, 38, 56, 143
Silva Mind Control Method, The, 20, 36, 38, 56, 143
Sports performance, improvement, 20 et seq
Sub-personalities, 100, 110
Synchronicity, 145, 152

T'ai Chi Ch'uan, 36, 99
Tantra, 63, 175
Tantra for the West, 62f, 65, 160, 195
Tantrism, 153
Tao (and equivalents), 47, 48, 55, 80, 152
Tao and Chinese Culture, The, 152, 153
Tao and Longevity, 165
Taoism, 80, 165
Tao of Art, The, 121f, 125
Tarot, 151
Tart, Charles, 146f
Thich Nhat Hahn, 83
Think-see, 41f
Through the Time Barrier, 132, 136, 137ff
Tibetan Book of the Dead, 188
Total Man, 118
Total Mind Power, 21, 30, 35, 36, 84
Towards a Psychology of Being, 99
Tulku, 155f, 172
Tulpa, 155f, 172

Unfolding Meaning, 29
Unitary Operational Thinking, 141f

Video tapes, 106
Visualization:
  controlled, 18
  defined, 16
  recollective, 18
  successful, 24f
  uncontrolled, 17

Watts, Alan, 80, 125, 166
Way of Zen, The, 80, 125

What We May Be, 19, 70, 71, 100, 109
Will, 24f
Willis, Ben, 121, 125
Wilson, Colin, 147, 150, 154, 159f
Wilson, Donald, 21, 30, 35, 36, 84, 87f
Witches, 150f
wu wei, 124ff

You're in Charge, 17, 72, 81, 90, 91, 158
Your Maximum Mind, 21, 84

Zen Flesh, Zen Bones, 80
Zen in the Art of Archery, 22, 124
Zohar, Danah, 132, 136–9, 142